Research Methods in
Design and Technology

Research Methods in Learning Design and Technology explores the many forms, both new and established, that research takes within the field of instructional design and technology (IDT). Chapters by experienced IDT researchers address methodologies such as meta-analysis, social media research, user experience design research, eye-tracking research, and phenomenology, situating each approach within the broader context of how IDT research has evolved and continues to evolve over time. This comprehensive, up-to-date volume familiarizes graduate students, faculty, and instructional design practitioners with the full spectrum of approaches available for investigating the new and changing educational landscapes. The book also discusses the history and prospective future of research methodologies in the IDT field.

Enilda Romero-Hall is Associate Professor of Education and Graduate Coordinator of the Instruction Design and Technology program at the University of Tampa, USA.

Research Methods in Learning Design and Technology

Edited by Enilda Romero-Hall

Routledge
Taylor & Francis Group

NEW YORK AND LONDON

First published 2021
by Routledge
52 Vanderbilt Avenue, New York, NY 10017

and by Routledge
2 Park Square, Milton Park, Abingdon, Oxon, OX14 4RN

Routledge is an imprint of the Taylor & Francis Group, an informa business

Library of Congress Cataloging-in-Publication Data
A catalog record for this title has been requested

ISBN: 978-0-367-20326-9 (hbk)
ISBN: 978-0-367-20328-3 (pbk)
ISBN: 978-0-429-26091-9 (ebk)

Typeset in Bembo
by Swales & Willis, Exeter, Devon, UK

To Diego, my cutie pie.

Contents

Acknowledgments

There are so many who I would like to acknowledge and thank for their support towards this edited volume; without their help and contribution, this project would not be completed. First, I would like to thank the University of Tampa, the members of the sabbatical committee, and Provost David Stern for supporting my sabbatical period to focus my energy and efforts towards coordinating and editing this book as well as writing two book chapters.

I would also like to thank the book chapter authors for their willingness to be part of this journey with me. Their expertise on the different topics shared will serve to advance our field, the knowledge of scholars, and serve as evidence of what we have accomplished and what there is to do moving forward, in terms of research methods in learning design and technology. I also much appreciate the book chapter authors' work ethic and excitement for this project.

Taking on editing a book is not an easy task. I am grateful for the editorial staff at Routledge Education and especially my editor Dan for his guidance throughout the process and various conversations about the content of the book. I would also like to thank my colleague Aimee Whiteside who shared her own experience editing a book and was always happy to answer any question that I sent her way.

At some point, while working on the book, I felt overwhelmed by the responsibility and anxious about the outcome. It was during this time that the confidence boosters from family, friends, former students, current students, and colleagues helped me put words into paper, send out emails, and get organized. Thank you to my partner, McFadden Hall, for his encouragement and pep talks. Also, thank you for reviewing the first and last chapters before submission.

A special thanks to the Association of Educational Communications and Technology (AECT) and colleagues who I have met throughout my years of participation in this conference. I want to acknowledge colleagues who I worked with as part of the AECT Research and Theory Division: Jozenia (Zeni) Colorado, David Moore, Marcus Childress, Lisa Yamagata-Lynch, Michael Grant, Ana-Paula Correia, George Veletsianos, E-Ling Hsiao, and Fei Gao. I am tremendously grateful to E-Ling and Fei who serve as co-editors with me on a journal special issue on the topic of "innovative research methods in instructional design and technology." The special issue was the propelling force that led me to work on this edited volume.

As a graduate student, I had the opportunity to work with Ginger Watson, whose knowledge of research methods helped spark my curiosity on the topic. We worked and published several research projects related to the use of eye-tracking and emotion face reading software in instructional design and technology research. Thank you, Ginger, for those experiences. Also, thank you to the Link Foundation Fellowship and the Old Dominion University Darden College of Education Dissertation Fellowship that helped fund these research projects.

Last, a huge thanks to the 31 reviewers who: (a) responded to my call for volunteers to review book chapters for this project and (b) provided very insightful feedback that assisted in the improvement and revisions of each book chapter included in this edited volume. Thanks to:

Fatih Ari
Okan Arslan
Ismahan Arslan-Ari
Pallavi Chhabra
Quincy Conley
Camille Dickson-Deane
Sarah Espinosa
Jose Flores
Wendy Ann Gentry
Michael M. Grant
Spencer P. Greenhalgh
Susie Gronseth
Marquis Holley
Tiantian Jin
Yong Ju Jung
Ahmed Lachheb
Heather Leary
Peter Leong
Defne Akıncı Midas
William S. Morris
Mary Ellen Muesing
Janos Olle
Heather Robinson
Dotty Sammons
Justin Sentz
Jill E. Stefaniak
Sonia Tiwari
Keri Duncan Valentine

Lucas Vasconcelos
Andrew Walker
Qing Zhang

I should also add that writing and editing this book during the COVID-19 pandemic is challenging, so I would like to acknowledge all scholars who, despite the circumstances, are still moving knowledge forward.

1 Research Methods in Learning Design and Technology

A Historical Perspective of the Last 40 Years

Enilda Romero-Hall

This book serves to combine knowledge related to research methodologies in the instructional design and technology (IDT) field. It will address questions such as: How have our research methodologies evolved? What are the methodologies that can be used to investigate traditional and new research environments? How can we apply innovative research methodologies to address questions related to learning, design, and technology? This book will provide IDT scholars with a solid foundation of the different methods that can be taken to investigate a research problem. This knowledge aids researchers in the understanding of the rationale for the application of specific procedures or techniques used to identify, select, process, and analyze information applied to understand a research question.

As researchers, in the IDT field, our research interests, learning environments, types of learners, challenges and experiences, and the form of content is changing. We need to prepare ourselves with a research toolkit that allows us to properly investigate this new educational landscape. However, before reviewing the different research methodologies presented in this book, it is important to provide some historical context of the evolution of educational research and, more specifically, research methods in the instructional design & technology field.

The 1980s: Positivistic versus Post-positivistic Views

In 1982, researchers discussed predictions for the future of educational research in the next decade. The predictions from educational researchers included: a) the potential rise of better research syntheses thanks to the "meta-analysis" method, b) wishes to focus less on the classification of humans and more on understanding central variables, processes, and concepts in the teaching and learning of students, c) the desire to have more ethics in which trade-offs and weakness of research settings are fully disclosed as standard practice, d) predictions involving the emergence of the "field of instructional psychology" and its focus, and e) hopes for improved training of research workers with an emphasis on the history of education, the philosophical issues that concern educators, methodologies of instruction, and the structure of educational systems (Farley, 1982). One particular prediction that Benjamin Bloom mentioned brought attention to the isolation and privacy of our research processes and dissemination (Farley, 1982). Bloom discussed that in other fields, such as physical and biological sciences, research efforts are more intensive. Knowledge among researchers and the work that they are doing is widespread and academics are working at the edge of the field. Whereas in education we have difficulty even knowing where the edges of the field are. Bloom predicted and suggested that education scholars should use group processes to probe more deeply into underlying issues and strategies (Farley, 1982). If you are familiar with concerns and issues with educational research, it will be clear to you that all of these predictions for the 1980s are still hopes and desires for research processes today.

Discussions in educational research that were often documented in the 1980s were related to the persistence of positivistic views and post-positivistic thoughts on educational research (Phillips, 1983), which in turn led to publications about the dogmas of our field (Howe, 1985). Positivistic philosophers a) were rigid believers that the scientific method could be applied to human affairs including the study of morals, b) had great hostility toward metaphysics, and c) adopted the verifiability principle which stated that something was meaningful if and only if it was empirically verifiable (Phillips, 1983). There were claims that positivism had died by the 1980s and that new and revolutionary accounts of the nature of science had emerged. However, it is well documented that many researchers felt that the legacy of positivism had not gone far enough (Howe, 1985; Phillips, 1983; Smith, 1983).

As Howe (1985) stated: "educational research had remained largely untouched by the epistemological advances that brought about the repudiation of logical positivism." Dogmas ingrained in educational research were argued and explored: quantitative versus qualitative and facts versus value (Howe, 1985; Smith, 1983). These dogmas and the beliefs of educational researchers led to serious and heated arguments, in which name-calling was not uncommon (i.e., "number crunchers versus storytellers"). During the 1980s various researchers published to share the perspectives on the dogmas previously stated and clarify perspectives (Howe, 1985; Smith, 1983). They hoped to dismantle assumptions about different research methods and focus researchers more on "what works" given the goal of the investigation.

To solidify the argument that moving away from positivist epistemological views was critical for educational researchers, Cziko (1989) shared in an essay several lines of reasonings related to the unpredictability of human behaviors and the importance of description and interpretation of educational phenomena. The factors guiding the unpredictability of human behaviors, according to Cziko (1989) included: individual differences, chaos, the evolutionary nature of learning and development, the role of consciousness and free will in human behavior, and the implications of quantum mechanics. These reasons and positions regarding educational research continued to evolve from the traditional views of research as experimentation versus the more realistic understanding of the complexities of educational environments (Brown, 1992; Schoenfeld, 1992b). This was not only a shift in epistemological views influencing methodology, but it was also a shift from laboratory research to classroom settings (Romero-Hall, Hsiao, & Gao, 2018).

The 1990s: Immerse and Investigate in the Real World of Teaching and Learning

By 1992, researchers in education, specifically in the learning science fields, were posing the question: "What do you do when the perspective, paradigms, and methods that you know fail to provide adequate explanations of the things you need to understand?" (Schoenfeld, 1992b). It was clear by then that educational research was evolving; researchers were full of desire to immerse and investigate in the real world of teaching and learning. In a special issue of the *Journal of the Learning Sciences* titled "Research Methods in and for the Learning Sciences," guest-edited by Alan Schoenfeld, researchers discussed new methods used to explore different situations, behaviors, and learning experiences (Brown, 1992; Saxe, 1992; Schoenfeld, 1992a). This special issue provided insights into the true complexities of research post-positivist times, beyond just qualitative versus quantitative. Brown (1992) shared the intricacies engineering innovative learning experience in inner-city classrooms while also understanding how to investigate learning communities and interpretation amongst learners. For Brown (1992) the methodological issues in this type of complex intervention studies included: a) cross-fertilization between the classroom and laboratory settings to enrich understanding the developmental phenomenon in question, 2) the decision between idiographic (single variable in many subjects) versus nomothetic (the throughout study of individual cases) approaches, and c) the data selection. Schoenfeld (1992a) examined methodological issues related to the analysis of videotapes of problem-solving sessions. Using two case studies, Schoenfeld (1992a) described "wrestling with the data" as well as issues related to theory building, validity, and reliability, among others. Last, Saxe (1992) described in detail a framework that he developed to better understand children's learning in cultural practices and educational activities. This framework was created due to the need to capture and analyze the dynamics of cognitive development in a unique community in ways that went beyond the traditional approach such as structural-development traditions of Jean Piaget and Heinz Werner (Saxe, 1992). What Saxe (1992) found was that traditional methods of researching cognitive development ignored "the interplay between unique sociocultural histories and the constructive cognitive activities of individuals" (p. 216).

The Early 2000s: We are More than Controlled Experiments

History teaches us that, to understand learners and their experiences (cognitive, physical, and emotional), researchers needed to evolve from traditional ideologies of research to a more intricate research method that carefully considers "context." For learning design and technology researchers this became particularly critical as complete, complex, and interactive learning environments became tokens of interest for researchers in the educational technology field. By 2002, research in the educational technology field had explored content (instructional design), format (message design), and interactions (simulations) in learning experiences (Winn, 2002). According to Winn (2002), the new age of research in educational technology would focus on learning environments. He specifically predicted a focal point on a) artificial learning environments, b) inscriptional systems, c) social aspects of learning, and d) distributed cognition in learning communities. For Winn (2002) this change in topics of research in the educational technology field meant that researchers also had to change their research questions and methods by "adjusting to the demands of studying increasingly more complex interactions between students and their environments" (p. 347). Winn (2002) stated that design experiments could be successful at determining effectiveness; however, just like Brown (1992), he believed that experiments can also distort the view of a setting where variables cannot be controlled.

In response to Winn (2002), Mayer (2003) wrote a seminal piece to clarify that recommendations for practice should be evidence-based using empirical research (ranging from controlled experiments to systematic observation in natural contexts). Mayer (2003) also expressed "research should be issue-driven, not method drive" (p. 362). Mayer (2003) highlighted the importance of this type of methodology by stating: "Controlled experiments offer an unsurpassed methodology for establishing the effectiveness of educational programs. The application of experimental methods to behavioral research is perhaps one of the greatest scientific advances of the twentieth century" (pp. 362–363). The idea that controlled experiments should be disregarded or criticized, as Winn (2002) had expressed previously, was troubling to Mayer.

This kind of back-and-forward argument about research methods in educational technology sets the stage for our academic discourse and the use of various research methodologies. Researchers in the educational technology field were encouraged to adequately consider the research question and engage in their investigations using the most appropriate method at their disposal (Hannafin, Orrill, Kim, & Kim, 2005; Reeves, Herrington, & Oliver, 2005; Richey & Klein, 2005; Ross, Morrison, & Lowther, 2005; Savenye & Robinson, 2005; Winn, 2003). In a special issue of the *Journal of Computing in Higher Education*, Ross et al. (2005) discussed extensively the different types of experimental designs, its advantages/disadvantages, and the potential threats to the internal validity of the experiment. Ross et al. (2005), just like Mayer (2003), expressed that experimental methods on educational technology are a powerful way of determining what works in education. However, in the same special issue, Reeves et al. (2005) encouraged education faculty to consider a design research approach. Some of the reasons for the use of design research included: a) its focus on a broad-based, complex problem, b) it integrates known and hypothetical design principles to render plausible solutions, c) it consists of rigorous and reflective inquiry to test and refine learning environments, d) it involves the continual refinement of protocols and questions, and there is a commitment to theory construction and explanation, among other reasons (Reeves et al., 2005). Others, such as Richey and Klein (2005) provided insights into the importance of developmental research, which seeks to create knowledge grounded on data systematically derived from practice. In particular, developmental research addresses areas such as product design and development, product evaluation, validation of tool or technique, model development, model use, and model validation. "It is research that is intricately connected to real-world practice" (Richey & Klein, 2005) and due to its complexity was construed of a mixed-method approach that could involve: case study, survey research, expert review, experimental research, interviews, replication, observations, document analysis, and others. Last, in support of post-positivist views in educational research and the use of qualitative methods in the educational technology research, Savenye and Robinson (2005) provided a comprehensive overview on the appropriate use of qualitative methods, its characteristics, the various types of qualitative methodologies, and assumptions that are often made about these types of research methods. Although extensive discussions about quantitative and qualitative comparisons had already occurred many years ago (Howe, 1985; Phillips, 1983), Savenye and Robinson (2005) aimed to share some of the challenges and opportunities that researchers should consider when conducting qualitative research. Even after years of discussions related to the importance of post-positivist views in educational research, Savenye and Robinson (2005) reiterate that researchers conducting qualitative inquiry faced challenges related to "proof of rigor" through generalizability, validity, and reliability imposed by those who strive to treat qualitative research with an experimental research mindset.

Perhaps one of the most devastating aspects of this revolving door of discussion about adequate use of research methods and the different paradigms was the skepticism that it created towards educational technology, its validity, and its impact in education settings (Hannafin et al., 2005). By 2005, despite thousands of investigations on the topic of educational technology, definite answers remained disturbingly elusive about the impact of technology to support individualization, improve efficiency, and improved access to learning experiences (Hannafin et al., 2005). According to Hannafin et al. (2005), contributions to the yielding of so many contradictory findings in educational technology literature included: "the emphasis on comparison research, emphasis on laboratory research, differences in

problem framing and research methodology, bias toward statistically significant effects and the primacy of individual disciplines" (p. 8). Recommendations to elevate educational technology research and its endeavors went far
beyond specific methodologies. Instead, to improve research quality he
proposed a framework for educational research that considered a deeper
understanding of levels of research and considerations of use. Similar recommendations were given by Klein, Martin, Tutty, and Su (2005) who during
the same time period published a study focused on the research methods,
processes, and issues taught to instructional design and technology graduate
students. The findings from the investigation revealed that instructional
design and technology graduate students were taught: a) a range of quantitative and qualitative methodologies in research courses and b) typical steps
for how to conduct a research study. However, the results of the study also
revealed that learning about the professional context of research was not to
be covered in depth in instructional design and technology research courses.
Moreover, the research processes taught less often in instructional design
research courses included: selecting a research design, sampling participants,
and developing data-collection instruments (Klein et al., 2005).

Today: Research Methods Galore

Over the last decade research in education and educational technology has
continued to grow and made important contributions to advance our
understanding of the study and ethical practice of facilitating learning and
improving performance (Romero-Hall et al., 2018). To do so, scholars
have relied on advances in educational technology research methods that
have sought to overcome more traditional techniques. This methodological
push forward has included research addressing questions related to types of
learning interactions (Jung, Zimmerman, & Pérez-Edgar, 2018), content
created, geolocation (Greenhalgh, Staudt Willet, Rosenberg, & Koehler,
2018), learners' and instructors' experiences (Dennen & Rutledge, 2018;
Gratch & Warren, 2018), to name a few. The variety of learning environments in which this research occurs continues to change at a rapid pace. As
stated by Romero-Hall et al. (2018) "we are no longer interested in the
learning outcomes, we also want to know how, where, and why learning
occurs" (p. 1).

To reiterate, our current research practice and literature reveal that we
continue to rely on traditional methods, but keep on pushing methodological boundaries to further explore topics of interest. In 1976 Gene Glass
initiated a research synthesis methodology called "meta-analysis." As stated
by N. L. Cage, meta-analysis aimed to estimate the effect size from
knowledge based on the number of results that go in the same direction
in a cluster of studies (Farley, 1982). Today meta-analysis, as well as meta-
synthesis, are used in educational technology research to more deeply
understand trends and patterns on research findings across multiple studies

(Leary & Walker, 2018). Similarly, qualitative research methods such as phenomenology (Valentine, Kopcha, & Vagle, 2018) and critical ethnography (Gratch & Warren, 2018) are not new. Yet, at present, non-descriptive phenomenologies can offer great approaches to the educational technology field by helping study and better understand ambiguous and hard to define phenomena in learning, design, and teaching experiences (Valentine et al., 2018). Likewise, critical ethnography in education now goes beyond traditional analysis of learning discourses for identity, power, relationship, and other systemic components (Gratch & Warren, 2018). Critical ethnography methods have morphed into Critical CinéEthnography (Gratch & Warren, 2018), which employs audio-visual analysis (in the digital experience and out of the class discussion) and analysis of learning artifacts.

Other methodologies such as mobile eye tracking are now used in educational technology research to understand learning processes by tracing a learner's gaze and attention as they move around in a particular location (Jung et al., 2018). This is an advancement from research using stationary eye-tracking studies in educational technology, which has already been used for research in gaming and computer-based simulated environments (Jung et al., 2018; Enilda Romero-Hall, Watson, & Papelis, 2014; Romero-Hall, Watson, Adcock, Bliss, & Adams Tufts, 2016). Another example of the adaptation of research methods is the practice of public internet data mining in educational research (Kimmons & Veletsianos, 2018) and particular research related to social media (Greenhalgh et al., 2018). As stated by Romero-Hall et al. (2018), "research on large datasets on public domain has posed a new opportunity for instructional design and technology topics. This methodology can lead to extracting knowledge and gaining an understanding of topics through complex, interdisciplinary, and multidimensional data".

There are many other emerging research methodologies used in education and educational technology research, such as art-based research (Culshaw, 2019), autoethnography (Romero-Hall et al., 2018), biometrics methods (Romero, 2014), action research (Arslan-Ari, Ari, Grant, & Morris, 2018), Q methodology (Walker, Lin, & McCline, 2018), and learning analytics, among others. In a research study conducted by West and Borup (2014), an analysis of research papers published in ten major journals in the educational technology field from 2001 to 2010 revealed that interpretative/qualitative papers comprised 26% of the total papers and inferential papers that focused primarily on descriptive statistics made up 22% of the total papers. These results appeared to show a balance between qualitative and quantitative, with other research methods emerging (West & Borup, 2014).

The goal of this book is to provide IDT researchers with knowledge and guidance on different methodologies that can help address their novel research questions. IDT scholars need to have a solid foundation of the different methods that can be taken to investigate a research problem. This foundation aids researchers in understanding the rationale for the application of specific procedures or techniques used to identify, select, process, and analyze information applied to understand a research question. The way a researcher approaches a question will have a profound effect on the way they construct and explore their investigation and the results that the inquiry will yield. Ideally, this chapter has served to share some of the histories of research methods in the learning design and technology field, understanding this discourse can potentially help us move forward and avoid duplicating settled arguments.

One last important matter before you move forward with reading the chapters presented in this book; *learning design and technology* is used as an umbrella term that refers to instructional design, instructional design and technology, educational technology, and instructional technology. All of these terms have been employed by practitioners, scholars, and professional organizations in our field to work towards a similar goal, "to study and ethical practice of facilitating learning and improving performance by creating, using, and managing appropriate technological processes and resources" (Definition and Terminology Committee of the Association for Educational Communications and Technology, 2007, p. 1).

References

Arslan-Ari, I., Ari, F., Grant, M. M., & Morris, W. S. (2018). Action research experiences for scholarly practitioners in an online education doctorate program: Design, reality, and lessons learned. *TechTrends*, *62*(5), 441–449. doi:10.1007/s11528-018-0308-3.

Definition and Terminology Committee of the Association for Educational Communications and Technology. (2007). Definition. In A. Januszewski & M. Molenda (Eds.), *Educational technology: A definition with commentary* (pp. 1–14). New York, NY: Routledge.

Brown, A. L. (1992). Design experiments: Theoretical and methodological challenges in creating complex interventions in classroom settings. *Journal of the Learning Sciences*, *2*(2), 141–178. doi:10.1207/s15327809jls0202_2.

Culshaw, S. (2019). The unspoken power of collage? Using an innovative arts-based research method to explore the experience of struggling as a teacher. *London Review of Education*, *17*(3), 268–283. doi:10.18546/LRE.17.3.03.

Cziko, G. A. (1989). Unpredictability and indeterminism in human behavior: Arguments and implications for educational research. *Educational Researcher*, *18*(3), 17–25. doi:10.2307/1174887.

Dennen, V. P. & Rutledge, S. A. (2018). The embedded lesson approach to social media research: Researching online phenomena in an authentic offline setting. *TechTrends*, *62*(5), 483–491. doi:10.1007/s11528-018-0315-4.

Farley, F. H. (1982). The future of educational research. *Educational Researcher*, *11*(8), 11–19. doi:10.2307/1175580.

Gratch, J. & Warren, S. J. (2018). Critical cinéethnographic methods: A new dimension for capturing the experience of learning in twenty-first century qualitative research. *TechTrends*, *62*(5), 473–482. doi:10.1007/s11528-018-0316-3.

Greenhalgh, S. P., Staudt Willet, K. B., Rosenberg, J. M., & Koehler, M. J. (2018). Tweet, and we shall find: Using digital methods to locate participants in educational hashtags. *TechTrends*, *62*(5), 501–508. doi:10.1007/s11528-018-0313-6.

Hannafin, M., Orrill, C., Kim, H., & Kim, M. (2005). Educational technology research in postsecondary settings: Promise, problems, and prospects. *Journal of Computing in Higher Education*, *16*(2), 3–22. doi:10.1007/BF02961472.

Howe, K. R. (1985). Two dogmas of educational research. *Educational Researcher, 14* (8), 10–18. doi:10.3102/0013189X014008010.

Jung, Y. J., Zimmerman, H. T., & Pérez-Edgar, K. (2018). A methodological case study with mobile eye-tracking of child interaction in a science museum. *TechTrends*, *62*(5), 509–517. doi:10.1007/s11528-018-0310-9.

Klein, J., Martin, F., Tutty, J., & Su, Y. (2005). Teaching research to instructional design and technology students. *Educational Technology*, *45*(4), 29–33. Retrieved June 23, 2020, from www.jstor.org/stable/44429219

Kimmons, R. & Veletsianos, G. (2018). Public internet data mining methods in instructional design, educational technology, and online learning research. *TechTrends*, *62*(5), 492–500. doi:10.1007/s11528-018-0307-4.

Leary, H. & Walker, A. (2018). Meta-analysis and meta-synthesis methodologies: Rigorously piecing together research. *TechTrends*, *62*(5), 525–534. doi:10.1007/s11528-018-0312-7.

Mayer, R. E. (2003). Learning environments: The case for evidence-based practice and issue-driven research. *Educational Psychology Review*, *15*(4), 359–366. doi:10.1023/A:1026179332694.

Phillips, D. C. (1983). After the wake: Postpositivistic educational thought. *Educational Researcher*, *12*(5), 4–12. doi:10.2307/1175133.

Reeves, T. C., Herrington, J., & Oliver, R. (2005). Design research: A socially responsible approach to instructional technology research in higher education. *Journal of Computing in Higher Education*, *16*(2), 96. doi:10.1007/BF02961476.

Richey, R. C. & Klein, J. D. (2005). Developmental research methods: Creating knowledge from instructional design and development practice. *Journal of Computing in Higher Education*, *16*(2), 23–38. doi:10.1007/BF02961473.

Romero, E. (2014). *Measuring cognition in computer-based instruction using an EEG: A review of the literature*. Paper presented at the EdMedia: World Conference on Educational Media and Technology 2014, Tampere, Finland. www.learntechlib.org/p/147828.

Romero-Hall, E., Aldemir, T., Colorado-Resa, J., Dickson-Deane, C., Watson, G. S., & Sadaf, A. (2018). Undisclosed stories of instructional design female scholars in academia. *Women's Studies International Forum*, *71*, 19–28. doi:10.1016/j.wsif.2018.09.004.

Romero-Hall, E., Hsiao, E. L., & Gao, F. (2018). The (re)adaptability of research methodologies in the instructional design & technology field. *TechTrends*, *62*(5), 424–426. doi:10.1007/s11528-018-0321-6.

Romero-Hall, E., Watson, G., & Papelis, Y. (2014). Using physiological measures to assess the effects of animated pedagogical agents in multimedia instruction. *Journal of Educational Multimedia & Hypermedia*, *23*(4), 359–384. Retrieved from http://esearch.ut.edu/login?url=http://search.ebscohost.com/login.aspx?direct=true&db=eft&AN=100297275&site=ehost-live.

Romero-Hall, E., Watson, G. S., Adcock, A., Bliss, J., & Adams Tufts, K. (2016). Simulated environments with animated agents: Effects on visual attention, emotion, performance, and perception. *Journal of Computer Assisted Learning, 32*(4), 360–373. doi:10.1111/jcal.12138.

Ross, S. M., Morrison, G. R., & Lowther, D. L. (2005). Using experimental methods in higher education research. *Journal of Computing in Higher Education, 16*(2), 39–64. doi:10.1007/BF02961474.

Savenye, W. C. & Robinson, R. S. (2005). Using qualitative research methods in higher education. *Journal of Computing in Higher Education, 16*(2), 65–95. doi:10.1007/BF02961475

Saxe, G. B. (1992). Studying children's learning in context: Problems and prospects. *Journal of the Learning Sciences, 2*(2), 215–234. doi:10.1207/s15327809jls0202_4.

Schoenfeld, A. H. (1992a). On paradigms and methods: What do you do when the ones you know don't do what you want them to? Issues in the analysis of data in the form of videotapes. *Journal of the Learning Sciences, 2*(2), 179–214. doi:10.1207/s15327809jls0202_3.

Schoenfeld, A. H. (1992b). Research methods in and for the learning sciences. *Journal of the Learning Sciences, 2*(2), 137–139. doi:10.1207/s15327809jls0202_1.

Smith, J. K. (1983). Quantitative versus qualitative research: An attempt to clarify the issue. *Educational Researcher, 12*(3), 6–13. doi:10.2307/1175144.

Valentine, K. D., Kopcha, T. J., & Vagle, M. D. (2018). Phenomenological methodologies in the field of educational communications and technology. *Tech-Trends, 62*(5), 462–472. doi:10.1007/s11528-018-0317-2.

Walker, B. B., Lin, Y., & McCline, R. M. (2018). Q methodology and Q-perspectives® online: Innovative research methodology and instructional technology. *TechTrends, 62*(5), 450–461. doi:10.1007/s11528-018-0314-5.

West, R. E. & Borup, J. (2014). An analysis of a decade of research in 10 instructional design and technology journals. *British Journal of Educational Technology, 45*(4), 545–556. doi:10.1111/bjet.12081.

Winn, W. (2002). Current trends in educational technology research: The study of learning environments. *Educational Psychology Review, 14*(3), 331–351. Retrieved from http://search.ebscohost.com/login.aspx?direct=true&db=pbh&AN=7045787&site=ehost-live.

Winn, W. (2003). Research methods and types of evidence for research in educational technology. *Educational Psychology Review, 15*(4), 367–373. doi:10.1023/A:1026131416764.

2 Interpretive and Postmodern Phenomenological Research Approaches

Opportunities for New Lines of Inquiry in the Field of Learning Design and Technology

Keri Duncan Valentine

Introduction

Phenomenology, as both a philosophical and methodological approach, investigates phenomena "as we live them rather than as we conceptualize or theorize them" (van Manen, 2014, p. 41). This is a significant distinction. Crossley (1996), for example, illustrates the problematics inherent with objectivist positions: "For objectivists, the inclination is towards 'scientific' methods ... these methods ignore the fact that the social world is meaningful to those who live in it, and they (the methods) impose their own, seemingly arbitrary meanings onto it" (pp. 74–75). At the same time, phenomenology should not be characterized as merely subjective, such as we see in narrative and other subjectivist orientations. Instead, phenomena mark the analytical focus, emphasizing the interrelatedness between subjects and objects as they manifest in the world, a world pregnant with culture, history, symbols, etc. Phenomenology is best characterized as a critical orientation. It "calls into question what is taken for granted. It is critique and grounds a critical methodology" (Crotty, 1998, p. 82).

Phenomenology first emerged as an epistemological, philosophical project concerning consciousness and was soon after taken up as an ontological project concerning being (e.g., existentialism, embodiment). Phenomenology is similar to postmodernism in that it resists the modernist, Enlightenment project to define reason and rationality as separate from culture and human experience. Hermeneutic phenomenologist Hans-Georg Gadamer, for example, argues that "Understanding, by its very nature ... is an occurrence in which history is operative" (2001, p. 45). This complex view of phenomena, such as their historical and cultural entwinements, informs both the philosophical and methodological approaches.

This chapter seeks to support researchers in the field of learning design and technology (LDT) to consider critical aspects and affordances of phenomenological inquiry. First, the philosophical foundations of phenomenology are traced to demonstrate the plurality of methodological approaches. Next, the chapter situates and advocates for interpretive and postmodern phenomenological approaches by considering foci that these forms of phenomenology might open up within LDT. Key considerations are explicated regarding data sources, analysis, and other research practices within these approaches.

Variations within Phenomenology

Phenomenology has a long history as both a philosophical and methodological approach, with variations of each emerging over the past century. As much has been written comparing the variant philosophical approaches in phenomenology (Moran & Mooney, 2002; Vagle, 2018; Valentine, Kopcha, & Vagle, 2018; van Manen, 2014), only a brief philosophical trajectory is offered to ground this chapter's methodological discussion. Edmund Husserl is credited as the "principal founder" of the phenomenological movement in philosophy (Beyer, 2018, para. 1). Breaking with the Cartesian tradition, Husserl criticized Descartes's method of "scientifically validating by deduction the existence of the world as corresponding to his ideas of it" (Jean-Marc Laporte, 1963, p. 340). Writing, "to the things themselves," Husserl, 1970 described consciousness as reaching out towards the world—consciousness is conscious of something. Methodologically, phenomena should be described as they are given to consciousness, and thus become manifest in lived experience.

Heidegger, Sartre, Merleau-Ponty, Gadamer, and others shifted the focus from "consciousness of" to "being in," investigating the ontological and hermeneutic aspects of phenomena such as tool use, perception, illness, method, and time. Even still, "to the things themselves" sustained as a call for a phenomenological investigation as Merleau-Ponty (1945/2002) articulated:

> To return to the things themselves is to return to that world which precedes knowledge, of which knowledge always *speaks*, and in relation to which every scientific schematization is an abstract and derivative sign-language, as is geography in relation to the country-side in which we have learnt beforehand what a forest, a prairie or a river is.
>
> (pp. ix–x)

Merleau-Ponty is conveying the relationship that humans have with their world—one of being in and to the world. Abstractions, such as models and scientific theories, are thus rooted in human experience. Even in the field of mathematics, Lakoff and Núñez (2000) show how mathematical systems emerged from the human experience with phenomena in the world.

In the following sections, three approaches for phenomenological inquiry are discussed: a hermeneutic approach, a reflective lifeworld approach, and a post-intentional phenomenological approach. While many methodological variations exist, the three discussed below are tied to well-known methodologists and each considers the ontological and hermeneutic foundations just described.

Van Manen's Hermeneutic Approach

van Manen (2014) emphasizes that "every possible human experience (event, happening, incident, occurrence, object, relation, situation, thought, feeling, and so on) may become a topic for phenomenological inquiry" (p. 38). He makes a point to argue for investigations of a phenomenon we take for granted or assume we understand to open up possibilities and potentialities, arguing for a complex perspective regarding appearance:

> The main task of phenomenological research is an interpretive description of the primordial meaning structures of lived experience—a graphic depiction of phenomena just as they give and show themselves in what appears or gives itself. In other words, what "appears" is not at all something apparent or clear-given. If it were, then phenomenology would not be necessary: we would simply see what it is that "appears."
>
> (p. 61)

Van Manen's hermeneutic approach would be useful to those seeking to understand a wide array of phenomena as they manifest in human relationships, in spaces, and even in literature.

van Manen (2014) traces many forms of phenomenology (e.g., ethical, feminist, ecological), articulating his own approach as a "hermeneutic or interpretive-descriptive phenomenology" (p. 26). His approach foregrounds wonder: "Phenomenological research begins with wonder at what gives itself and how something gives itself. It can only be pursued while surrendering to a state of wonder" (p. 27). He recently investigated the phenomenon of pedagogical tact, creating a text that opens up educational moments such as immediacy, worry, and even the "faceless" student (2015, p. 74). Van Manen views phenomenology as an approach that "cannot be fitted to a rule book, an interpretive schema, a set of steps, or a systematic set of procedures" (p. 29). However, he does offer guidance concerning possibilities for data sources, data analysis, and especially writing up phenomenological research. While data sources and analysis will be detailed later in this chapter, it is essential to note that van Manen conceptualizes phenomenological analysis and writing as occurring together in the research project.

Dahlberg, Dahlberg, and Nyström's Reflective Lifeworld Approach

As the title of Dahlberg, Dahlberg, and Nyström's (2008) book suggests, their approach can be characterized as a reflective lifeworld approach where the practice of researcher openness with the phenomenon is emphasized. Drawing heavily on Merleau-Ponty's (1968, 2002) embodied phenomenology and especially his notion of "the flesh of the world," Dahlberg et al. emphasize the lived world as embodied—a connection between mind, body, and society. They underline the flesh's hidden nature and see the researcher's role as opening up phenomenon as they manifest in the lived, embodied world of humans: "As humans, we live as subjects in and through our bodies. All understanding, our memory, perception, emotional and cognitive relations to the world, is embodied" (p. 45). A central activity in Dahlberg et al.'s approach is to remain open to the phenomenon, attempting to show what is oftentimes invisible. This is achieved in part through a practice they term "bridling." Bridling refers to the researcher holding back understanding in an attempt to let the phenomenon show itself, in other words, "to have the patience to wait for the phenomenon to reveal its own complexity rather than imposing an external structure on it, such as the dogmatic use of theories or models" (p. 112).

The reflective lifeworld approach would be useful to those seeking to understand phenomena as they manifest bodily in one's experience (e.g., living with an illness, moving in augmented reality). Nyström, Dahlberg, and Carlsson (2003), for example, used the reflective lifeworld approach to investigate "non-caring encounters at an emergency care unit" (p. 761). They were able to explicate the ways in which nurses and patients adapt to organizational expectations regarding efficiency, highlighting a lack of presence on the part of nurses. Recommendations emerging from their study suggest the need to focus on caring competencies in nurse education. In this way, phenomenological research findings can inform the work of designers by illuminating phenomenon as an interconnected system of beings embodied in contexts, such as the emergency care unit.

Vagle's Post-Intentional Approach

Vagle (2018) conveys phenomenology's aims, distinguishing phenomenology from constructivist and representational approaches: "phenomenologists set out to study how things are being and becoming—not how individuals construct things nor how the mathematical sciences represent things" (p. 23). Vagle's (2018) methodological approach, post-intentional phenomenology, conceptualizes phenomenon as being "produced and provoked." Drawing on Deleuze and Guattari's (1988) notion of "lines of flight," these phenomena are always in a state of becoming, "taking shape" as contexts, beings, researchers, histories, etc. converge and repel. This living and active notion of phenomena foregrounds their complexity and the fact that any understanding stemming from a phenomenological investigation will be necessarily partial, temporal, and entangled with social, political, cultural, and historical contexts.

Post-intentional phenomenology would be useful to those seeking to understand the complex, fleeting, and power-laden nature of phenomena. Vagle (2019) recently highlighted the way in which a post-intentional phenomenological approach "might produce social change, however great or small" (para. 1). This argument rests on the idea that phenomena are embraced "as social and not as belonging to the individual . . . experiences are 'shot through' the world" (Vagle, 2018, p. 46). In this way, researchers using a post-intentional phenomenological approach would account for the ways in which social "systems," "habits," and "practices" play a role in producing and provoking phenomena. Almost 30 years ago, Patti Lather (1992) indicated the ways in which technology is deeply intertwined with social concerns: "the profound effect that electronic mediation exerts on the way we perceive ourselves and reality is occurring in a world marked by gross maldistribution of power and resources" (p. 88). A post-intentional phenomenological approach would be a viable way to investigate this exertion of technology, especially considering the bodily, social, economic, cultural, and even political dimensions of humans living with and through technology.

Possible Lines of Inquiry in Learning Design and Technology

Phenomenology's aim is primarily one of seeking understanding and meaning regarding lived phenomenon, which includes those involved in learning design and technology. This aligns with the goals of basic research as Stokes (1997) articulates, as the quest for fundamental understanding. In LDT, we are also concerned with applied research, guided by a consideration of use. These concerns are evidenced by iterative design research/design-based research projects that seek to inform both theory and iterative design. While phenomenology might be characterized as a quest for understanding, phenomenological studies also contribute to characterizations of use, such as creating social change, educational reform, and design considerations. van Manen's (2015) study of pedagogical tact, for example, portrayed teacher–student interactions, such as facelessness, in ways that call for changes in education that differ from more achievement-oriented aims. In this way, phenomenology is a viable approach to inform critical and emancipatory work.

In addition to aligning to the research interests in LDT, phenomenological approaches afford researchers opportunities to investigate phenomena concerned with learning design and technology, such as the manifestation of design activity or experiences being in augmented reality. In the sections below, possible LDT phenomena researchers might consider are detailed. While dimensions of LDT are discussed separately, phenomenology can support researchers who want to investigate overlaps as well.

Learning

As learning is a complex activity, manifesting across contexts, with others, and mediated by tools and culture, there are many ways to frame, ground, and investigate the event. While a proliferation of research exists regarding psychological learning constructs (e.g., motivation, transfer, disposition), there is little that speaks to the phenomenological nature of *being in/living through* moments of learning. While narrative inquiry can detail the life story of a particular person, phenomenology differs in that it is oriented to the lived phenomenon (not individuals). Rather than begin an investigation with a psychological construct or measurement, even a "problem to be solved or a question to be answered," phenomenology "almost always starts with wonder or passes through a phase of wonder ... Wonder is the disposition that has a dis-positional effect: it dislocates and displaces us" (van Manen, 2014, p. 37). Rather than ask if a student learned a concept, phenomenology would seek to understand the way learning phenomena emerge in the world.

It is this "dis-positional" effect that motivated a series of phenomenological investigations by Valentine and Kopcha (2014, 2016, in press). Investigating learning in a middle school mathematics classroom started from a place of wonder and led to studying moments of shift in perspective, problematization activity, and embodiment as experienced by learners. While the learning environment design was informed by learning theories and domain-specific considerations—Cognitive Flexibility Theory (Spiro, Coulson, Feltovich, & Anderson, 1988) and Realistic Mathematics Education (Freudenthal, 1973)—the post-intentional phenomenological study that followed was motivated by wonder related to shift and problematization. This way of approaching investigations of learning can reframe investigations as involving more than measures of proficiency, disposition, and other psychological measures. Valentine and Kopcha (2014), for example, showed how learners' experiences investigating relations between dimensions (0D, 1D, 2D, 3D, 4D) emerged as an "ontological trying on" of dimensions, in part by imagining what it might be like to see, eat, and move as a different dimensional creature in various dimensional spaces. Davis (1994) investigated the phenomenon of teacher listening in a mathematics classroom, opening up the complex relation between students and teachers during moments of learning. I imagine many phenomena related to learning would benefit from a phenomenological lens, such as pedagogical moments and lived struggle.

Design

Phenomenological approaches, focused on understanding the way phenomena emerge as lived, is well-suited for informing iterative design-based research and considering the design of educational technologies.

Post-intentional phenomenological approaches are especially helpful for informing design work guided by a critical, social justice, or emancipatory lens. Owen (2007) emphasized that designers need to account for human and environmental concerns in addition to considering optimization—otherwise the "best" design on paper could contribute to inaccessibility, environmental contamination, etc. By investigating phenomenon associated with one's design, such as the way learners' struggle manifests in a designed learning environment, one is better positioned to consider next iterations. Valentine and Bolyard (2019), for example, investigated moments of shift while learning mathematics on the part of elementary pre-service teachers. While previous research conceptualized shifts as a single event, the phenomenological investigation revealed the tentative and temporal nature of lived shift, as well as opening up the way shifts manifest in relations with other people and with mathematical objects.

Phenomenological investigations might support designers to consider drawing on a variety of design lenses (interpretive, critical, emancipatory). Just as "teaching and learning mathematics are not politically neutral activities" (Gutiérrez, 2012, 2013), design is also an entangled, non-neutral activity, compellingly conveyed by Winograd and Flores (1986). They foreground the embodied and ethical relations in design:

> All new technologies develop within the background of a tacit understanding of human nature and human work. The use of technology in turn leads to fundamental changes in what we do, and ultimately in what it is to be human. We encounter the deep questions of design when we recognize that in designing tools we are designing ways of being.
>
> (p. xi)

Regardless of the designer or design-based researcher's aims, understanding how one's design opens up or constricts ways of being should be taken seriously.

Technology

Amiel and Reeves (2008) contend, "educational technology research aimed at examining the influence of tools in the educational process has offered little systematic advice to the practitioner" (p. 30). They argue for a shift in the way technology is both conceived and investigated: "recognizing technology as a *process* has implications for how educational technologists conduct research" (p. 30). As a value-laden process, they highlight "the complex interaction between technological interventions, the roles of educational institutions such as schools and universities, the purposes of education, and the meaning of research" (p. 32). Phenomenological approaches, especially post-intentional phenomenology, can support investigations that seek to understand technology in this way. Phenomenological approaches grounded in existential and embodied perspectives have the potential to open up the nature of lived spaces mediated by technology and even the social and cultural aspects of living, learning, and communicating with technology. Ihde (1993), for example, used "postphenomenology" to investigate technology as a cultural instrument. He argued strongly that "technologies must be understood *phenomenologically*, i.e., as belonging in different ways to our experience and use of technologies, as a human–technology relation, rather than abstractly conceiving of them as mere objects" (p. 34). He attends to several such human–technology relations: embodied, hermeneutic, alterity, and background.

Examples of current phenomenological investigations related to technology can be found in Valentine and Jensen (2016) as well as in Jensen, Valentine, and Case (2019), both focused on video game play experiences. The 2016 investigation sought to understand the ways in which perspectival shifts emerge for players in indie video games. A postphenomenological lens opened up connections between the game space, the game characters, and the player. The authors found that perspectival mechanics, such as the ones in *Fez* (Polytron Corporation, 2013), required players to "simultaneously transform the environment, the objects in the environment, and one's egocentric reference frames, illustrating the complex nature intrinsic within video game spaces" (p. 309). The investigation was able to open up how these perspectival mechanics in video games are both created and experienced, connecting the design of indie games to the more significant DIY movement.

Jensen et al. (2019) recently considered the phenomenon of play in the location-based, augmented reality game *Pokémon GO* (Niantic & The Pokémon Company, 2016). They show how *Pokémon GO* offers players access to a "Pokélayer," an "imaginary possibility space made real by the game" (p. 100). For the players in the study, "this playful experience was often the most potent when it intertwined with daily life events" (p. 100). As technologies change how people communicate, advocate, learn, and play, there are many possible phenomena worthy of exploration. For example, what might a phenomenological investigation into #MeToo (Brown, 2018) and #WhyIDidntReport (Baty, 2018) open up about the ways social media exposes and shapes lived trauma? While this possible investigation falls in line with cultural and media studies, it also speaks to how technologies mediate healing and activism.

As shown in the learning design and technology sections above, many opportunities exist for new lines of inquiry in the field. For those interested in exploring additional ways that phenomena in learning design and technology have been explored using phenomenological approaches, Kennedy's (2016) dissertation provides a review of 65 phenomenological research studies. She finds that most use descriptive (29) and interpretive (32) phenomenological approaches. The remaining four draw on postmodern phenomenological approaches, grounded in both Ihde (1993) and Vagle (2014).

Methodological Considerations: Data Sources, Analysis, and the Role of Reflexivity

Conducting hermeneutic, reflective lifeworld or post-intentional phenomenological research is challenging. This is due in part because of the complex (and evolving) philosophical foundations informing methodological choices, the commitment needed to maintain a patient and reflexive practice, and the iterative, dynamic nature of the data collection, analysis, and writing process. While there are several possible approaches for carrying out a phenomenological investigation, phenomenologists do not consider methods as fixed (Gadamer, 1994; Vagle, 2018; van Manen, 2014). van Manen (2014) states that phenomenological research "cannot be fitted to a rule book, an interpretive schema, a set of steps, or a systematic set of procedures" (p. 29). At the same time, there are several commitments each of the methodologists described in this chapter adhere to when investigating phenomenon as they are lived (and not as participants interpret them); maintaining patience and openness by engaging in a bridling or post-reflexive practice throughout all phases of the investigation; and engaging in multiple stages of data analysis using holistic and fine-grain cycles. The sections below detail methodological possibilities for gathering and analyzing data as well as considerations for a reflexive practice. The aim is to convey possible ways these phenomenological commitments might be carried out.

Data Sources

Phenomenological research views "the experience [as] the ultimate bearer of meaning" rather than "theory, linguistic formulation, or abstractive construction" (van Manen, 2014, p. 65). Any data source that provides access to phenomena as lived, "which presents itself directly—unmediated by thought or language," is a possible data source in phenomenological research (van Manen, 2014, p. 42). While eliciting lived-experience descriptions in written form and through interviews is a common way to access lived phenomenon, Vagle (2018) and van Manen (2014) articulate several other data sources that allow researchers to glean phenomenological insights. These include observations, media (e.g., Twitter's #MeToo thread), arts-based sources (e.g., photo-elicitation, visual, and performance arts), and even fictional writing. As phenomena are always in the process of becoming, data is always *a* possible experience. However, these possible experiences make singularly knowable (van Manen, 2014). Additional data might come from cultural sources, historical sources, language, literary and aesthetic sources, phenomenological sources, and social scientific sources (van Manen, 2019). There are no limits for phenomenological inquiry as long as it supports researchers to "open a phenomenon of interest" (Vagle, 2018, p. 86).

Whole-Part-Whole Analysis

The unit of analysis in phenomenology is "the phenomenon and the intentional meanings that run through and 'make up' the phenomenon's very fabric" (Vagle, 2018, p. 78). Valentine et al. (2018) describe in more detail intentional meanings and the phenomenological notion of intentionality. However, it will suffice to state here that intentionality, regardless of phenomenological perspective, locates meaning in the connections between people, things, ideas, attitudes, objects, and the world (e.g., conscious of, being in)—rather than in any one of these as isolated. Vagle (2018) further adds that in the post-intentional phenomenological approach, "the unit of analysis is not only seen as something an individual experiences but also as a social apparatus" (p. 140).

When analyzing phenomenological data in the interpretive and reflective lifeworld approaches, van Manen (2014), Vagle (2018), and Dahlberg et al. (2008) each advocate for some form of a whole-part-whole analysis process. This involves attending to the text or data source as a whole (without immediately analyzing), followed by a series of line-by-line readings, and then a return to the larger data set (and the broader phenomenon) to make sense of the phenomena across particular manifestations. If researchers choose to engage with Dahlberg et al.'s (2008) process, they will likely be on the lookout for patterns of meaning; with van Manen (2014), themes. Table 2.1, elaborates on a possible whole-part-whole process indicative of interpretive and reflective lifeworld approaches as Vagle (2018) describes.

Analysis in Post-intentional Phenomenology

In Vagle's (2018) post-intentional phenomenological approach, phenomena "flee, elude, flow, and leak," and as researchers, we "focus on *how things connect* rather than on *what things are*" (pp. 128–129). Vagle's post-intentional phenomenological approach to analysis consists of three parts: deconstructing the wholes in the data set, thinking with theory, and drawing on post-reflexive journaling activity as part of the analytic process. With this analytic approach, the researcher engages in one round of line-by-line reading and then proceeds to deconstructing the wholes. To deconstruct the wholes, Vagle uses Deleuze and Guattari's (1987) notion of lines of flight to recommend "two analytic 'noticings' . . . actively look for ways that knowledge 'takes off'" and "distinguish lines of flight from other lines operating on us and the phenomenon" (pp. 157–158). Within these two noticings, he poses a series of questions to consider, such as:

- What doesn't seem to fit? If I follow this "mis-fit" notion, idea, insight, perspective, what might I learn about the phenomenon that is not yet thinkable? (p. 157)

Table 2.1 Whole-Part-Whole Process Detailed in Vagle (2018)

Analytic Steps	Description of Process
Step 1: Holistic Reading of Entire Text	A holistic reading of the entire text refers to "getting attuned" to all data sources such as transcripts, observations, and other artifacts (p. 110). Getting attuned is a way of reading through the data without note taking. The aim is to consider "the whole material-gathering event" before spending time with individual data sources (p. 110).
Step 2: First Line-by-Line Reading	The line-by-line reading refers to "careful note-taking and marking of excerpts that appear to contain initial meanings" for each data source (p. 110). During the first line-by-line reading, the researcher might start by chunking the text, such as an anecdote or story from an interview that articulates a particular experiential moment important to the phenomenon. Vagle recommends inserting "margin notes that might be questions (e.g., How does this influence her recognition of [the student's] understanding?) at times and statements (e.g., potential meaning 'having an idea in your head') at other times" (p. 110). During the first line-by-line reading, and subsequent readings, the researcher should also engage in post-reflexive journaling (or bridling) where thoughts related to the phenomenon or process are captured. This "allows one to harness what is being read and thought" (p. 110).
Step 3: Follow-Up Questions	After the first line-by-line reading, the researcher should "review margin notes in order to craft follow-up questions for each participant. These questions should be designed to clarify intentional meanings that one predicts, at the early stages of analysis, might be important to describe/interpret/represent the phenomenon" (pp. 110–111).
Step 4: Second Line-by-Line Reading	The second line-by-line reading entails "articulating the meanings, based on the markings, margin notes, and the follow-up with research participants" (p. 111). At this stage, it is beneficial to create a document for each participant that will "contain all of the potential parts that the researcher thinks might contribute to the phenomenological text" (p. 111).
Step 5: Third Line-by-Line Reading	During the third line-by-line reading, the research should write though "analytic thoughts about each part" for "each participant's interview/description/observation" (p. 111).
Step 6: Subsequent Readings	Subsequent readings involve "reading across individual participants' phenomenological material, with the goal of looking for what van Manen would most likely call 'themes' ... Once you begin to see themes/patterns of meaning/meaning units you should give them preliminary titles" (p. 111). During this process, analytic thoughts might be both added and deleted.

- Where might I have retreated to either/or thinking? (p. 158)
- Where might I appear "certain" of what something means? (p. 158)
- Where might I have extended to something creative and intriguing, but then backed off to something a bit more safe? (p. 158)
- Where might I appear "uncertain" of what something means? (p. 158)

Deconstructing the wholes is followed by thinking with theory, as Jackson and Mazzei (2012) demonstrate, and then analyzing post-reflexions through a process of unpacking. It is important to note that this process is an iterative one where the researcher should feel free to move between the analytic activities described above.

The Role of Theory in the Analysis

Vagle (2018) and van Manen (2014) talk in depth about the role of theory in the phenomenological analysis. While theories "should not be used to determine or test how humans experience the world" (Vagle, 2018, p. 81), theories are part of the world, and thus phenomena. They should be brought to bear during the later stages of analysis. van Manen (2014) purports three uses for theory in phenomenology: (1) "to show where the promise of theory fails to remain fulfilled," (2) "bring in theory where theory and phenomenology intersect in the understanding of human phenomena," and (3) "phenomenological reflection and analysis itself is sometimes referred to as theorizing and theory" (p. 67). Vagle articulates considerations for researchers as they think with theory. Most notable is to be open to shifting the theories that you think with, as those that influenced the beginning stages of the study might no longer make sense to the phenomenological data. Additionally, theories should not be viewed as something to insert into the data analysis, but "*thinking with theory* means that you have puzzled a lot over what the theoretical concept does and means" (p. 159).

The Role of Post-reflexivity in Analysis

Vagle's (2018) notion of post-reflexivity refers to the practice of "exploring how [prior knowledge, assumptions, and beliefs about the phenomenon] play a part in producing the phenomenon ... Post-reflexing happens before, during, and after phenomenological material is gathered" (p. 153). Rooted in the phenomenological practices of bracketing and bridling, post-reflexivity attempts to keep the researcher engaged with their prejudices (in a broad sense) and limited lenses throughout the research process to allow the phenomenon to reveal itself better. Post-reflexive thoughts also play a role in the data analysis process, as these "contain all sorts of important 'startings' of your interpretations" (p. 159). The researcher might choose to reengage in these earlier starts, bringing phenomenological material and theories together in an analytic act. This way of approaching phenomenological analysis allows researchers to maintain an open stance to consider the myriad ways in which phenomena are "being shaped, produced, and provoked" (p. 159).

Conclusion

This chapter sought to advocate for and situate interpretive and postmodern phenomenological research approaches in the field of learning design and technology. These approaches can support researchers to investigate phenomena as lived and embodied, as produced by political structures, and shed light on aspects of phenomenon we tend to take for granted. While these approaches are challenging to learn and implement, labor-intensive, and sometimes difficult to publish, there is value in phenomenological insights. In a pursuit to understand our world, ourselves, and phenomena in the world, phenomenological approaches offer researchers an invitation to wonder, expose contradictions and assumptions, and lead to further questions.

References

Amiel, T. & Reeves, T. C. (2008). Design-based research and educational technology: Rethinking technology and the research agenda. *Journal of Educational Technology & Society, 11*(4), 29–40.

Baty, E. (2018, September 21). People on Twitter are sharing powerful #WhyIDidntReport stories about their sexual assaults. Retrieved August 1, 2019, from Cosmopolitan website www.cosmopolitan.com/politics/a23366420/why-i-didnt-report-assault-hashtag-donald-trump/.

Beyer, C. (2018). Edmund Husserl. In E. N. Zalta (Ed.), *The Stanford encyclopedia of philosophy* (Summer 2018). Retrieved from. https://plato.stanford.edu/archives/sum2018/entries/husserl/.

Brown, D. (2018, October 13). 19 million tweets later: A look at #MeToo a year after the hashtag went viral. Retrieved August 1, 2019, from USA TODAY website: www.usatoday.com/story/news/2018/10/13/metoo-impact-hashtag-made-online/1633570002/.

Crossley, N. (1996). *Intersubjectivity: The fabric of social becoming.* Thousand Oaks, CA: Sage Publications Inc.

Crotty, M. (1998). *The foundations of social research: Meaning and perspective in the research process.* Thousand Oaks, CA: Sage.

Dahlberg, K., Dahlberg, H., & Nyström, M. (2008). *Reflective lifeworld research.* Lund, Sweden: Studentlitteratur AB.

Davis, B. A. (1994). Mathematics teaching: Moving from telling to listening. *Journal of Curriculum and Supervision, 9*(3), 267–283.

Deleuze, G. & Guattari, F. (1987). *A thousand plateaus: Capitalism and schizophrenia* (B. Massumi, Trans.). London: The Athlone Press Ltd.

Freudenthal, H. (1973). *Mathematics as an educational task.* Dordrecht, Holland: D. Reidel.

Gadamer, H.-G. (1994). *Truth and method* (2nd revised ed.; J. Weinsheimer & D. G. Marshall, Trans.). New York: Continuum.

Gadamer, H.-G. (2001). *Gadamer in conversation* (R. E. Palmer, Ed. & Trans.). New Haven: Yale University Press.

Gutiérrez, R. (2012). Context matters: How should we conceptualize equity in mathematics education? In B. Herbel-Eisenmann, J. Choppin, D. Wagner, & D. Primm (Eds.), *Equity in discourse for Mathematics education: Theories, practices, and policies* (pp. 17–33). New York, NY: Springer.

Gutiérrez, R. (2013). The sociopolitical turn in mathematics education. *Journal for Research in Mathematics Education, 44*(1), 37–68.

Husserl, E. (1970). *Logical investigations* (Vol. 2; J. N. Findlay, Trans.). London: Routledge & Kegan Paul. (Original work published 1901).

Ihde, D. (1993). *Postphenomenology: Essays in the postmodern context.* Evanston, IL: Northwestern University Press.

Jackson, A. Y. & Mazzei, L. A. (2012). *Thinking with theory in qualitative research: Viewing data across multiple perspectives.* New York, NY: Routledge.

Jean-Marc Laporte, S. J. (1963). Husserl's critique of Descartes. *Philosophy and Phenomenological Research, 23*(3), 335–352.

Jensen, L. J., Valentine, K. D., & Case, J. P. (2019). Accessing the Pokélayer: Augmented reality and fantastical play in Pokémon Go. In R. M. Branch, H. Lee, & S. S. Tseng (Eds.), *Educational media and technology yearbook* (Vol. 42, pp. 87–103). New York, NY: Springer.

Kennedy, J. V. (2016). *Being, belonging, and becoming in immersive complexity: A post-intentional phenomenological analysis of connectedness in doctoral students' personal learning networks* (Doctoral dissertation, The University of Minnesota). Retrieved from https://conservancy.umn.edu/bitstream/handle/11299/183356/Kennedy_umn_0130E_17591.pdf?sequence=1.

Lakoff, G. & Núñez, R. E. (2000). *Where mathematics comes from: How the embodied mind brings mathematics into being.* New York, NY: Basic Books.

Lather, P. (1992). Critical frames in educational research: Feminist and post-structural perspectives. *Theory into Practice, 31*(2), 87–99.

Merleau-Ponty, M. (1968). *The visible and the invisible* (C. Lefort Ed.; A. Lingis, Trans.). Evanston, IL: Northwestern University Press.

Merleau-Ponty, M. (2002). *Phenomenology of perception* (C. Smith, Trans.). New York, NY: Routledge Classics. (Original work published 1945).

Moran, D. & Mooney, T. (Eds.). (2002). *The phenomenology reader.* New York, NY: Routledge.

Niantic & The Pokémon Company. (2016). *Pokémon Go* [IOS, Android]. San Francisco, CA: Niantic.

Nyström, M., Dahlberg, K., & Carlsson, G. (2003). Non-caring encounters at an emergency care unit – A life-world hermeneutic analysis of an efficiency-driven organization. *International Journal of Nursing Studies, 40*(7), 761–769.

Owen, C. (2007). Design thinking: Notes on its nature and use. *Design Research Quarterly, 2*(1), 16–27.

Polytron Corporation. (2013). *Fez* [PC and Mac game]. Montreal, Canada: Trapdoor.

Spiro, R. J., Coulson, R. L., Feltovich, P. J., & Anderson, D. K. (1988). *Cognitive flexibility theory: Advanced knowledge acquisition in ill-structured domains* (Technical Report No. 441). Champaign, IL: University of Illinois, Center for the Study of Reading.

Stokes, D. E. (1997). *Pasteur's quadrant*. Washington, DC: The Brookings Institution.

Vagle, M. D. (2014). *Crafting phenomenological research*. New York, NY: Routledge.

Vagle, M. D. (2018). *Crafting phenomenological research* (2nd ed.). New York, NY: Routledge.

Vagle, M. D. (2019). Post-intentional phenomenology and studies of social change in teaching. In *Oxford research encyclopedia of education*. Retrieved from https:// oxfordre.com/education/view/10.1093/acrefore/9780190264093.001.0001/acre fore-9780190264093-e-350?rskey=bE7koy&result=4.

Valentine, K. D. & Bolyard, J. (2019). Lived moments of shift in prospective elementary teachers' mathematical learning. *Journal for Research in Mathematics Education, 50*(4), 436–463.

Valentine, K. D. & Jensen, L. J. (2016). Jamming econo: The phenomenon of perspectival shifts in indie video games. In K. D. Valentine & L. J. Jensen (Eds.), *Examining the evolution of gaming and its impact on social, cultural, and political perspectives* (pp. 309–342). Hershey, PA: IGI Global.

Valentine, K. D. & Kopcha, T. J. (2014). Middle school learners' ontological "trying on" of dimensions: A phenomenological investigation. In J. L. Polman, E. A. Kyza, D. K. O'Neill, I. Tabak, W. R. Penuel, A. S. Jurow, . . . L. D'Amico (Eds.), *Learning and becoming in practice: The International Conference of the Learning Sciences (ICLS) 2014, Volume 2* (pp. 745–752). Boulder, CO: International Society of the Learning Sciences.

Valentine, K. D. & Kopcha, T. J. (2016). The embodiment of cases as alternative perspective in a mathematics hypermedia learning environment. *Educational Technology Research and Development, 64*(6), 1183–1206.

Valentine, K. D. & Kopcha, T. J. (in press). Manifestations of middle school learners' problematization activity as an embodied phenomenon. *Journal for Research in Mathematics Education*.

Valentine, K. D., Kopcha, T. J., & Vagle, M. D. (2018). Phenomenological methodologies in the field of educational communications and technology. *Tech-Trends, 62*(5), 462–472.

van Manen, M. (2014). *Phenomenology of practice: Meaning-giving methods in phenomenological research and writing*. Walnut Creek, CA: Left Coast Press.

van Manen, M. (2015). *Pedagogical tact: Knowing what to do when you don't know what to do*. Walnut Creek, CA: Left Coast Press, Inc.

van Manen, M. (2019, August 2). Sources of meaning. Retrieved August 2, 2019, from Phenomenology Online website: www.phenomenologyonline.com/ inquiry/sources-of-meaning/.

Winograd, T. & Flores, F. (1986). *Understanding computers and cognition: A new foundation for design*. Norwood, NJ: Ablex Publishing Corporation.

3   Mobile Eye-tracking for Research in Diverse Educational Settings

Yong Ju Jung, Heather Toomey Zimmerman, and Koraly Pérez-Edgar

Introduction

Mobile eye-tracking (MET) is a technology that captures visual information (e.g., gaze, eye-movements, pupil dilations) in the moment as people move through different settings. Traditional eye-tracking has contributed to educational research by allowing researchers to analyze learning activities conveyed through one's eyes, such as focused attention, engagement, and emotional reactions (Lai et al., 2013; Rayner, 1998). However, traditional eye-tracking can only be used in limited settings since it requires learners to be stationary. MET can overcome such limitations—allowing for eye-tracking to be utilized as a research tool in diverse, innovative, and authentic educational settings by Learning Design and Technology (LDT) researchers and practitioners. This chapter aims to highlight the potential of MET as a research method and discuss how it can be incorporated into impactful, rigorous LDT research in diverse settings.

What Can Mobile Eye-tracking Data Contribute to LDT Research?

Eye-tracking's Contributions to Educational Research

To understand MET's contributions to LDT, educational researchers need to understand how eye-tracking information, in general, can contribute to what we know about human learning. Eye-tracking has been widely used in psychological research since the 1970s (Rayner, 1998), but its application to educational research has rapidly increased since the late 2000s (Lai et al., 2013). Eye-tracking data's primary contributions include (1) precise information related to learners' cognitive and emotional engagement; (2) the production of moment-by-moment information throughout a person's learning processes; (3) the capture of learners' interactions with learning resources and technologies.

Precise Measures of Cognitive and Emotional Engagement

Eye-tracking technology enables researchers to track people's fixations (gaze) and saccades (eye movements between fixations) that can evidence perception and attention, especially when people are performing specific tasks (Rayner, 1998, 2009). Eye-tracking collects multiple measures simultaneously: temporal measures (time and duration of gaze), spatial measures (locations, distances, and directions of gaze and eye movement), and count measures (frequency of gaze and eye movement) (Lai et al., 2013). Also, some eye-trackers capture pupil dilation. Pupils continuously change in size as individuals interact with stimuli. Changes in pupil size are systematically triggered when people are confronted with emotional stimuli (e.g., surprising events) or cognitively challenging problems (Pomplun & Sunkara, 2003; Wang, 2011). These measures can be interpreted as either cognitive or emotional indicators of learning and engagement (see Table 3.1 for more examples). In sum, via diverse measures, eye-tracking provides psychological and physiological information about learners' cognitive and emotional engagement, which can be understood as an important learning outcome that cannot be sufficiently obtained through surveys, interviews, or video recordings (Lai et al., 2013).

Moment-by-Moment Learning Processes

Another benefit of eye-tracking is the real-time continuity of eye-related data (Rayner, 1998, 2009). Rather than measuring learners' engagement across several time-points or their learning outcomes at the end of an experience, eye-tracking can provide precise, moment-by-moment information about learning processes (Hyönä, 2010; Lai et al., 2013). For example, Jamet (2014) used eye-tracking to look for differences in attention paths among undergraduate students with, and without, provided cues as they engaged with a computer-based presentation. By analyzing the moment-by-moment gaze information, he found that students with the cueing presentation paid more attention to important/relevant content throughout the course. Likewise, eye-tracking can help researchers obtain precise insights about paths of engagement and transitions of attention throughout learning processes.

Interactions with Learning Tools

Since the 2010s, eye-tracking has increasingly been used to investigate learners' interactions with new learning tools and elucidate the effects of specific instructional strategies (Hyönä, 2010; Lai et al., 2013). Because eye-tracking can provide rich information about which representations or features of the environment or stimuli attracted learners' visual attention, it has particularly contributed to research examining computer-based multimedia

Table 3.1 Examples of using eye-tracking measures (using either stationary or mobile eye-tracking) in LDT-related research

Eye-tracking measures	Educational interpretation with example studies
Fixation time (duration) and/or count (frequency)	• Cognitive loads or complexity of cognitive processing when learners are asked to solve a problem (e.g., T.K. Wang, Huang, Liao, & Piao, 2018; Romero-Hall et al., 2013) • Learners' choice of attention and duration of engagement with specific learning resources when multiple resources and stimuli are provided (e.g., Jung, Zimmerman, & Pérez-Edgar, 2018; Renshaw, Stevens, & Denton, 2009) • Attention distribution (e.g., Kiili & Ketamo, 2010)
Fixation paths	• Attention paths when scanning different resources before making a choice (e.g., Mayr, Knipfer, & Wessel, 2009; Jung et al., 2018) • Order of information processing when dealing with a problem (e.g., Duchowski et al., 2000)
Gaze transition	• Sense-making by integrating information from different resources (e.g., Harley, Poitras, Jarrell, Duffy, & Lajoie, 2016; Meißner, Pfeiffer, Pfeiffer, & Oppewal, 2019) • Reaction (e.g., faster gaze shift) to curiosity-based activities (Gottlieb, Oudeyer, Lopes, & Baranes, 2013)
Pupil diameter dilation	• Cognitive loads when dealing with different tasks (e.g., J. Wang, 2011) • Emotional reaction to interesting stimuli (e.g., J. Wang, 2011)

or game learning (Hyönä, 2010; Romero-Hall, Watson, Adcock, Bliss, & Adams Tufts, 2016; van Gog & Scheiter, 2010). In a game-based learning environment with a video game (*Tomb Raider*), Renshaw et al. (2009) collected eye-tracking data during undergraduate students' game activities and revealed that, contrary to what students expressed during their post-interviews, the students actually did not necessarily follow the verbal probes. Kiili and Ketamo (2010) adapted eye-tracking to observe how students (ages 10–11) distributed their attention across several areas of interest (AOI; e.g., a virtual character's eyes, classroom binder feature) while they engaged with problem-based game learning about mathematics and geography. The researchers also used eye-tracking to assess whether and how long students took to react to critical feedback for the game. They found that some students failed to notice the feedback. Such information about the real-time visual interactions can help researchers to test their interventions and further develop specific educational resources.

Limitations of Traditional Eye-tracking

Despite these benefits listed above, traditional eye-tracking has some weaknesses due to its structural nature. First, traditional eye-tracking is stationary, so learners need to be geographically fixed in a single location, and they typically cannot move their heads and bodies beyond a limited range of motion or change positions. Doing so will cause the equipment to lose track of the eyes. Having learners stay still may not be possible in many educational settings. In particular, in informal environments, where learning happens as learners are mobile (Sharples, Taylor, & Vavoula, 2005) or on the move (Headrick Taylor, 2017), the best opportunities for learning may require movement. Second, traditional eye-tracking is often set up on a computer screen, so it cannot capture learners' visual interactions with targets outside of the screen. Learning can happen beyond the square screen, even with stationary computers. Third, traditional eye-tracking captures no or limited information about contexts surrounding learners, despite the importance of considering contextual and situated information in learning (e.g., Brown, Collins, & Duguid, 1989; Greeno, 1998, 2006).

Mobile Eye-tracking: Adding More Authenticity and Investigating Learning *in Situ*

The development of *mobile* eye-tracking (MET) complements the limitations of traditional eye-tracking by expanding the reach of eye-tracking into authentic learning settings. MET allows researchers to collect not only precise but also nuanced and authentic information related to learners' gaze, eye-movements, and pupil dilations *in situ* (Pérez-Edgar, Fu, & MacNeill, in press). This mobility allows for dynamic data to be collected by (a) using eye-tracking even when learners move around, (b) identifying less-limited, more diverse areas of interest (AOI) beyond a predetermined scene, and (c) collecting contextual information along with eye-tracking data.

Learning while Moving within or across Space(s)

MET's most prominent feature is adding mobility to eye-tracking so that dynamic data can be captured within one or across multiple settings. Before the introduction of MET, most eye-tracking research in LDT took place in computer-based or game-based environments that required learners to stay seated as they watched the same screen the whole time (e.g., Renshaw et al., 2009; Romero-Hall et al., 2016; Kiili & Ketamo, 2010). However, MET allows researchers to follow learners outside of lab-based (or stationary) environments and move into the diverse types of educational environments people really inhabit. For example, Foulsham, Walker, and Kingstone (2011) used MET to compare different scanning strategies and gaze distributions between walking on campus and watching a first-person view video of someone walking. Figure 3.1 also demonstrates another case of MET used to collect moment-by-moment information related to a child's attention and engagement at a museum.

Also, MET technology is continuously developing and moving toward wireless collection systems. Early MET versions were wired (e.g., MET glasses had to be physically connected to a portable computer for data transmission). Such wires may cause data loss because they can be accidentally unplugged as learners move about (Jung et al., 2018). They can also be bulky for young children. However, more recent MET tools enable the use of wireless data transmission through WiFi or Bluetooth (e.g., Franchak, Kretch, Soska, & Adolph, 2011). In other words, MET is getting more feasible for *mobile* learners.

Diverse Targets of Attention and Engagement

While traditional eye-tracking limited the targets of learners' attention to specific locations (e.g., within the computer screen), MET allows learners to look at targets beyond a screen—not only objects but also other people

Figure 3.1 A child wearing a mobile eye-tracker and carrying the tablet PC (in the backpack) while exploring hands-on exhibits in a museum

surrounding them. MET can capture more diversified AOIs than traditional eye-tracking, which allows learners to move their eyes as they would
do in real life. For example, with a virtual simulation environment for
nursing education, Romero-Hall et al. (2016) used stationary eye-tracking
and predetermined learners' AOIs (e.g., three virtual patients' heads, their
bodies, pop-up questions) that were presented only in the simulation.
MET, however, is not restricted to a specific screen, so it can capture the
diverse targets with which learners visually interact. If the researchers had
MET in this simulation environment, they could have also measured visual
information about how multiple students interacted with each other while
sharing the same computer and solving the same simulated problems—as
they would really do in a real emergency with colleagues. MET can also be
utilized in settings with more varied physical and social subjects to interact
with. In our study at a museum (Jung et al., 2018), various types of AOIs
were identified—museum exhibits, other visitors, family, guide map—to
understand a child's sociotechnical interactions.

Contextual and Nuanced Information Derived from MET

Many MET devices are head-mounted equipment comprised of two eye-
cameras: one or two cameras looking back to track a person's pupil(s) and
another camera looking forward to record person-centered point-of-view
scenes (e.g., Kassner, Patera, & Bulling, 2014). These front-and-back
recordings can be integrated into a video data stream that provides eye-
tracking indicators (e.g., dots for fixations and lines for gaze paths) on the
person-centered video recordings. As such, MET data show eye-tracking
information incorporated with contextual information (Eghbal-Azar &
Widlock, 2012; Fu, Nelson, Borge, Buss, & Pérez-Edgar, 2019). The
person-centered video recordings of MET not only contain detailed
information about the learning contexts but also indicate the potential
targets of the person's eye-movements, which can give more nuanced data
associated with learners' choices of AOI. As shown in Figure 3.2, MET
data layers the person's view (right-side), which would help researchers to
understand more situated information regarding where the child was gazing
and pointing to. The scenes collected from MET provide a different view-
point from the data captured when using a traditional third-person-view
camera configuration solely (e.g., camcorders) (left-side).

For Which LDT Research Themes Can Mobile Eye-tracking Be Used?

Designing Diversified Learning Technologies and Environments

MET can benefit researchers in understanding how people learn in diverse
types of educational settings and designing better affordances of educational

Figure 3.2 A screenshot from the merged video recordings of MET data (right-side) and third-person-view camera recording (left-side) of Celine's (pseudonym) museum exploration with her family. This child was wearing eye-tracking equipment while pointing to the areas she would explore and scanning exhibits (red dots and lines indicate the fixation and eye-movements of the child in the yellow box)

materials in LDT, above and beyond stationary computer-based settings. We suggest using MET for research in diverse technologically enhanced environments, including hybrid computer-supported settings, augmented reality (AR) and virtual reality (VR), museums, and maker spaces.

Hybrid Computer-supported Settings

MET can advance research in hybrid environments where learners are engaged with both virtual (digital) and physical worlds at the same time. For example, MET was used in an afterschool club where elementary school students learned collaborative design thinking by utilizing papers and pencils, LEGO blocks, and a video game installed in laptop computers (see Jung, Yan, & Borge, 2016 more about the club). Their interactions occurred through both the virtual and real worlds. Children verbally talked to each other or moved around to see what their peers were doing as they virtually built artifacts in Minecraft. MET can help to investigate such multiple layers of learners' interactions, including on and off screens.

AR and VR

MET can be used to advance immersive learning environments using VR and AR. Some VR (3D) glasses can incorporate MET, as Duchowski et al. (2000) used eye-tracking to investigate how learners located their gaze to detect problems during virtual training in a simulated aircraft. Such research illustrates the potential for MET to explore visual patterns of problem-solving and engagement in diverse forms of VR educational settings. With AR technology, Harley et al. (2016) used MET to examine how learners visually interacted with the Google Earth Display (showing present scenes of historic places) and their mobile AR app (showing historical figures from historic places) for an indoor experiment. By measuring gaze transition between the two devices, the researchers explored how learners compared information from each device and engaged in sense-making about historical differences across locations.

Object-based Museums

Because of its mobile nature, studies situated in museums have used MET to capture engagement as people move around and explore different exhibits. For instance, MET was used to explore visitors' gaze patterns across exhibits (e.g., Mayr et al., 2009) or behavioral ways of scanning exhibits (e.g., Eghbal-Azar & Widlock, 2012). We also used MET with a ten-year-old child and examined the patterns of his choices over multiple museum exhibits and the pathways of his engagement with each exhibit (Jung et al., 2018). In museum studies, data about gaze allocation and paths from MET are particularly helpful in understanding visitors' choices and behaviors (e.g., how learners scanned and selected specific exhibits, how they engaged with exhibits, or how they read and used information from text instruction). Such data can improve the design and presentation of exhibits.

Makerspaces

In a makerspace, learners may search for information, explore different resources and ingredients they can use, and discuss with other people about what artifacts to make and how to make them. As learners utilize multiple tools and elements (e.g., Figure 3.3) throughout sketching, designing, and/or creating their own artifacts, MET can help explore when and how they utilize specific materials and how their visual interactions with and across diverse tools are connected to their final products.

Social and Sociotechnical Interactions

MET provides detailed and nuanced data about the social and physical targets a learner interacts with. This feature can help support researchers exploring the social and technical interactions of learners. We suggest using MET to investigate learners' interactions across multiple technical resources and teachers' interactions with students and teaching tools in a classroom.

Interactions across Multiple Resources

Traditional eye-tracking technology has revealed patterns of online learners' social interactions, such as learners' collaboration and discussion with their peers in Massive Open Online Course (MOOC) environments (Sharma et al., 2015a). MET can expand researchers' focus on online

Figure 3.3 Celine and her mother were wearing MET devices and exploring different materials and resources (e.g., iPad and clays) to initiate their making project

collaboration by incorporating more diverse forms of collaboration, including hybrid and face-to-face interactions beyond the computer screen. In particular, it can detect eye-movements across various educational materials (e.g., learners can read paper articles, use mobile devices, or talk to other people in person during a computer-based online activity). Also, MET can capture learners' in-person social interactions; for example, MET was used to explore child–parent interactions as well as child–exhibit interactions in a museum (Jung et al., 2018). MET can show how learners interact across diverse materials and with other people as they would do in the real world.

Teacher Interaction in Classrooms

MET can be used in school-based classroom settings. It can help to investigate teachers' cognitive and emotional activities in classrooms or their ways of interacting with students. For example, MET can assess and compare expert and novice teachers' gaze patterns and distributions on their students during their classes (Cortina, Miller, McKenzie, & Epstein, 2015). Also, MET can measure variations in teachers' degree of cognitive load as they facilitate innovative activities (e.g., computer-supported collaborative activities) in a classroom (Prieto, Sharma, Wen, & Dillenbourg, 2015). These real-time eye-tracking measures of teachers in their classrooms can benefit understanding teachers' authentic interactions with students and instructional tools and provide more precise feedback for teacher education.

Personalized Learning Materials and Learning Analytics

Eye-tracking itself can be an instructional material that teaches self-awareness because reflecting on one's own MET data can provide a learner with insights into personalized learning processes (van Gog & Scheiter, 2010). Sommer, Hinojosa, and Polman (2016) used stationary eye-trackers to collect youths' eye-tracking footage, showed the footage back to the students to promote their data literacy, and found increases in youths' metacognitive awareness. Likewise, MET can serve as an instructional tool with which people can learn about their visual attention patterns in mobile or place-based educational settings. Furthermore, recent studies have also attempted to develop adaptive multimedia environments that can prompt different materials based on eye-movements (indicating information processing) in real-time (e.g., Scheiter et al., 2019). Therefore, promising advances may help researchers embrace learning analytics to collect and analyze MET data in real-time to develop personalized, adaptive learning materials for more diverse activities.

Overall Processes of MET Application

In this section, we overview the steps and elements that researchers need to consider throughout the processes of preparing, collecting, and analyzing MET data. Because this chapter does not aim to provide a meticulous guide, and specific how-to varies across different MET technologies, we do not offer precise details for each step.

Preparing Devices

Different mobile eye-trackers have been developed for research or marketing purposes (e.g., Pupil Core®, iMotions®, Tobii Pro®). Each eye-tracker brand needs software to sync and merge eye-tracking footage and point-of-view recordings. As an example, Pupil Labs (Kassner et al., 2014) provide free software (i.e., Pupil Capture and Pupil Player) to collect and process MET data through their devices. Depending on the brand, researchers may need to prepare a tablet, portable computer, or PDA to be connected to the eyeglasses with or without a wire; appropriate software should be installed on the computer. Also, batteries need to be fully charged, and the memory capacity needs to be sufficient for the rich data, especially since MET data often requires a substantial storage capacity and processing speed.

Considering Data Triangulation

For eye-tracking data, researchers commonly incorporate supplemental data sources (such as stationary camera video recordings) that capture an overall view of the environment (e.g., Fu et al., 2019; Jung et al., 2018). Because

MET does not record a person's facial expressions and gestures unless within the participant's visual field, having another video camera can complement the MET data, also researchers can prepare a separate audio recorder and attach it to the computer or eyeglasses so that they can add verbal interactions to MET data.

Collecting Data

It takes additional time to use MET equipment because researchers must assist participants in wearing the MET devices and then performing calibration. If using a wired version of MET technology, researchers should check to see if the eyeglasses and the tablet are well connected and working. If it is a wireless version, researchers must check their Internet connections. Audio recorders need to be attached. Appropriate software (e.g., PUPIL Capture®) and the recording function on the tablet computer need to be engaged before participants start their activity.

Researchers need to be trained on how to calibrate the eye-tracker. Calibration is used for matching the positions of the person's pupil with the eye-tracking system's standard scale. When calibration is not accurate, collected eye-tracking footage does not indicate actual fixation and saccades, which would harm the validity of the data. Kassner et al. (2014) specified four methods of calibrating: Screen marker calibration (using nine point animation), manual marker calibration (using a concentric, moving marker), natural feature calibration (using natural features within the scene), and camera intrinsic calibration (calculating camera intrinsics). The methods, however, can vary across different devices and software. Calibration takes five to 15 minutes, depending on the expertise of the MET practitioner and the research subject.

Processing Data

Processing and preparing MET data is more complicated than other forms of video-based data because the collected raw data must be processed through appropriate software (e.g., PUPIL Player) to sync and merge two data streams. Special software aligns the back-facing eye-tracking footage from the eye camera with the front-facing point-of-view scenes. Audio data should also be combined with eye-tracking data. The resultant MET data are formatted as video recordings of point-of-view scenes that are overlaid with circles and lines of different colors, which indicate the targets of the participant's gaze (see Figure 3.2).

Researchers may consider collecting supplemental video data and merge it with MET data, so that they have one video record displaying both scenes (as Figure 3.2 shows). Video editing software (e.g., Final Cut Pro X®, iMovie®) can be used to merge these data (e.g., Fu et al., 2019; MacNeill, 2019).

Analyzing Data

MET data can be analyzed in diverse ways based on research questions and purposes. Most eye-tracking studies (both stationary and mobile) used quantitative approaches—by coding AOIs, counting gaze duration or frequency, and conducting statistical analyses (e.g., ANOVA). Such approaches allowed LDT researchers to find statistical evidence for spontaneous participant behavior or intervention effects (e.g., Romero-Hall et al., 2016). However, because MET data contain rich information regarding the participant's social and environmental contexts, it can also be analyzed in interpretivist, qualitative ways by adapting microethnography, interaction analysis, or multimodal analysis techniques (e.g., Jung et al., 2018).

For analysis, studies have used software including, but not limited to, Datavyu (e.g., Fu et al., 2019), OpenSHAPA (e.g., Franchak et al., 2011), Tobii Pro Glasses Analyzer (e.g., Rainoldi, Neuhofer, & Jooss, 2018), and V-Note (e.g., Jung et al., 2018). Many studies use manual coding to identify AOIs. However, some researchers have developed advanced technology to reduce the time and effort of coding. For example, 3D marker tracking was used to sync the locations in a virtual world with the objects in the real-world (Pfeiffer & Renner, 2014). Machine learning techniques have also been used to automatically code MET data (Zemblys, Niehorster, Komogortsev, & Holmqvist, 2018).

Example Analysis: Case Study of Celine's Situational Interest in a Museum

This section demonstrates an example analysis from a case study of Celine's situational interest during her museum exploration with her mother and younger sister. Celine's family was invited to an hour-long family STEM learning session at a science museum where they explored museum exhibits and then engaged with making activities. During the session, Celine wore the wired version of the PUPIL mobile eye-trackers.

We used MET data to identify evidence of Celine's situational interest during her museum exploration. Situational interest is a relatively short-term interest that is more contingent on external stimuli in contrast to individual interest, which is more stable (Hidi & Renninger, 2006). The development of situational interest involves two phases: it can first be newly *triggered* by the learner's exposure to novel stimuli, and can then be *maintained* throughout certain experiences (Dohn, 2011, 2013; Hidi & Renninger, 2006). We conducted a qualitative interaction analysis on Celine's visual interactions (from MET data) and verbal discourse (from attached audio recording) by adapting the coding framework developed in our previous study (Jung, Zimmerman, & Land, 2019; Table 3.2). Using this framework, we identified visual and verbal evidence of Celine's triggered situational interest (e.g., surprise after visual interactions) and maintained situational interest (e.g., focused attention after triggered situational interest).

Table 3.2 Coding framework adapted from Jung et al. (2019)

Situational interest phases	Verbal and visual evidence from Celine's MET data
Triggered situational interest	• When Celine verbally expressed surprise, feeling of enjoyment, and/or curiosity right after visually interacted with certain exhibits
Maintained situational interest	• When Celine's attention was focused on certain exhibits for more than a minute after having triggered situational interest • When Celine repeatedly talked about certain exhibits or subjects after having triggered situational interest

For example, our findings with MET data showed that Celine's situational interest was triggered by noticing an exhibit of multiple rocks and then maintained by observation activity, particularly with an assistive tool. Once Celine noticed that there were rocks and expressed curiosity, saying, "Hmmm, mm?" she approached the exhibit closer. Our MET data showed that her visual attention was targeted to the rocks from a distance (Figure 3.4, left) along with the verbal expression of curiosity, which could indicate triggered situational interest. After Celine got closer to the exhibit, she used a magnifier for closer observation and investigation of the rocks. Our MET data showed that she verbally hummed sweetly while she closely observed the rocks through the magnifier (focused attention on the rocks with positive emotion; Figure 3.4, right), which shows her situational interest was maintained throughout the observation activity.

This example analysis shows that MET data can be utilized for research about interest, which was associated with both emotional and cognitive engagement, by allowing researchers to analyze the learner's visual and verbal interactions at the same time. Also, this analysis implies that MET was used to identify AOIs from some distance, which may be influential in investigating how the learner's attention moves within three-dimensional space (beyond a flat monitor screen).

Additional Considerations Related to MET

Before making their methodological choices, researchers need to acknowledge the potential challenges of MET and how to minimize or overcome them. One primary challenge is the cost. Currently, most mobile eye-trackers cost more than $1,000 (Farnsworth, 2019). Also, MET software and hardware (e.g., laptop, tablet PC) may add to the overall research

Figure 3.4 Celine's MET data. Her attention was focused on the rocks from a distance when she first found them (left). Her attention was sustained on the rocks as she observed them through the magnifier (right)

budget. However, some companies (e.g., PUPIL Labs) provide open-source MET software and many offer discounts for academic purposes.

Another challenge lies with MET glasses. Participants already wearing their glasses may not be able to wear additional glasses. Moreover, wearing MET glasses can be heavy, especially for children (Jung et al., 2018), which may interfere with their learning. Like some regular glasses, some participants may find that their MET glasses slide down the nose, which also influences the data quality. Researchers need to keep these in mind when recruiting participants and minimize any potential discomfort of MET glasses.

Furthermore, researchers need to consider that eye information, especially pupil dilations, can be affected by factors other than cognitive or emotional reactions. Pupil diameters change depending on lighting conditions, so measuring and interpreting pupil dilations in settings having non-consistent lighting (e.g., outdoor) may be challenging. Thus, enough understanding of the setting's physical conditions that may influence eye-information is necessary.

However, with technological development, many of these challenges may be mitigated in the future. In the trend of LDT research from investigating the effect of a specific technology or teaching method in controlled settings to exploring authentic learning processes in diverse contexts (e.g., Winn, 2002), precise, rich, and nuanced information of MET can advance the understanding of cognitive, emotional, and social aspects of learning.

References

Brown, J. S., Collins, A., & Duguid, P. (1989). Situated cognition and the culture of learning. *Educational Researcher*, 18(1), 32–42.

Cortina, K. S., Miller, K. F., McKenzie, R., & Epstein, A. (2015). Where low and high inference data coverage: Validation of CLASS Assessment of mathematics instruction using mobile eye tracking with expert and novice teachers. *International Journal of Science and Mathematics Education, 13*(2), 389–403.

Dohn, N. B. (2011). Situational interest of high school students who visit an aquarium. *Science Education, 95*(2), 337–357. doi:10.1002/sce.20425.

Dohn, N. B. (2013). Situational interest in engineering design activities. *International Journal of Science Education, 35*(12), 2057–2078. doi:10.1080/09500693.2012. 757670.

Duchowski, A. T., Shivashankaraiah, V., Rawls, T., Gramopadhye, A. K., Melloy, B. J., & Kanki, B. (2000). Binocular eye tracking in Virtual Reality for inspection training. *Proceedings of the Eye Tracking Research and Applications Symposium 2000*, 89–96.

Eghbal-Azar, K., & Widlock, T. (2012). Potentials and limitations of mobile eye tracking in visitor studies: Evidence from field research at two museum exhibitions in Germany. *Social Science Computer Review, 31*(1), 103–118.

Farnsworth, B. (2019, July 18). Eye tracker prices – An overview of 20+ eye trackers [Blog post]. Retrieved from https://imotions.com/blog/eye-tracker-prices/.

Foulsham, T., Walker, E., & Kingstone, A. (2011). The where, what and when of gaze allocation in the lab and the natural environment. *Vision Research, 51*(17), 1920–1931.

Franchak, J. M., Kretch, K. S., Soska, K. C., & Adolph, K. E. (2011). Head-mounted eye tracking: A new method to describe infant looking. *Child Development, 82*(6), 1738–1750.

Fu, X., Nelson, E. E., Borge, M., Buss, K. A., & Pérez-Edgar, K. (2019). Stationary and ambulatory attention patterns are differentially associated with early temperamental risk for socioemotional problems: Preliminary evidence from a multimodal eye-tracking investigation. *Development and Psychopathology, 31*, 971–988.

Gottlieb, J., Oudeyer, P. Y., Lopes, M., & Baranes, A. (2013). Information-seeking, curiosity, and attention: Computational and neural mechanisms. *Trends in Cognitive Sciences, 17*(11), 585–593.

Greeno, J. G. (1998). The situativity of knowing, learning, and research. *American Psychologist, 53*(1), 5–26.

Greeno, J. G. (2006). Learning in activity. In R. K. Sawyer (Ed.), *The Cambridge handbook of the learning sciences* (pp. 79–96). NY: Cambridge University Press.

Harley, J. M., Poitras, E. G., Jarrell, A., Duffy, M. C., & Lajoie, S. P. (2016). Comparing virtual and location-based augmented reality mobile learning: Emotions and learning outcomes. *Educational Technology Research and Development, 64* (3), 359–388.

Headrick Taylor, K. (2017). Learning along lines: Locative literacies for reading and writing the city. *Journal of the Learning Sciences, 26*(4), 533–574.

Hidi, S. & Renninger, K. A. (2006). The four-phase model of interest development. *Educational Psychologist, 41*(2), 111–127. doi:10.1207/s15326985ep4102_4.

Hyönä, J. (2010). The use of eye movements in the study of multimedia learning. *Learning and Instruction, 20*(2), 172–176.

Jamet, E. (2014). An eye-tracking study of cueing effects in multimedia learning. *Computers in Human Behavior, 32*, 47–53.

Jung, Y. J., Yan, S., & Borge, M. (2016). Problems with different interests of learners in an informal CSCL setting. In C.-K. Looi, J. Polman, U. Cress, & P. Reimann (Eds.), *Transforming Learning, Empowering Learners: The International Conference of the*

Learning Sciences (ICLS) 2016, Volume 2 (pp. 878–881). Singapore: International Society of the Learning Sciences.

Jung, Y. J., Zimmerman, H. T., & Land, S. M. (2019). Emerging and developing children's situational interests during tablet-mediated biology education activities at a nature center. *Science Education, 103*, 900–922. doi:10.1002/sce.21514

Jung, Y. J., Zimmerman, H. T., & Pérez-Edgar, K. (2018). A methodological case study with mobile eye-tracking of child interaction in a science museum. *Tech-Trends, 62*(5), 509–517.

Kassner, M., Patera, W., & Bulling, A. (2014). Pupil: An open source platform for pervasive eye tracking and mobile gaze-based interaction. In *Proceedings of the 2014 ACM International Joint Conference on Pervasive and Ubiquitous Computing* (pp. 1151–1160). Adjunct Publication.

Kiili, K., & Ketamo, H. (2010). Eye-tracking in educational game design. In B. Meyer (Ed.), *Proceedings of the 4th European Conference on Games Based Learning* (pp. 160–167). Copenhagen, Denmark: Academic Publishing Limited.

Lai, M. L., Tsai, M. J., Yang, F. Y., Hsu, C. Y., Liu, T. C., Lee, S. W. Y., . . . Tsai, C. C. (2013). A review of using eye-tracking technology in exploring learning from 2000 to 2012. *Educational Research Review, 10*(88), 90–115.

MacNeill, L. (2019). *Attention processes in context: A multi-method assessment of how parenting and temperament contribute to the development of attention.* (PhD Dissertation), The Pennsylvania State University, University Park, PA.

Mayr, E., Knipfer, K., & Wessel, D. (2009). In-sights into mobile learning: An exploration of mobile eye tracking methodology for learning in museums. In G. Vavoula, N. Pachler, & A. Kukulska-Hulme (Eds.), *Researching mobile learning: Frameworks, tools and research designs* (pp. 189–204). Oxford, England: Peter Lang.

Meißner, M., Pfeiffer, J., Pfeiffer, T., & Oppewal, H. (2019). Combining virtual reality and mobile eye tracking to provide a naturalistic experimental environment for shopper research. *Journal of Business Research, 100*, 445–458. doi:10.1016/j.jbusres.2017.09.028

Pérez-Edgar, K., Fu, X., & MacNeill, L. (in press). Navigating through the experienced environment: Insights from mobile eye-tracking. *Current Directions in Psychological Science.* https://osf.io/qawc4/.

Pfeiffer, T., & Renner, P. (2014). EyeSee3D: A low-cost approach for analysing mobile 3D eye tracking data using augmented reality technology. In *Proceedings of the Symposium on Eye Tracking Research and Applications* (pp. 195–202). New York, NY: ACM.

Pomplun, M. & Sunkara, S. (2003). Pupil dilations as an indicator of cognitive workload in human-computer interaction. In *Proceedings of the International Conference on HCI* (pp. 542–546).

Prieto, L. P., Sharma, K., Wen, Y., & Dillenbourg, P. (2015). The burden of facilitating collaboration: Towards estimation of teacher orchestration load using eye-tracking measures. In O. Lindwall, P. Häkkinen, T. Koschman, P. Tchounikine, & S. Ludvigsen (Eds.), *Exploring the Material Conditions of Learning: The Computer Supported Collaborative Learning (CSCL) Conference 2015*, Volume 1. Gothenburg, Sweden: The International Society of the Learning Sciences.

Rainoldi, M., Neuhofer, B., & Jooss, M. (2018). Mobile eyetracking of museum learning experiences. In B. Stangl & J. Pesonen (Eds.), *Information and communication technologies in tourism 2018* (pp. 473–485). Jönköping, Sweden: Springer International Publishing AG.

Rayner, K. (1998). Eye movements in reading and information processing: 20 years of research. *Psychological Bulletin, 124*(3), 372–422.

Rayner, K. (2009). Eye movements and attention in reading, scene perception, and visual search. *Quarterly Journal of Experimental Psychology, 62*(8), 1457–1506.

Renshaw, T., Stevens, R., & Denton, P. D. (2009). Towards understanding engagement in games: An eye-tracking study. *On the Horizon, 17*(4), 408–420.

Romero-Hall, E.J. (2013).Training Effects of Adaptive Emotive Responses from Animated Agents in Simulated Environments(doctoral dissertation). Old Dominion University, Norfolk, VA.

Romero-Hall, E., Watson, G. S., Adcock, A., Bliss, J., & Adams Tufts, K. (2016). Simulated environments with animated agents: Effects on visual attention, emotion, performance, and perception. *Journal of Computer Assisted Learning, 32*(4), 360–373.

Scheiter, K., Schubert, C., Schüler, A., Schmidt, H., Zimmermann, G., Wassermann, B., ... Eder, T. (2019). Adaptive multimedia: Using gaze-contingent instructional guidance to provide personalized processing support. *Computers and Education, 139*, 31–47.

Sharples, M., Taylor, J., & Vavoula, G. (2005). Towards a theory of mobile learning. *Proceedings of mLearn, 1*(1), October, 1–9.

Sharma, K., Caballero, D., Verma, H., Jermann, P., & Dillenbourg, P. (2015a). *Looking AT versus looking THROUGH: A dual eye-tracking study in MOOC context.* In the proc. of the Computer Supported Collaborative Learning 205 (pp. 260–267). International Society of the Learning Sciences, Inc. [ISLS].

Sommer, S., Hinojosa, L., & Polman, J. L. (2016). Utilizing eye tracking technology to promote students' metacognitive awareness of visual STEM literacy. In C. K. Looi, J. Polman, U. Cress, & P. Reimann, *Transforming learning, empowering learners: The International Conference of the Learning Sciences (ICLS) 2016*, Volume 2 (pp. 1231–1232). Singapore: International Society of the Learning Sciences.

van Gog, T. & Scheiter, K. (2010). Eye tracking as a tool to study and enhance multimedia learning. *Learning and Instruction, 20*(2), 95–99.

Wang, J. T.-Y. (2011). Pupil dilation and eye tracking. In M. Schulte-Mecklenbeck, A. Kuenberger, & J. G. Johnson (Eds.), *The handbook of process-tracing methods for decision research: A critical review and user's guide* (pp. 185–204). London, UK: Psychology Press.

Wang, T. K., Huang, J., Liao, P. C., & Piao, Y. (2018). Does augmented reality effectively foster visual learning process in construction? An eye-tracking study in steel installation. *Advances in Civil Engineering, 2018*, 1–12.

Winn, W. (2002). Current trends in educational technology research: The study of learning environments. *Educational Psychology Review, 14*(3), 331–351.

Zemblys, R., Niehorster, D. C., Komogortsev, O., & Holmqvist, K. (2018). Using machine learning to detect events in eye-tracking data. *Behavior Research Methods, 50*(1), 160–181.

4 Treating Research Studies as Our Primary Subject

Using Meta-Analysis and Meta-Synthesis to Conduct Systematic Reviews

Heather Leary and Andrew Walker

Introduction

Research synthesis aims to understand and aggregate a group of primary research studies to identify gaps in the literature, integrate research findings, and develop scientific knowledge (Cooper, 2009, 2016). There are many forms of research synthesis, with more recent methodologies or systematic reviews attempting to limit the potential for bias. For example, meta-analysis techniques try to control bias and reduce the statistical imprecision of synthesis work (Chalmers, Hedges, & Cooper, 2002). With the emphasis being placed on how a study was conducted, reported outcomes, and best practice suggestions, meta-analysis and meta-synthesis provide systematic methodologies to collect and report data across multiple studies, and systematic reviews provide a rigorous process for synthesizing and generating theoretical frameworks (Finfgeld-Connett, 2016). All of these methods with their results can assist researchers, practitioners, and policymakers to make informed decisions on various topics in education.

There are many types of synthesis methods, including quantitative (meta-analysis), qualitative (meta-ethnography and qualitative meta-synthesis), and mixed-methods (meta-synthesis) approaches for analyzing collected data (see Figure 4.1). These various forms of synthesis are widely used in medicine and psychology, and increasingly in education research, especially when growing numbers (e.g., hundreds) of empirical research studies cannot be easily summarized using narrative review (Gurevitch, Koricheva, Nakagawa, & Stewart, 2018; Higgins, 2016).

For IDT, the need to discuss and engage in systematic reviews to provide essential updates on research findings in specific topics relevant to the field is pressing. Reeves and Oh (2017) analyzed research articles published in the *Educational Technology Research and Development* journal to determine the evolution of research in the field over a 25-year period. They report that between 1989 and 1994, 40% of the published articles consisted of literature reviews, but by 2009–2014 that number decreased to only 8%. Given the large volume of research literature and the propensity

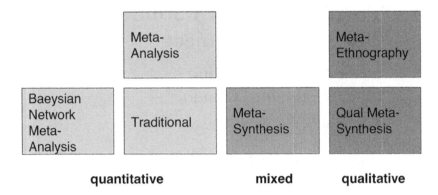

Figure 4.1 Relationships among meta-analysis and meta-synthesis methods

for change in the broader IDT field, we run a real risk of missing important trends and gaps in the existing literature base. With lower numbers of literature reviews being published, the different types of meta-reviews described here can provide an insight for the needs of the IDT field, increased rigor, and a depth of understanding beyond narrative review that is more a form of data collection and analysis.

The purpose of this chapter is to illustrate systematic review methods that can be used to gain a deeper understanding of the kinds of multiple treatment designs and rich qualitative methods common to IDT settings. The traditional meta-analysis, Bayesian network meta-analysis, and qualitative meta-synthesis approaches are summarized. Meta-synthesis (mixed method) and meta-ethnography are briefly described as well (Barnett-Page & Thomas, 2009; Finfgeld, 2003; Finfgeld-Connett, 2010). A high-level comparison of meta-analysis and qualitative meta-synthesis is provided in Table 4.1 to compare and contrast the two techniques.

Research Synthesis Methodologies

Traditional meta-analysis is several decades old, originating in part from Gene Glass (1976), wanting to counter a narrative review of psychotherapy. It's difficult to point to single articles since the technique is so in-depth. There are two early recommended texts. The first is Cooper and Hedges (1994), which is a good robust overview and still a useful reference for things like search strategies, formulating research questions, and walking through synthesis examples. It breaks down with modern techniques, particularly when it comes to publication bias. A modern take, which clarifies the dangers of approaches like vote counting to address publication bias, can be found in Borenstein, Hedges, Higgins, and Rothstein (2009). For a good discussion of the basic idea behind network meta-analysis,

Table 4.1 Comparing and contrasting meta-analysis and qualitative meta-synthesis features

Meta-Analysis	Qualitative Meta-Synthesis
Positivist, deductive.	Post-positivist, inductive.
Has an end goal of theory validation and refinement, illuminating knowledge gaps.	Has an end goal of theory building as well as identification of knowledge gaps.
Begin with identifiable and replicable search terms. Treat primary research as a population study (all available research articles).	Depending on the research questions may include random, population, or purposeful sampling of existing research.
Inclusion criteria include ability to calculate an effect size alongside specific criteria for the review which should include research quality.	Inclusion criteria include the research questions, theory underlying the work, and clear methods.
Data include study characteristics, quantitative results—ideally raw data.	Data include qualitative findings inclusive of the study's context, methods, analysis, researcher position, framework, and data sources.
Analysis can consist of aggregation of effect sizes, overall summary and subgroup analysis, analysis of variance.	Analysis can consist of key findings within a context discussed through ethnography, grounded theory, case study, phenomenology, or discourse analysis.
Results are generalizable, representative and ideally cohesive. Explaining variance through further recoding.	Results consist of new theory, encompass common as well as abnormal phenomena, remain unfinished until applied in a new setting.
Quality is a function of a review that is transparent, replicable, and based on a cohesive set of studies.	Quality is a function of triangulation from scholars, data sources, or contexts. Good reviews have supporting evidence that go back to direct quotes from primary research, have an audit trail and are clear about their own researcher's positionality.

building up a network of direct and indirect comparisons see (Goring et al., 2016). Those interested in conducting their Bayesian network meta-analysis should also read (Bhatnagar, Lakshmi, & Jeyashree, 2014; Lam & Owen, 2007; Law, Jackson, Turner, Rhodes, & Viechtbauer, 2016). Readers are also referred to Belland, Walker, and Kim (2017b), which is not only a meta-analysis in our field on computer-based scaffolding but also contains supplemental material showing how to conduct the analysis. Meta-analysis is a continually evolving space. Fortunately, the methodologists who are driving new analysis techniques are eager to implement them as packages in R, or in WinBUGS both of which are free tools.

To begin to understand and use meta-synthesis, many seminal manuscripts explain the process. In 2005, Walsh and Downe published a literature review describing meta-synthesis, its purpose, and the stages or process of doing meta-synthesis work. They provide an overview of the state of meta-synthesis work and include references to many articles written previously about meta-synthesis. These previous writing give information on what meta-synthesis is and how to go about using it to review qualitative research (Finfgeld, 2003; Sandelowski, Docherty, & Emden, 1997; Thorne, Jensen, Kearney, Noblit, & Sandelowski, 2004), as well as information on the issues involved in meta-synthesis work (Sandelowski et al., 1997) and reflections on using this method (Thorne et al., 2004). Since the 2005 literature review, additional articles have been published continuing to explain meta-synthesis and pushing the capabilities of the method, examined with a critical eye on the value and usefulness as an interpretive method (Zimmer, 2006), challenges associated with the method and its theoretical contributions (Bondas & Hall, 2007), clarifying the process and contributing to the development of the method (Finlayson & Dixon, 2008), and what, if any, generalizability and transferability elements are associated with the method (Finfgeld-Connett, 2010). Over some time, what meta-synthesis is, how to use it, challenges related to it, and the historical roots of the method are described.

Meta-Analysis

Meta-analysis uses a statistical analysis evaluating studies together to gain an understanding of the magnitude of similarities and differences in the reported outcomes (Borenstein et al., 2009; Cooper, 2016; Glass, 1976, 2000). Building on the foundation of a narrative review, a typical meta-analysis has several standard features: search strategy transparency including inclusion and exclusion criteria, a clear problem statement indicating why a review is necessary, questions that the review is attempting to address, a critique of existing work, and the generation of new knowledge as an outcome of the review process (Boote & Beile, 2005; Torraco, 2016). From there, in a quantitative meta-analysis, a researcher will engage in structured coding of study features, beginning with calculating an effect size for each outcome. Generally, effect sizes are an effort to quantify the relationships between variables on a standard scale such as Pearson's r or the differences between groups such as Cohen's d, Hedges' g, or an odds ratio. Researchers might also classify the research methods, threats to validity, and critical constructs in the area of literature. Each categorical, ordinal, or continuous variable is then used in subsequent analyses to look for summary effects or trends in the existing literature. Meta-analysis is becoming a standard means to quantitatively synthesize empirical literature (Lipsey & Wilson, 2001). Traditional and network meta-analysis are the two main types (Higgins & Green, 2008).

Traditional Meta-Analysis (TMA)

In a traditional meta-analysis, the options include a fixed-effect model and a random-effect model comparing the differences between the treatment of interest, such as problem-based learning, and a common control group. For a fixed-effect, it is assumed that each study included is examining the same phenomenon and that a single true effect size exists. In a random-effect model, each study is considered to have its own effect size. Researchers might choose a random-effect model if studies compare a wide range of grade levels, ability levels, or variations in the treatment. In both cases, fixed and random-effect models result in a weighted mean of effect sizes. The more precise an individual effect size, the more weight it will be given in the mean (Borenstein et al., 2009).

There are several possible effect sizes to use in a meta-analysis. Correlations that explore relationships between two variables, or frequency data for two variables like alcoholism and domestic abuse (Lipsey & Wilson, 2001). One of the most common effect sizes is based on mean differences between a treatment and control group and could use anything from a mean, standard deviation, and sample size, to a t-test, F-statistic, or even a p-value (Cooper & Hedges, 1994). As an emerging trend, single case study designs common to special education can be quantified as well (Barton, Pustejovsky, Maggin, & Reichow, 2017). Any single study may contain one or more outcomes of interest as long as each outcome compares a treatment group with a control group. For example, coding sheet presenting some of the data collected from a traditional meta-analysis (Belland, Walker, Kim, & Lefler, 2017a) see Figure 4.2. This data includes identifying data (the ID assigned by the authors and APA citation), tracking

	A	B	C	D	E	F	G
1	uid	2) apaCitation	3) effectName	4) codedBy	7) treatmentName	8) controlName	9) lectureYes
16	20390002	(Beal et al., 2010)	ITS vs Comparison - Average math Skills	consensus	ITS Users High Math Skills	Comparison High Math Skills	yes
17	20390001	(Beal et al., 2010)	ITS vs Comparison - Low math Skills	consensus	ITS Users Low Math Skills	Comparison Low Math Skills	yes
18	10790001	(Belland, 2009)	argument evaluation test - average achieving	consensus	experimental = connection log	control - no connection log	no
19	10790002	(Belland, 2009)	argument quality - high achieving exc vs high control	consensus	experimental = connection log (Class D)	control - no connection log (Class A)	no
20	10790004	(Belland, 2009)	argument quality - low achieving exC vs low control	consensus	experimental = connection log (Class E)	control - no connection log (Class B)	no
21	17250002	(Butz et al., 2006)	Cohort 2 - Exam #3	consensus	Interactive Multimedia Intelligent Tutoring	control	yes
22	17250001	(Butz et al., 2006)	Combined (Cohort 1 - course lab #4 & Cohort 2 - course lab	consensus	Interactive Multimedia Intelligent Tutoring	control	yes
23	17250003	(Butz et al., 2006)	Combined (Cohort 1 - IMITS Problem #5 & Cohort 3 -	consensus	Interactive Multimedia Intelligent Tutoring	control	yes
24	10080002	(Chang et al., 2001)	bilogy achievement - Construct by self	consensus	Construct on scaffold	paper and pencil	no
25	10080001	(Chang et al., 2001)	biology achievement - Construct by self	consensus	Construct on scaffold	paper and pencil	no
26	14480002	(Chang, Quintana, & Krajcik, 2009)	T1 (Designing, interpreting and evaluating) versus T3	consensus	T 1 (Designing, interpreting, and evaluating)	T3 (Viewing and Interpreting)	no
27	14480001	(Chang, Quintana, & Krajcik, 2009)	T1 (Designing, interpreting and evaluating) versus T3	consensus	T1 (Designing, interpreting, and evaluating)	T3 (Viewing and Interpreting)	no
28	14480004	(Chang, Quintana, & Krajcik, 2009)	T2 (Designing and interpreting) versus T3	consensus	T2 (Designing and interpreting)	T3 (Viewing and Interpreting)	no

Figure 4.2 Coding sheet for Belland et al. (2017a)

data (the coded by information indicating consensus), and data extracted from the articles (the effect name, treatment name, and control name).

Note that authors conducting a meta-analysis need to deal with a variety of essential considerations. Outcomes may be subject to publication bias, which should be both tested and potentially accounted for. Variations in study quality should be addressed, and if studies have multiple outcomes, then reviewers need to decide on independence. Findings might be combined and represented as a single outcome; reviewers may choose the most representative result given the context of the review, or they may select, as Belland et al. (2017a) did, to consider each outcome individually.

Outcomes for a traditional meta-analysis (see Figure 4.3) will generally report a summary effect size and perhaps subgroup effect sizes, often with a forest plot. For example, Belland et al. (2017a) examined the impact of computer-based scaffolding. One of the coding categories was the problem-centered pedagogy that was used alongside the scaffolding. The overall effect ($g = 0.46$) clearly favors computer-based scaffolding. For each subgroup or paired intervention, the effect size (Hedges' g) is generally similar to wide variations of precision. The one exception is project-based learning, where the effect size estimate was so high ($g = 1.33$) that it was not pictured in the visualization.

Traditional meta-analyses have been utilized in several IDT related areas. Specific examples include the promise of technology-enhanced mathematics instruction (Young, 2017) and relatively disappointing outcomes associated with learner control in technology-based environments (Karich, Burns, & Maki, 2014).

While important and able to provide a good overview, summary, and analysis of subgroup differences, using a traditional meta-analysis has critical challenges. Traditional analysis is subject to publication bias and also

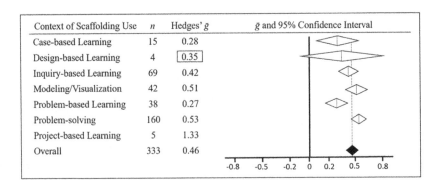

Figure 4.3 Outcomes for the paired problem-centered pedagogy from Belland et al. (2017a)

requires a control and treatment group design. For a variety of reasons, randomized control trials may not be feasible. For example, in medical research, some studies use a placebo, but others may look at a standard treatment (Lumley, 2002) for ethical reasons. In educational research, multiple treatment studies are even more prevalent.

Bayesian Network Meta-analysis (BNMA)

Bayesian Network Meta-analysis (BNMA) expands the traditional model by allowing for multiple treatment studies with or without a control. This will enable reviews to follow a common evolution in research. In computer-based scaffolding, study authors stopped comparing computer-based scaffolds to control conditions because they knew they were effective. Instead, authors started to look at the conditions under which computer-based scaffolds might optimize. These multiple treatment studies cannot be used in traditional meta-analysis, but they can be incorporated into a BNMA. In Figure 4.4, both the control and treatment groups are listed on individual rows and coded for pre-post gain scores. Some studies (Beal, Arroyo, Cohen, & Woolf, 2010) have both treatment and control groups, and others (Bulu & Pedersen, 2010) have only treatment groups.

All of these direct comparisons (Puhan et al., 2014), either between treatment variations or between a treatment and control, are then used to form a network of comparisons (Lumley, 2002; Puhan et al., 2014). Each node is a problem-centered pedagogy (project-based learning, problem-solving, inquiry-based learning, design-based learning, modeling/visualization, or control) with a corresponding number of outcomes from various studies. This information can then be used to inform and estimate the indirect (Puhan et al., 2014) comparison of no change and adding scaffolds for which there are no direct comparisons. Much like a traditional meta-analysis, a range of effect sizes can be used, including log-odds ratios

	A	B	C	D	E	F	G	
1	uid	2) apaCitation	3) codedBy	4) effectName	includeOutco	6) treatmentType	7) contextOfUse	8) conditio
20	20390004	(Beal et al., 2010)	Consensus	Comparison - High math Skills	yes	Control	problem solving	students ha three days i
21	20390003	(Beal et al., 2010)	Consensus	Comparison - Low math Skills	yes	Control	problem solving	students ha three days i
22	20390005	(Beal et al., 2010)	Consensus	half ITS-half small group tutoring	yes	Treatment	problem solving	students sp software, ar
23	20390001	(Beal et al., 2010)	Consensus	ITS - Low math Skills	yes	Treatment	problem solving	students us the regular
24	20390002	(Beal et al., 2010)	Consensus	ITS - High math Skills	yes	Treatment	problem solving	students us the regular
25	20390006	(Beal et al., 2010)	Consensus	Small group tutoring	yes	Control	problem solving	"Students ir four math s Comparisor
26	12660001	(Bulu & Pederson, 2010)	Consensus	Domain-General Continuous	yes	Treatment	problem solving	Students w over the co They were :
27	12660003	(Bulu & Pederson, 2010)	Consensus	Domain-General Faded	yes	Treatment	problem solving	Students w over the co They were :
28	12660002	(Bulu & Pederson, 2010)	Consensus	Domain-Specific Continuous	yes	Treatment	problem solving	Students w over the co They were :
29	12660004	(Bulu & Pederson, 2010)	Consensus	Domain-Specific Faded	yes	Treatment	problem solving	Students w over the co They were :

Figure 4.4 Coding sheet for Walker, Belland, Kim, and Lefler (2016)

(Lumley, 2002). In the case of Belland, Walker, and Kim (2017b) mean differences expressed as gain scores were used.

One important consideration is the level of cohesion within the network of comparisons (Lumley, 2002). If there is disagreement among a set of trials, much like an examination of publication bias, then researchers should determine if there is a meaningful subset of outcomes that should be examined separately. Puhan et al. (2014) add that reviewing the quality of the evidence is important as well, and recognizing that quality may vary within the network. In Belland et al. (2017b), the Cochrane Collaboration risk of bias tool (Higgins et al., 2011) for assessing study quality was employed.

Network meta-analysis uses direct comparisons from traditional meta-analysis but also allows for indirect comparisons (Salanti, Giovane, Chaimani, Caldwell, & Higgins, 2014) by using an inferential approach to analysis. NMA does require a common treatment (such as a control group) for all direct comparisons. Alternatively, a Bayesian approach can be used (Bhatnagar et al., 2014). Scholars will need to choose between an informed prior distribution based on previous reviews and assumptions about the phenomenon of interest or use a non-informed prior distribution and examine fit statistics. The result is not inferential but rather population-level statistics, expressing variability as a credible interval rather than a confidence interval.

The results of a BNMA are expressed in multiple ways. In contrast to a traditional meta-analysis, a single summary effect size is not possible since a common comparison is not available across all outcomes. Instead, results are first expressed as the pre-post gains for all individual pedagogies relative to a control condition of zero (see Figure 4.5). Project-based ($g = 1.21$) and problem-solving ($g = 0.86$) approaches paired with scaffolds both show substantial gains over students who received no scaffolding. Still, the credible interval for project-based learning is quite large. By contrast, inquiry-based learning with scaffolding appears to offer no real improvement ($g = 0.00$) over control conditions. Next, pairwise comparisons examine the differences between individual treatments. Many of these pairwise comparisons have wide credible intervals suggesting that more evidence is needed to make claims but there are promising contrasts, such as project-based learning as a better-paired intervention than inquiry-based learning ($g = 1.21$).

Finally, results include the ranking probability for each treatment (Puhan et al., 2014) in two different forms (see Table 4.2). The easiest to interpret is the probability that any one treatment will be ranked first among the possible alternatives and is expressed as a percentage. For each subsequent rank, a cumulative probability is calculated and then averaged. The ranking is thus the average rank for each problem-centered pedagogy. Looking at a combination of ranking and probability of the best can be crucial. In this case, there is no clear winner on ranking on four pedagogies that are close

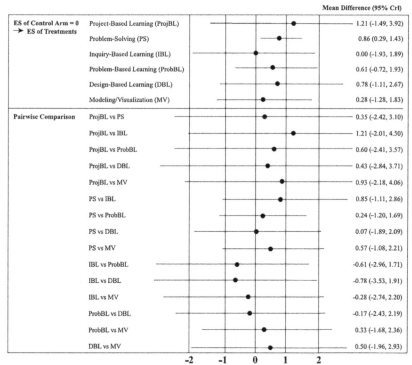

Mean Difference (95% CrI)

ES of Control Arm = 0 → ES of Treatments	Project-Based Learning (ProjBL)	1.21 (-1.49, 3.92)
	Problem-Solving (PS)	0.86 (0.29, 1.43)
	Inquiry-Based Learning (IBL)	0.00 (-1.93, 1.89)
	Problem-Based Learning (ProbBL)	0.61 (-0.72, 1.93)
	Design-Based Learning (DBL)	0.78 (-1.11, 2.67)
	Modeling/Visualization (MV)	0.28 (-1.28, 1.83)
Pairwise Comparison	ProjBL vs PS	0.35 (-2.42, 3.10)
	ProjBL vs IBL	1.21 (-2.01, 4.50)
	ProjBL vs ProbBL	0.60 (-2.41, 3.57)
	ProjBL vs DBL	0.43 (-2.84, 3.71)
	ProjBL vs MV	0.93 (-2.18, 4.06)
	PS vs IBL	0.85 (-1.11, 2.86)
	PS vs ProbBL	0.24 (-1.20, 1.69)
	PS vs DBL	0.07 (-1.89, 2.09)
	PS vs MV	0.57 (-1.08, 2.21)
	IBL vs ProbBL	-0.61 (-2.96, 1.71)
	IBL vs DBL	-0.78 (-3.53, 1.91)
	IBL vs MV	-0.28 (-2.74, 2.20)
	ProbBL vs DBL	-0.17 (-2.43, 2.19)
	ProbBL vs MV	0.33 (-1.68, 2.36)
	DBL vs MV	0.50 (-1.96, 2.93)

-2   -1   0   1   2

95% CrI: The range of 95% probability that the true value of θ falls within the credible region

Figure 4.5 Main effect and pairwise comparisons between main effects from Belland et al. (2017b)

Table 4.2 Ranking and probability of the best paired intervention used with scaffolding

Problem-centered instructional model	Ranking	Probability of the best
Project-based learning	2.81	44%
Problem solving	2.89	10%
Design-based learning	3.4	22%
Problem-based learning	3.7	11%
Modeling/visualization	4.55	7%
Inquiry-based learning	5.08	6%

together (2.81–3.7)—considering only the probability that pedagogy is first favored project-based learning (44%).

Given that it does well with ranking and probability of the best, it might be a recommended pairing for scaffolding but recall that the credible interval is quite large. It is perhaps better given all of these results (main effect, pairwise, ranking, and the probability of the best) to recommend either avoiding or improving the use of inquiry-based learning and modeling/visualization than promote the use of any other paired pedagogy but other than these areas scaffolds perform well.

A BNMA can be a challenging analysis technique involving critical and, at times, controversial decisions, such as employing an informed prior or non-informed prior distribution. However, the ability to include a substantially different set of research studies opens doors for quantitative meta-analysis that might otherwise remain closed. For those interested in how to conduct a BNMA using mean gains, Belland et al. (2017b) contains supplemental materials including a sample data set and video walkthrough of formatting data and analysis using Lunn et al.'s (2009) WinBUGS software tool. While BNMA is relatively new to education research, in general, it is quite new to IDT research, with the only known cases both focused on computer-based scaffolding (Belland et al., 2017b). Robust areas of research such as computer-assisted language learning, game-based learning where there are lengthy existing reviews may benefit significantly from modifying the scope of studies that can be included using BNMA.

Meta-Synthesis

Meta-synthesis examines a group of studies focused on a similar topic or phenomenon to produce generalizable results (Finfgeld, 2003; Finfgeld-Connett, 2014; Walsh & Downe, 2005). In contrast to meta-analysis (see Figure 4.1), typically meta-synthesis is an integration of results from qualitative studies to interpret (not aggregate) the findings and results. This method uses an inductive examination of patterns and concepts in a more hermeneutic fashion, for the refinement of new knowledge and theories (Finfgeld-Connett, 2010; Finlayson & Dixon, 2008; Lachal, Revah-Levy, Orri, & Moro, 2017). Many meta-synthesis investigations translate isolated qualitative findings meaningfully to inform research, theory, and practice.

There are a variety of types of meta-synthesis methods, including mixed-methods meta-synthesis (Paterson, Thorne, Canam, & Jillings, 2001), meta-ethnography (Noblit & Hare, 1988), and qualitative meta-synthesis (Sandelowski et al., 1997). Each of these methods strive to report findings that result in theory building, theory explication, or descriptive study, interpretation, and generalizability (Finfgeld-Connett, 2010, 2014).

Often, there is confusion distinguishing meta-synthesis and narrative literature reviews or systematic literature reviews (Finfgeld-Connett, 2010; Thorne et al., 2004). Literature reviews situate a reader in the context of what has been previously studied, while meta-synthesis uses sophisticated methods of inductive interpretation to report summative findings or new theory (Finfgeld-Connett, 2010). Meta-synthesis brings together and then breaks down the findings of multiple studies. It is a complete and rigorous study aiming to produce new findings that are more substantive together than as individual studies, which can clarify concepts and patterns (Finfgeld, 2003).

As with all rigorous research methods, meta-synthesis begins with research questions, which drive the entire process, including who is part of the research team, the type of synthesis study conducted, how broad or narrow the search for literature is (defining the inclusion and exclusion criteria), the analysis methods (if collecting and analyzing ethnographic studies, analysis methods used in ethnography is a good choice for the meta-ethnography), and the purpose for the research (e.g., theory building, interpretation). For IDT, relying on a focused topic and strong research questions is imperative. This guides the search terms used, which databases to search in, specific journals to collect studies from, as well as aids in selecting the appropriate analysis methods to use.

Typically, single qualitative studies don't report on generalizability, but the nature of meta-synthesis allows for some latitude in this area. When systematic sampling, triangulation, audit trails, single study quality, and other rigorous qualitative methods are employed, meta-synthesis research findings are enhanced and can provide tentative generalizable ideas, which of course need to then be rigorously and independently tested in new situations and settings (Finfgeld-Connett, 2010).

With many published studies in IDT being entirely qualitative in design, using qualitative meta-synthesis to focus on identifying gaps in the literature and where to focus future research would be valuable. Researchers and practitioners in IDT would also benefit from rigorous research that provides more generalizable results and the means to more deeply understand trends and patterns in research findings across multiple studies.

Mixed-Methods Meta-Synthesis

Historically known as meta-study or sometimes a systematic review, a mixed-methods meta-synthesis uses quantitative and qualitative methods to approach an increased understanding of a concept. Combining quantitative and qualitative studies requires a researcher to use a meta-analysis method and then a qualitative meta-synthesis method, with a final synthesis step of uniting the findings together. Harden (2010) provides an example of and process for using a mixed-methods meta-synthesis method. Figure 4.6 is a sample coding sheet from a mixed-methods meta-synthesis focused on

Meta-analysis citation	Visualization type /Subject	Question or hypothesis (aim)	Notes	Sample	Variables coded	Outcome and Findings	d
(Armstrong, 1991)	Computer based simulations /Interdisciplinary	Are achievements of students taught via computer simulation significantly different from achievements of students taught using traditional methods?	Focused on the effectiveness of computer-based instruction vs. traditional instruction; the impact of instruction, implementation, and student characteristics on outcomes; studies included from 1983-1991	43	Five categories: types of comparison groups, instructional features, implementation features, student characteristics, research and methodology features; see appendix A for specifics	Low-level thinking, high-level thinking, and retention could be combined to represent an overall assessment of cognitive achievement; noteworthy is the lack of difference between low-level and high-level thinking outcomes, making the author wonder why simulations are necessary	0.29
(Cunninghm, 1988)	Computer generated instructional graphics /Interdisciplinary (ex. geometry, physics, chemistry, etc.)	Analyze problems underlying the instructional graphics processes presented in literature	Focused on characteristics of electronic visual displays utilized in education. Representational graphics were most widely used graphic level, while the animated graphics were the most efficiently used.	24 of 37 8 of 37 5 of 37	Methodological features, hardware, software, graphics features, year	Mix of positive and negative effects, probably due to hardware capabilities; there was no statistically significant relationship between the instructional treatment modalities and student aptitudes in achievement scores; students preferred textual information without a high level of pictorial enhancements	0.33-0.099
(Ginns, 2005)	Modality effect (graphical material presented visually, textual information, auditory /Interdisciplinary (ex. History, botany, algebra)	Hypothesis 2-high element interactivity vs low element interactivity	Presenting materials in multiple formats-auditory for textual, visual for graphical-hypothesize more effective than than all visual; looked at level of interactivity; looked at pacing of presentation (self or system)	39 effects	Level of interactivity, pacing of presentation, form o foutcome variate, broad field of study, type of testing, age group, form of multiple modality presentation (pg 9-10)	Favorable; the overall modality effect was moderated by element interactivity, with larger effects for high element interactivity materials than low element interactivity materials	High = .6-2 Low = .10
(Hoffler & Luetner, 2007)	Animation vs. static pictures / Interdisciplinary	When are dynamic displays more effective than static pictures? Computer based vs video based animations	Identify the factors responsible for successful learning with animations; survey of the studies comparing these two forms; analyzes which form may be superior in learning outcomes and under what conditions	76 pairwise comp. effects	Features of animation version (video-based vs computer-based), realism of the animation, representational vs decorational animations), annotated with text, signaling cues, subject domain, type of knowledge (learning goal), time learner used, year, sample	Advantage of non-interactive animations to static pictures; this advantage becomes particularly evident under specific combinations of instructionally relevant circumstances. When visualization is intended to play a decorational, rather than a representational role, animationsa re not superior to static pictures; inconclusive	Comp.= .36 video = .76

Figure 4.6 Example coding sheet from a mixed-method meta-synthesis (Leary et al., 2010)

existing meta-analyses and their reported findings, including the stated effect sizes and main findings (Leary, Shelton, & Walker, 2010).

In IDT, few manuscripts use mixed-methods meta-synthesis (or meta-study). For example, Heller (1990) used techniques associated with meta-studies when examining the role of hypermedia in education, and Mumtaz (2000) found that teachers need to be convinced that technology will increase student motivation and interest.

Meta-Ethnography

As an alternative to meta-analysis, Noblit and Hare (1988) first introduced meta-ethnography with the intent to put together textual and more interpretative research. This type of synthesis involves the translation of concepts collected from single studies into each other. Findings from the studies are compared, also known as reciprocal translational analysis, and contradictions between and among single studies, or lines-of-argument, are explored and explained using refutational synthesis to build a whole picture (Barnett-Page & Thomas, 2009). Taquero (2011) reports research results from using meta-ethnography and reciprocal translational analysis, discovering that the process revealed the relationships among the individual studies, making the translation and synthesis of them clear and logical. We discovered one meta-ethnography article in the IDT literature that reviewed qualitative studies focused on strategies to prepare pre-service teachers with technology integration (Tondeur et al., 2012). It would be refreshing for the IDT field to use this method more so that the concepts and actions in IDT might be translated, synthesized, and viewed differently.

Qualitative Meta-Synthesis

In qualitative meta-synthesis, a whole picture of the data is sought so it can be interpreted and understood. This involves describing the collection of individual parts of qualitative research to help draw this whole picture (Finlayson & Dixon, 2008). In qualitative meta-synthesis, the search criteria are critical. They need to be exhaustive, even though only recently have researchers discussed their methodological steps, highlighting differences and mutual understanding for conducting qualitative meta-synthesis (Ludvigsen et al., 2016).

As noted above, search criteria and what studies to include in a qualitative meta-synthesis are determined by the focus of the research questions. Also included are date ranges and other precise inclusion criteria established by the researchers to fit the purpose and aims of the synthesis. The studies included can be anywhere from five to over 100, and there is no hard rule on the number of studies needed to conduct a qualitative meta-synthesis. But the most important part of inclusion in the synthesis always goes back to the quality of the studies. What this means has changed over the years as qualitative meta-synthesis is used more and more, but it is commonly agreed that a more inclusive approach provides opportunities not to overlook essential findings or introduce unnecessary bias (Sandelowski & Barroso, 2003).

Finlayson and Dixon (2008) provide a list of guidelines for a researcher (or the reviewer) to begin conducting meta-synthesis, including being comfortable with the philosophy of synthesizing separate qualitative research studies, some experience with qualitative research, an interest in the topic being studied, clear and articulated objectives for the study, carefully crafted research questions that lead easily into searching and sampling of studies, criteria for how the individual studies will be appraised, and a plan for synthesizing the studies together. If aiming to build theory, sometimes grounded theory analysis is the correct choice, while seeking for a broad understanding of themes leads a researcher to use a thematic network analysis (Attride-Stirling, 2001).

After studies are chosen for inclusion, just as in meta-analysis, data from these studies need to be coded. Figure 4.7 shows a coding sheet for a qualitative meta-synthesis focused on integrating arts into science, technology, engineering, and mathematics. In contrast to the mixed-methods meta-synthesis, this example and portion of a coding sheet include only qualitative data.

The next step is to choose the analysis method and work on synthesizing the findings together and visually representing findings when possible. For example, in thematic coding, a visualization with basic codes, organizing themes, and global themes (see Figure 4.8) presents varying themes and can highlight different patterns or gaps in the research being studied. Thus, a specific topic explored through multiple empirical studies can be integrated and synthesized for deeper understanding.

Like meta-study and meta-ethnography, few meta-synthesis studies in IDT exist. The articles found that use meta-synthesis do not differentiate on a specific meta-synthesis method in the manuscript. For example, Lin (2015) conducted a meta-synthesis on the effectiveness of computer-mediated communication, and Liu, Cornish, and Clegg (2007) also used meta-synthesis but neither provide more detail than that. We suggest that authors provide more detail on the specific type of meta-synthesis they are conducting, and we call for more meta-synthesis work to be conducted in IDT. With so much qualitative research being conducted in IDT, it is important to synthesize these findings, so future research surges forward.

Appropriate Contexts for Various Review Techniques

It can be overwhelming to choose between various review techniques, so the following flowchart is provided (see Figure 4.9). Note that while the flowchart appears to be a straightforward set of rules, the practical application is much

Citation	Type of manuscript (lit review, empirical research, editorial)	Medium (visual art, dance, music, crafts, computer design, etc.)	Grade level (elementary, secondary, higher ed)	How they define the A (art, creativity, innovation, design, etc.)	RQs or Purpose	Focus (teacher, students, women/girls, minorities)	Discipline of focus (math, science, engineering, etc.)	Main findings	Implications for practice
Daugherty, M. K. (2013). The Prospect of an "A" in STEM Education. Journal of STEM Education: Innovations and Research, 14(2), 10–15.	Literature review	Arts	K-12	Arts (design thinking, creativity, visual arts, dance, etc.)	To argue there is a place for the A in STEM.	teacher, administrators	STEM	It is clear that art education has a great deal to offer the movement of STEM education Storksdieck noted that in science, art can be seen as a different way of seeing the world, or a heuristic that leads to a different understanding of the world. Studio thinking includes habits of mind that are important not only for the arts, but most other disciplines.	
DeFauw, D. L., & Saad, K. (2014). Creating Science Picture Books for an Authentic Audience. Science Activities: Classroom Projects and Curriculum Ideas, 51(4), 101–115.	Program description	Visual art, language art	Secondary)	Visual arts, language arts/writing, creativity	Describe a program of writing a book to demonstrate student knowledge of biology for elementary age students.	teacher	Science	By creating a picture book, students experience the writing process, understand how to share their learning with an authentic audience, and create an artifact that demonstrates their understanding of content knowledge.	The picture book project can be extended to other literacy tasks to support learning such as poems, blogs, or letters that probably take less time to complete. Cross-curricular teaming between content area and English language arts teachers at the secondary level would be beneficial.
DesPortes, K., Spells, M., & DiSalvo, B. (2016). The MoveLab: Developing Congruence Between Students' Self-Concepts and Computing. Proceedings of the 47th ACM Technical Symposium on Computing Science Education - SIGCSE '16, 267–272.	Empirical research	Dance	Secondary	Creativity, dance	What characteristics of a learning environment help students develop congruence between their self-concept and the disciplines of computing and dance?	African American and Hispanic girls	Technology, computing (computer science)	We found that creating multiple roles for participation, fostering a socially supportive community, and integrating student values within the curriculum led to students forming congruence between their self-concept and the disciplines of computing and dance.	Within these interdisciplinary learning environments it is important to respect the students' values while understanding their perspectives of the disciplines. Educators can then help students learn in ways that fit within their value system.

Figure 4.7 Sample coding sheet for a qualitative meta-synthesis

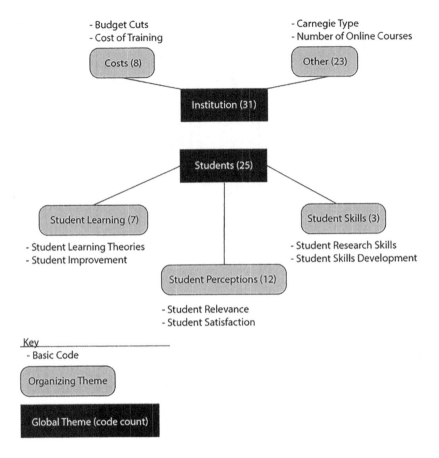

Figure 4.8 Example of a thematic network visualization

more emergent. When delving into an area of literature, new primary research may emerge. It may also take a combination of analysis techniques and multiple reviews to address the research questions you are pursuing.

There are correlational and odds ratio (for comparisons like chi-squared) techniques for both traditional meta-analysis and Bayesian network meta-analysis. BNMA originated with log-odds ratios in pharmaceutical research. For this chapter, we have limited discussion to examinations of mean differences. Readers are referred to Fields (2001) for a debate on correlations with traditional meta-analysis and Greco, Landoni, Biondi-Zoccai, D'Ascenzo, and Zangrillo (2016) for a discussion of BNMA with bivariate outcomes. There are also major methodological decisions for both TMA and BNMA. Fixed vs. random effects are outlined in Figure 4.9 because it is often misunderstood as a decision to be made at the time of analysis. It is

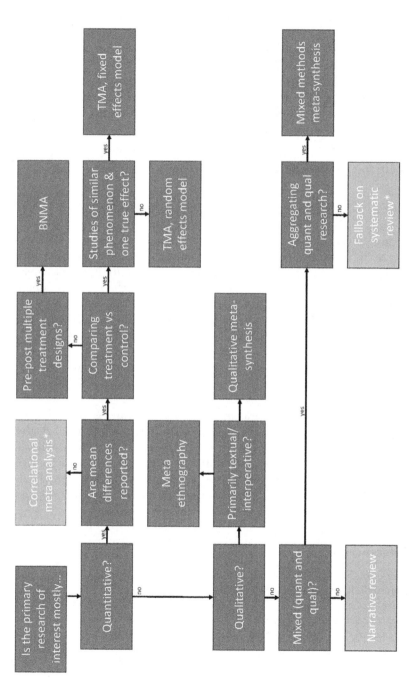

Figure 4.9 Flowchart to choose between various review techniques. Narrative, correlational, odds–ratio, and systematic reviews are not covered as part of this chapter

most appropriate as an a-priori decision based on the nature of the studies being coded. A systematic review is separated from the decision tree structure because it is a suitable fallback technique regardless of the underlying nature of the primary research, and because all of the review techniques discussed are a form of a systematic review. Systematic reviews can be useful to characterize the primary populations of study, methodologies, and analysis techniques employed, and to highlight gaps in the literature. The implied and most urgent gap to report is insufficient reporting of quantitative analyses or overreliance on purely descriptive research designs.

Need and Value of Research Syntheses

While meta-analysis has existed for some time, recent innovations like Bayesian Network Meta-analysis (Lam & Owen, 2007) and Qualitative Meta-Synthesis (Finlayson & Dixon, 2008) are useful tools for analyzing the research literature that pervades educational research generally, and IDT research specifically. Both provide an avenue to rigorously piece together and summarize research findings to push research and practice forward. As noted above, at least in terms of Educational Technology Research and Development (ETR&D) publications, we have seen a dramatic decrease in the number of literature reviews. Yet this is precisely the work both in ETR&D and other educational technology journals that is most often cited (Reeves & Oh, 2017).

For the IDT field to continue moving forward and to gain deeper understandings of the many topics realized, the use of new methods is necessary. Whether meta-analysis, meta-synthesis, or the preliminary work of mapping or scoping reviews (Grant, 2009) to cover emerging research or determine gaps in the review literature, much work is needed. These review methodologies, which can adapt to the increase of mixed methods research and account for the interest in primary research methodologies like design-based research (McKenney & Reeves, 2012), will be critical. Treating the literature review, not just as a narrative, but as a form of data collection and analysis will be important in expanding what we know about the IDT field, as well as defining and refining theory.

References

Attride-Stirling, J. (2001). Thematic networks: An analytic tool for qualitative research. *Qualitative Research, 1*(3), 385–405.

Barnett-Page, E. & Thomas, J. (2009). Methods for the synthesis of qualitative research: A critical review. ESRC National Centre for Research Methods, Social Science Research Unit, Institute of Education, University of London, London, 01/09.

Barton, E. E., Pustejovsky, J. E., Maggin, D. M., & Reichow, B. (2017). Technology-aided instruction and intervention for students with ASD: A meta-analysis using novel methods of estimating effect sizes for single-case research. *Remedial and Special Education, 38*(6), 371–386.

Beal, C. R., Arroyo, I., Cohen, P. R., & Woolf, B. P. (2010). Evaluation of animalwatch: An intelligent tutoring system for arithmetic and fractions. *Journal of Interactive Online Learning, 9*(1), 64–77.

Belland, B., Walker, A., Kim, N., & Lefler, M. (2017a). Synthesizing results from empirical research on computer-based scaffolding in STEM education: A meta-analysis. *Review of Educational Research, 82*(2), 309–344.

Belland, B., Walker, A., & Kim, N. (2017b). A Bayesian network meta-analysis to synthesize the influence of contexts of scaffolding use on cognitive outcomes in STEM education. *Review of Educational Research, 87*(6), 1042–1081.

Bhatnagar, N., Lakshmi, P. V. M., & Jeyashree, K. (2014). Multiple treatment and indirect treatment comparisons: An overview of network meta-analysis. *Perspectives in Clinical Research, 5*(4), 154–158. doi:10.4103/2229-3485.140550.

Bondas, T., & Hall, E. O. (2007). Challenges in approaching metasynthesis research. *Qualitative Health Research, 17*(1), 113–121.

Boote, D. N. & Beile, P. (2005). Scholars before researchers: On the centrality of the dissertation literature review in research preparation. *Educational Researcher, 34*(6), 3–15. doi:10.3102/0013189X034006003.

Borenstein, M., Hedges, L. V., Higgins, J. P. T., & Rothstein, H. R. (2009). *Introduction to meta-analysis.* Chichester, UK: Wiley.

Bulu, S. & Pedersen, S. (2010). Scaffolding middle school students' content knowledge and illstructured problem solving in a problem-based hypermedia learning environment. *Educational Technology Research & Development, 58*(5), 507–529.

Chalmers, I., Hedges, L. V., & Cooper, H. (2002). A brief history of research synthesis. *Evaluation & the Health Professions, 25*(1), 12–37.

Cooper, H. (2009). *Research synthesis and meta-analysis: A step-by-step approach (Applied social research methods).* Thousand Oaks, CA: Sage Publications.

Cooper, H. (2016). *Research synthesis and meta-analysis: A step-by-step approach* (5th ed.). Thousand Oak, CA: Sage Publications.

Cooper, H. & Hedges, L. V. (1994). *The handbook of research synthesis.* New York: Russell Sage Foundation.

Fields, A. (2001). Meta-analysis of correlation coefficients: A Monte Carlo comparison of fixed-and random-effects methods. *Psychological Methods, 6*(2), 161–180.

Finfgeld, D. L. (2003). Metasynthesis: The state of the art – so far. *Qualitative Health Research, 13*(7), 893–904.

Finfgeld-Connett, D. (2010). Generalizability and transferability of meta-synthesis research findings. *Journal of Advanced Nursing, 66*(2), 246–254.

Finfgeld-Connett, D. (2014). Metasynthesis findings: Potential versus reality. *Qualitative Health Research, 24*, 1581–1591. doi:10.1177/1049732314548878.

Finfgeld-Connett, D. (2016). The future of theory-generating meta-synthesis research. *Qualitative Health Research, 26*(3), 291–293.

Finlayson, K. & Dixon, A. (2008). Qualitative meta-synthesis: A guide for the novice. *Nurse Researcher, 15*(2), 59–71.

Glass, G. V. (1976). Primary, secondary, and meta-analysis of research. *Educational Researcher, 5*(10), 3–8.

Glass, G. V. (2000). *Meta-analysis at 25.* www.gvglass.info/papers/meta25.html.

Goring, S. M., Gustafson, P., Liu, Y., Saab, S., Cline, S. K., & Platt, R. W. (2016). Disconnected by design: Analytic approach in treatment networks having no common comparator. *Research Synthesis Methods, 7*(4), 420–432. doi:10.1002/jrsm.1204.

Grant, M. J. (2009). A typology of reviews: An analysis of 14 review types and associated methodologies. *Health Information and Libraries Journal, 26*(2), 91–108.

Greco, T., Landoni, G., Biondi-Zoccai, G., D'Ascenzo, F., & Zangrillo, A. (2016). A Bayesian network meta-analysis for binary outcome: How to do it. *Statistical Methods in Medical Research, 25*(5), 1757–1773. doi:10.1177/0962280213500185.

Gurevitch, J., Koricheva, J., Nakagawa, S., & Stewart, G. (2018). Meta-analysis and the science of research synthesis. *Nature, 555*, 175–182.

Harden, A. (2010). Mixed-methods systematic reviews: Integrating quantitative and qualitative findings. *Focus Technical Brief, 25*, 1–8.

Heller, R. (1990). The role of hypermedia in education: A look at the research issues. *Journal of Research on Computing in Education, 22*, 431–441.

Higgins, J. P. & Green, S. (Eds.). (2008). *Cochrane handbook for systematic reviews of interventions.* Chichester, UK: John Wiley & Sons Ltd. Retrieved from doi: 10.1002/9780470712184.

Higgins, J. P. T., Altman, D. G., Gøtzsche, P. C., Jüni, P., Moher, D., Oxman, A. D., . . . Sterne, J. (2011). The Cochrane Collaboration's tool for assessing risk of bias in randomised trials. *BMJ, 343*. Retrieved from www.bmj.com/content/343/bmj.d5928.

Higgins, S. (2016). Meta-synthesis and comparative meta-analysis of education research findings: Some risks and benefits. *Review of Education, 4*(1), 31–53.

Karich, A. C., Burns, M. K., & Maki, K. E. (2014). Updated meta-analysis of learner control within educational technology. *Review of Educational Research, 84*(3), 392–410.

Lachal, J., Revah-Levy, A., Orri, M., & Moro, M. R. (2017). Metasynthesis: An original method to synthesize qualitative literature. *Frontiers in Psychiatry, 8*, 1–9.

Lam, S. K. H. & Owen, A. (2007). Combined resynchronisation and implantable defibrillator therapy in left ventricular dysfunction: Bayesian network meta-analysis of randomised controlled trials. *BMJ, 335*(7626), 925–928.

Law, M., Jackson, D., Turner, R., Rhodes, K., & Viechtbauer, W. (2016). Two new methods to fit models for network meta-analysis with random inconsistency effects. *BMC Medical Research Methodology, 16*. doi:10.1186/s12874-016-0184-5.

Leary, H., Shelton, B. E., & Walker, A. (2010). Rich visual media meta-analyses for learning: An approach at meta-synthesis. *Paper presented at the American Educational Research Association annual meeting*, Denver, CO.

Lin, H. (2015). A meta-synthesis of empirical research on the effectiveness of computer-mediated communication (CMC) in SLA. *Language Learning & Technology, 19*(2), 85–117. Retrieved from http://llt.msu.edu/issues/june2015/lin.pdf.

Lipsey, M. & Wilson, D. (2001). *Practical meta-analysis (Applied social research methods).* Thousand Oaks, CA: Sage Publications.

Liu, Y., Cornish, A., & Clegg, J. (2007). ICT and special educational needs: Using meta-synthesis for bridging the multifaceted divide. In Y. Shi, G. D. van Albada, J. Dongarra, & P. M. A. Sloot (Eds.), *Computational Science – ICCS 2007. ICCS 2007. Lecture notes in Computer Science, vol 4490.* Berlin, Heidelberg: Springer.

Ludvigsen, M. S., Hall, E. O. C., Meyer, G., Fegran, L., Aagaard, H., & Uhrenfeldt, L. (2016). Using Sandelowski and Barroso's meta-synthesis method in advancing qualitative evidence. *Qualitative Health Research, 26*(3), 320–329.

Lumley, T. (2002). Network meta-analysis for indirect treatment comparisons. *Statistics in Medicine, 21*(16), 2313–2324. doi:10.1002/sim.1201

Lunn, D., Spiegelhalter, D., Thomas, A., & Best, N. (2009). The BUGS project: Evolution, critique and future directions. *Statistics in Medicine, 28*(25), 3049–3067.

McKenney, S. & Reeves, T. C. (2012). *Conducting educational design research*. London: Routledge.

Mumtaz, S. (2000). Factors affecting teachers' use of information and communications technology: A review of the literature. *Journal of Information Technology for Teacher Education, 9*(3), 319–342.

Noblit, G. W. & Hare, R. D. (1988). *Meta-ethnography: Synthesizing qualitative studies*. London: Sage.

Paterson, B. L., Thorne, S. E., Canam, C., & Jillings, C. (2001). *Meta-study of qualitative health research: A practical guide to meta-analysis and meta-synthesis*. London: Sage.

Puhan, M. A., Schünemann, H. J., Murad, M. H., Li, T., Brignardello-Petersen, R., Singh, J. A., . . . Guyatt, G. H. (2014). A GRADE working group approach for rating the quality of treatment effect estimates from network meta-analysis. *BMJ, 349*, g5630.

Reeves, T. & Oh, E. (2017). The goals and methods of educational technology research over a quarter century (1989–2014). *Educational Technology Research & Development, 65*(2), 325–339.

Salanti, G., Giovane, C. D., Chaimani, A., Caldwell, D. M., & Higgins, J. P. T. (2014). Evaluating the quality of evidence from a network meta-analysis. *Plos One, 9*(7), e99682.

Sandelowski, M. & Barroso, J. (2003). Toward a metasynthesis of qualitative findings on motherhood in HIV-positive women. *Research in Nursing and Health, 26*(2), 153–170.

Sandelowski, M., Docherty, S., & Emden, C. (1997). Quality metasynthesis: Issues and techniques. *Research in Nursing and Health, 20*, 365–371.

Taquero, J. M. (2011). A meta-ethnographic synthesis of support services in distance learning programs. *Journal of Information Technology Education: Innovations in Practice, 10*, 157–179.

Thorne, S., Jensen, L., Kearney, M. H., Noblit, G., & Sandelowski, M. (2004). Qualitative metasynthesis: Reflection on methodological orientation and ideological agenda. *Qualitative Health Research, 14*(10), 1342–1365.

Tondeur, J., van Braak, J., Sang, G., Voogt, J., Fisser, P., & Ottenbreit-Lewftwich, A. (2012). Preparing pre-service teachers to integrate technology in education: A synthesis of qualitative evidence. *Computers & Education, 59*(1), 134–144.

Torraco, R. J. (2016). Writing integrative literature reviews: Using the past and present to explore the future. *Human Resource Development Review, 15*(4), 404–428.

Walker, A., Belland, B., Kim, N., & Lefler, M. (2016). Searching for structure: A Bayesian network meta-analysis of computer-based scaffolding research in STEM education. Paper presented at the American Educational Research Association, San Antonio, TX.

Walsh, D. & Downe, S. (2005). Meta-synthesis method for qualitative research: A literature review. *Methodological Issues in Nursing Education, 50*(2), 204–211.

Young, J. (2017). Technology-enhanced mathematics instruction: A second-order meta-analysis of 30 years of research. *Educational Research Review, 22*, 19–33.

Zimmer, L. (2006). Qualitative meta-synthesis: A question of dialoguing with texts. *Journal of Advanced Nursing, 53*(3), 311–318.

5 Considerations for Using Social Media Data in Learning Design and Technology Research

Spencer P. Greenhalgh, Matthew J. Koehler, Joshua M. Rosenberg, and K. Bret Staudt Willet

Introduction

Since their emergence in the early-to-mid 2000s, social media platforms have quickly established themselves as phenomena of interest for Learning Design and Technology (LDT) researchers. Indeed, in Van Osch and Coursaris's 2015 review of 610 articles on social media published between 2004 and 2011, they found that 13.9% were focused on *Education and Learning*, more than on any other topic. In addition to providing new phenomena for educational researchers to study, the emergence of new technologies also offers new ways for researchers to collect and analyze data (Mishra, Koehler, & Greenhow, 2016). In short, when using social media platforms for teaching and learning, "people leave traces of their identity, their actions, and their social relations" (Welser, Smith, Fisher, & Gleave, 2008, p. 116). This means that social media data can often be unobtrusively collected as an authentic representation of educational practices within these platforms. Our purpose in this chapter is, therefore, to suggest considerations for the use of social media data in LDT research. These considerations are intended to help LDT professionals use social media data to produce research that is rigorous, rich, and—importantly—ethical.

We also recognize limits to the focus and approach we have adopted in this chapter. First, it is entirely possible to study social media *phenomena* without using social media *data*. However, we do not consider these approaches in this chapter, we welcome (and regularly cite) them, as they make contributions that analyzing these data cannot. Second, we refrain from providing a step-by-step technical overview of how projects using social media data could or should be completed. Social media platforms and research tools are numerous, diverse, and continuously changing—even with considerably more space, we would struggle to provide enough detail and ensure enough longevity to make a technical walkthrough useful. Third, although the considerations we suggest are applicable to social media data understood broadly, we are most familiar with Twitter data, which will be evident throughout the chapter. This overrepresentation of Twitter is characteristic of all social media research (Tufekci, 2014), but we nonetheless emphasize that our suggestions should be considered in the context of the specific platform being studied. Finally, as our chat logs and email conversations would attest, there is considerable room for debate and disagreement around the proper way to conduct this research—our goal is not to describe *the right way* to work with social media data so much as it is to scaffold researchers' efforts to find *a proper way* for their context. In short, we avoid giving specific *answers* in this chapter, preferring instead to draw LDT researchers' attention to *questions* they should be asking as they use social media data in their research.

We have organized our discussion of these considerations into six broad steps:

- Conducting Ethical Research;
- Framing the Research;
- Organizing the Research Process;
- Collecting Data;
- Analyzing Data; and
- Writing, Sharing, and Publicizing Research.

Although we present these steps as distinct and in approximate chronological order, it is highly unlikely (and even inadvisable) that researchers would complete them in strict order or as independent decisions. Indeed, we present Conducting Ethical Research as a "first" step only because it should be considered throughout the entire research process. Furthermore, we have regularly collected interesting data before formally framing or organizing a research project (when doing so has not conflicted with ethical considerations). Finally, as Peng and Matsui (2017) have noted in the context of data science, research is an iterative process, with each step potentially inviting a re-evaluation of the previous ones.

LDT research involving social media data is characterized by a mix of innovation and established tradition. None of the steps listed above is unique to this kind of research, but the considerations we list under each step are likely new—or of additional importance—for scholars exploring the use of social media data in LDT research. On a similar note, readers will notice that we avoid traditional distinctions between "quantitative" and "qualitative" research in this chapter. Methodological developments with obvious applications to social media research—such as computational text analysis and ethnographic approaches to digital trace data (see Selwyn, 2019)—have blurred the distinctions usually associated with these terms. We, therefore, prefer to describe a given study using: (a) the four considerations described in the Framing the Research section, (b) the distinction made between "obtrusive" and "unobtrusive" methods in the Collecting Data section, and (c) the distinction made between "human" and "machine" methods in the Analyzing Data section.

Conducting Ethical Research

Social media data challenge traditional understandings of "human subject research" and the "common rule" (U.S. Department of Health and Human Services, 2018) that have traditionally guided researchers and institutional oversight in the United States. Thus, depending on their institution and their research design, LDT researchers working with social media data may experience different levels of oversight or receive conflicting guidance (see Vitak, Proferes, Shilton, & Ashktorab, 2017).

Even if an institutional body does not consider an analysis of social media data to be "human subjects research," social media data constitute a human phenomenon and thus demand ethical reflection. We argue, therefore, that regardless of oversight, the primary responsibility for the ethical study of social media data lies with the researchers themselves. Furthermore, we join a growing consensus of researchers in suggesting that thorough consideration of ethical principles situated in a specific research phase and context—rather than a one-size-fits-all "checklist" approach—is critical to ensure responsible and ethical digital research (e.g., franzke, Bechmann, Zimmer, & Ess, 2020). Indeed, here we reiterate the emphasis from franzke et al. (2020) and Krutka, Heath, and Staudt Willet (in press) that ethical considerations begin with asking and answering critical questions. In this section, we draw from efforts by the Association of Internet Researchers (franzke et al., 2020); Fiesler and Proferes (2018); Golder, Ahmed, Norman, and Booth (2017); Moreno, Goniu, Moreno, and Diekema (2013); Sloan, Quan-Haase, Kitchin, and Beninger (2017); Suomela, Chee, Berendt, and Rockwell (2019); and Townsend and Wallace (2016) to identify the following, selected ethical principles that should influence LDT researchers' decisions of what data to collect, how to analyze it, and how to present findings:

Public vs. Private: Some social media platforms make users' data fully public, whereas others impose privacy restrictions. However, Proferes's (2017) survey of Twitter users' beliefs about how the platform works demonstrated that many social media users do not fully understand—or truly consent to—who can see their posts.

Harms and Benefits: A researcher must identify potential harms and benefits and adapt research strategies to reduce harms—including those resulting from unexpected publicity. For example, LDT researchers may be interested in social media's role in teacher activism (e.g., Krutka, Asino, & Haselwood, 2018). However, identifying teachers who participate in online activism in research on the subject could indirectly lead to professional or political reprisals against those teachers.

Vulnerability: Considerations of harms and benefits must be made with the understanding that some individuals and groups are especially vulnerable in social media spaces, mainly when research focuses on sensitive topics.

Anonymity: Researchers may try to avoid harm by "anonymizing" data (e.g., quoting a post without identifying its author). However, "anonymized" data often retain enough information to identify individuals—for example, searching the Internet for the text from a public social media post reproduced "anonymously" in research may allow someone to identify the author.

Consent: Researchers must often decide the extent to which participants should provide consent to access social media contexts; collect data from those contexts; and store, share, or publish excerpts from collected data. Proferes and Walker (2020) summarize some of the diverse opinions and practices of social media researchers in a helpful paper focused on this topic.

Legal Considerations: Local, national, and international laws concerning privacy, copyright, and conduct of research—as well as the terms of service agreements for social media platforms (cf. SIGCHI Ethics Committee, 2017)—may impact the collection, storage, and sharing of data.

Framing the Research

Social media data present new opportunities for LDT researchers, but these data do not speak for themselves. Rather, "interpretation [remains] at the center of data analysis" (boyd & Crawford, 2012, p. 668). We therefore suggest that researchers remain attentive to the following considerations that may influence their study and interpretation of social media data:

Paradigms and Assumptions: LDT research is characterized by a plurality of paradigms, including "positivism, interpretivism, critical theory, feminism, post-modernism, and design-based research" (Kimmons & Johnstun, 2019, p. 2). Each represents a different set of accepted understandings, methods, values, and expectations for research. Social media research in LDT can adopt any of these paradigms, and researchers benefit from explicitly examining, exploring, and declaring their paradigmatic assumptions.

Research Design, Methods, and Modes of Inquiry: Researchers must consider both research design (overall structure) and methods (processes, procedures, tools, and analyses). Together, these form *modes of inquiry* that "employ different standards of evidence for ... the validity and reliability of claims, and make different kinds of value commitments" (Penuel & Frank, 2016, p. 16). Social media data can be approached using any established mode of inquiry (e.g., Creswell, 2014; Remler & Van Ryzin, 2015), from a randomized control trial investigating educational outcomes of social media use to an ethnography of a social media learning community. We recommend Sloan and Quan-Haase's (2017) *The SAGE Handbook of Social Media Research Methods* for a detailed overview of issues and innovations in research design, methods, and modes of inquiry in social media research.

Conceptual Frameworks: Researchers should guide their inquiry with a *conceptual framework* that indicates "what to pay attention to, what difficulties to expect, what questions to ask, and how to approach problems" (Wenger, 1998, p. 9). Ngai, Tao, and Moon (2015) found that 30 different conceptual framings, theories, or models were used in 46 studies of social media. There are also many frameworks unique to education or LDT research that may also be helpful, and the choice of a conceptual framework is therefore not easy—but remains important. Indeed, Staudt Willet, Koehler, and Greenhalgh (2017) demonstrated that researchers employing different conceptual frameworks may be interested in different elements of the same social media data set and may interpret that data in different ways.

Phenomena and Units of Analysis: A single collection of social media data may include all of the following features (and perhaps more): (a) content of posts, (b) characteristics of posts, (c) characteristics of individuals, (d) activity of individuals, (e) interactions between individuals, (f) networks or communities formed by groups, and (g) connections between groups. Within a given study, LDT researchers may be interested in just one of these *phenomena* or may wish to consider several of them; however, it is unlikely that they will be able to consider all of them within a single research project. Thus, LDT researchers must necessarily delineate one or more target *phenomena*—this delineation will indicate one or more *units of analysis*, each of which has implications for research design, analysis, and conceptual framing. Researchers' choice of a phenomenon may be guided by established theory and research or inspired by new conventions and phenomena that have organically emerged from social media contexts (e.g., boyd, Golder, & Lotan, 2010).

Organizing the Research Process

The novel affordances of social media data and innovations in social media research methods reinforce the importance for LDT researchers in carefully organizing the research process.

Software: Most social media research requires—or is aided by—the use of specialized software for collecting or analyzing data. We suggest evaluating software in terms of *control, simplicity, cost,* and *training*. As a general (but far from absolute) rule, the more *control* a tool allows over the collection and analysis of data, the less *simple* it is to use—these features tend to exist in a reciprocal tension. Because the tools offering the finest control are often available at low, or no, *cost* (programming languages such as R, Python, and PHP can be used for free), we generally recommend these approaches as an ideal to strive for. However, we recognize that they also require more *training* not often provided to LDT scholars (Kimmons & Veletsianos, 2018) and therefore also recommend considering the use of specialized software like the researcher-focused *Netlytic* (https://netlytic.org; see also Gruzd, Mai, & Kampen, 2017), which allows for advanced analysis despite a relatively low cost and technical threshold. Similarly, we have long found Hawksey's Twitter Archiving Google Sheet (https://tags.hawksey.info), which is free and requires no programming, to be helpful for data collection and some simple analysis.

Storing Data: It is often relatively simple to collect large amounts of social media data, creating a need for careful storage and organization. As they respond to this need, LDT researchers should carefully consider the security and privacy that is (not) offered by a given storage solution. Furthermore, LDT researchers may be interested in storage platforms (e.g., Open Science Framework repositories; https://osf.io) that facilitate sharing data with collaborators, peer reviewers, and even the public, though this also requires careful attention to security and privacy.

Workflows: Social media researchers should establish workflows— common and ongoing understandings of *who* is doing *what, when* (and *why*)—even when working alone. Scheduling research tasks is especially important because social media platforms may place restrictions on how much historical data can be collected—or how much contemporary data can be collected within a particular timeframe. Workflows should also involve validating data collection and analysis. In one study (Rosenberg, Greenhalgh, Wolf, & Koehler, 2017), we experienced a data gap because our workflow did not include any supervision of an automated data collection process; human supervision could have noticed an important change in how a learning community was operating that our automated process was incapable of detecting. Multiple researchers should, therefore, regularly review and audit the data, code, and pro- cesses associated with a project.

Documentation: Those adopting positivist approaches to LDT inquiry may be interested in documenting their work so that other education researchers can reproduce their studies (van der Zee & Reich, 2018), whether in a different context or to confirm the contributions of the original study. However, even if supporting reproducibility is judged to be inappropriate given chosen ethical principles (e.g., because sharing data from the original study would reveal personal information) or unnecessary given a chosen research paradigm, careful documentation of the research process will be of great value to the social media researcher. The ready availability of social media data may make it necessary for researchers to manage several files, and seemingly trivial technical details can have a significant impact on how phenomena are operationalized or data are analyzed. Thus, carefully and thoroughly recording decisions (e.g., commenting code, writing memos, etc.) will help researchers accurately represent—and convincingly defend—their findings. Maintaining access to older versions of files (e.g., through version control software like Git, which is most accessible through services like GitHub; https://github.com) will allow for understanding and auditing previous decisions, and tools like R Markdown (https://rmarkdown.rstudio.com/) allow researchers to document their work (and even write manuscripts) by embedding analyses (e.g., the output from statistical tests) into text documents.

Collecting Data

The use of social media leaves behind many different kinds and scales of data, ranging from meaningful minutiae to staggering amounts of "big data." We have previously discussed the importance of identifying a phenomenon of interest (or unit of analysis), which will provide LDT researchers with initial guidance for what (and how much) social media data to collect. In this section, we identify three additional considerations related to collecting data:

Obtrusive or Unobtrusive: Much social media data can be collected *unobtrusively* (i.e., without alerting participants or thereby influencing the data; Lee, 2015). This has advantages in terms of authenticity and accuracy—particularly since participants do not always provide accurate accounts of their social media activity, as evidenced by Junco's (2013) finding that college students tended to overestimate the amount of time they spent on Facebook. However, unobtrusive methods can only report observable phenomena, and LDT researchers may wish to add obtrusive data collection to their research to better understand their participants. For example, Greenhow, Gleason, Marich, and Staudt Willet (2017) supplemented a collection of doctoral students' tweets with a survey of those students, which provided additional insight into their experience with Twitter. Furthermore, obtrusive methods—such as Gleason's (2018) request for participants' Twitter archives—may provide access to social media data that cannot be obtained through unobtrusive methods.

Process: Social media data may be collected in a number of ways. When using obtrusive methods, researchers will follow more traditional processes of contacting research participants directly and obtaining data from them. When using unobtrusive methods, researchers will most often collect data through a platform's *application programming interface* (API), whether directly (by writing their code) or indirectly (by using third-party software that accesses the API). Platforms sometimes change how their API works or what it provides access to, which may create obstacles for researchers; for more on this subject, we recommend

Bruns and Burgess's (2016) now-partial history of researchers' responses to changes in the Twitter API. Other techniques may also be used to unobtrusively collect data, though they are associated with concerns about reliability (in the case of manually collecting or copying data) or violating terms of service agreements (in the case of *web scraping*—i.e., programmatically collecting data that has been formatted for an end-user). In yet other cases, a third party has already collected social media data, and researchers may ask permission to access that data. For example, Gao and Li (2017) and Xing and Gao (2018) asked to access tweets archived by the organizers of a weekly synchronous chat. Similarly, Carpenter, Tani, Morrison, and Keane (2018) accessed Participate's archive of past Twitter chats from hundreds of different hashtags (see https://archive.participate.com/) to compare teachers' use of 16 different education-related Twitter hashtags.

Quantity: Different quantities of data are useful for answering different research questions. Large-scale studies incorporating "big data" are helpful for observing connections and trends, but small data are better for understanding specificity and motives (Latzko-Toth, Bonneau, & Millette, 2017). Given the sheer amount and availability of social media data, it is not uncommon for researchers to have access to—or even intentionally collect—more data than they actually need; in this case, they will need to decide how to sample, subset, or otherwise limit the data they have collected prior to their analysis. These concerns are not limited to social media research (e.g., Glesne, 2016; Remler & Van Ryzin, 2015), but social media researchers should also make this decision based on the phenomenon or unit of analysis that the researchers have previously decided on. For example, Greenhow, Li, and Mai (2019) were interested in social media use *during a specific educational event* (a conference) and therefore limited their data by a time frame; in contrast, Carpenter, Kimmons, Short, Clements, and Staples (2019) were focused on *a specific kind of social media user* (teachers) and eliminated data from other users. On social media platforms that allow for reposting others' material, LDT researchers have articulated compelling reasons to both retain duplicate material (e.g., because reposts serve as the amplification of a theme; Greenhalgh, Rosenberg, & Wolf, 2016) and remove it from the data (e.g., because reposts do not add new topics to a discussion; Gao & Li, 2017) while preparing for analysis.

Analyzing Data

In this section, we identify considerations that LDT researchers must make as they analyze social media data. Whatever decisions they make, researchers should both acknowledge that any analysis comes with a degree of uncertainty and take steps to establish the trustworthiness of their research. Naturally, this concern is not unique to social media research, and LDT researchers may consult one of several resources to guide their efforts (e.g., Creswell, 2014; Creswell & Miller, 2000; Maxwell, 2013; Remler & Van Ryzin, 2015). The following considerations are more specific to the analysis of social media data:

Spam: Before analyzing social media data, researchers must determine what to do with spam, which can be understood as "undesirable text, whether repetitive, excessive or interfering" (Brunton, 2013, p. xxii). Carpenter, Staudt Willet, Koehler, and Greenhalgh (2019) noted that educational researchers may take varied approaches to spam depending on their research goals. For example, researchers may eliminate spam from their analysis if their goal is to accurately represent learning activity or compare learning activity across contexts. In contrast, researchers focused on investigating participants' experiences of social media are more likely to retain spam content (i.e., to represent that experience fully).

Machine vs. Human Analysis: Social media data is often structured in a standardized way that facilitates *machine analysis*; indeed, machine techniques such as sentiment analysis, topic modeling, and classification algorithms allow researchers to approximate the kinds of analyses traditionally requiring human effort. For example, Greenhalgh, Staudt Willet, Rosenberg, and Koehler (2018) found that machine analysis could reasonably infer Twitter users' geographic location based on unobtrusively collected data, presenting several practical advantages over human analysis of obtrusively collected data. However, *human analysis* of data can account for nuance and meaning in ways that even the most advanced machine analyses cannot match. Researchers' choice between machine- or human-driven methods should, therefore, be driven by considerations of the *amount* of data researchers went to analyze (with more substantial amounts making human analysis impractical) and the *degree of nuance* desired (with higher levels of nuance being beyond the capability of machine analysis). Innovative combinations of machine and human analyses—such as Nelson's (2017) *computational grounded theory*—allow researchers to leverage the advantages of both approaches.

Networks: The networked aspect of social media platforms and education researchers' interest in interpersonal interaction invites LDT scholars to employ network analyses to understand social media activity (e.g., Rosenberg et al., 2019). Within network analysis, researchers may decide to focus on processes of *influence* (e.g., how ideas spread and affect individuals) or *selection* (e.g., how someone decides who to interact with). When representing networks visually, researchers must make choices about what features to highlight (e.g., how often users contribute, how frequently two users interact, or demographic information about users).

Disseminating Research

This step includes considerations related to *writing* the results of social media research studies as well as *sharing* and *publicizing* the final products. Although these issues are not unique to social media researchers—for a broader discussion of open science practices in education research, see van der Zee and Reich (2018)—some considerations stand out in this specific context:

Sharing Data: As previously described, some of the advantages of doing research based on social media data include their relative availability and authenticity. Given these advantages, it is logical for researchers to wish to share these data with others—whether as examples in written manuscripts (to support a study's assertions) or as publicly available data sets (to allow others to complete similar studies). Although the former goal is logical—and the latter laudable—we urge caution and recommend that researchers do so with the considerations in the Conducting Ethical Research section in mind.

Sharing Code: Collecting and analyzing social media data requires sustained attention to technical detail, and many education researchers do not have access to the technical training that is necessary to be aware of all the nuances involved in these processes (Kimmons & Veletsianos, 2018). Thus, while we urge caution before sharing social media *data* with other education researchers, we see few—if any—disadvantages to researchers' open sharing of the *code* they develop (indeed, our own research has long depended on software that other scholars have developed and shared). Sharing code helps communicate detailed methodological decisions, allows communities of scholars to validate findings (even without sharing data), helps others build upon the work, and can help establish standards for the rigor and quality of social media research in the field of LDT. Platforms such as GitHub (https://github.com) and the Open Science Framework (https://osf.io) facilitate the sharing of code online; however, the full benefits of sharing code are dependent on the documentation strategies that we have previously described.

Publishing and Publicizing Research: One interesting aspect to doing social media research is that social media themselves can help researchers publish and publicize their findings—a phenomenon called "social scholarship" (see Greenhow, Gleason, & Staudt Willet, 2019). In addition to blogs and other general-audience social media platforms, there are a number of academic-focused platforms that may be of use to LDT researchers seeking to promote and share their work; however, we encourage careful evaluation of the business models, privacy policies, and other practices of these platforms before using them. More importantly, researchers should consider whether and how to share their findings with social media users or communities whose data made that research possible. This is important not only in the context of ongoing considerations of what constitutes ethical relationships with those who contribute to research (Maxwell, 2013; Selwyn, 2019) but also given that social media users have expressed particular interest in learning about research based on their data (Fiesler & Proferes, 2018).

Conclusion

The ready availability of social media data provides many opportunities—but also considerable challenges—for LDT researchers. LDT research, social media platforms, and research tools are all diverse, not to mention continually evolving. Thus, scholars interested in using social media data in their research should familiarize themselves with the broad considerations that guide effective research in this domain—not just detailed walkthroughs of how to complete a specific task. In this chapter, we have described some of the key considerations associated with six critical steps in social media-focused LDT research: Conducting Ethical Research; Framing the Research; Organizing the Research Process; Collecting Data; Analyzing Data; and Writing, Sharing, and Publicizing Research. These considerations allow for numerous valid approaches to social media research and help researchers avoid the arguably more-numerous pitfalls they could encounter.

References

boyd, d. & Crawford, K. (2012). Critical questions for big data: Provocations for a cultural, technological, and scholarly phenomenon. *Information, Communication & Society, 15*(5), 662–679. doi:10.1080/1369118X.2012.678878.

boyd, d., Golder, S., & Lotan, G. (2010). Tweet, tweet, retweet: Conversational aspects of retweeting on Twitter. In *Proceedings of the 43rd Annual Hawai'i International Conference on System Sciences.* Los Alamitos, CA: IEEE Computer Society.

Bruns, A. & Burgess, J. (2016). Methodological innovation in precarious spaces: The case of Twitter. In H. Snee, C. Hine, Y. Morey, S. Roberts, & H. Watson (Eds.), *Digital methods for social science: An interdisciplinary guide to research innovation* (pp. 17–33). New York, NY: Palgrave Macmillan.

Brunton, F. (2013). *Spam: A shadow history of the Internet.* Cambridge, MA: MIT Press.

Carpenter, J., Tani, T., Morrison, S., & Keane, J. (2018, March). Exploring the education Twitter hashtag landscape. In E. Langran & J. Borup (Eds.), *Proceedings of Society for Information Technology & Teacher Education International Conference 2018* (pp. 2230–2235). Association for the Advancement of Computing in Education (AACE).

Carpenter, J. P., Kimmons, R., Short, C. R., Clements, K., & Staples, M. E. (2019). Teacher identity and crossing the professional-personal divide on Twitter. *Teaching and Teacher Education, 81.* doi:10.1016/j.tate.2019.01.011.

Carpenter, J. P., Staudt Willet, K. B., Koehler, M. J., & Greenhalgh, S. P. (2019). Spam and educators' Twitter use: Methodological considerations and challenges. *TechTrends.* doi:10.1007/s11528-019-00466-3.

Creswell, J. W. (2014). *Research design: Qualitative, quantitative, and mixed methods approaches* (4th ed.). Thousand Oaks, CA: SAGE.

Creswell, J. W. & Miller, D. L. (2000). Determining validity in qualitative inquiry. *Theory into Practice*, *39*(3), 124–130. doi:10.1207/s15430421tip3903_2.

Fiesler, C. & Proferes, N. (2018). "Participant" perceptions of Twitter research ethics. *Social Media and Society*, *4*, 1. doi:10.1177/2056305118763366.

franzke, A. S., Bechmann, A., Zimmer, M., & Ess, C., & the Association of Internet Researchers (2020). *Internet Research: Ethical Guidelines 3.0*. Retrieved from https://aoir.org/reports/ethics3.pdf.

Gao, F. & Li, L. (2017). Examining a one-hour synchronous chat in a microblogging-based professional development community. *British Journal of Educational Technology*, *48*, 332–347. doi:10.1111/bjet.12384.

Gleason, B. (2018). Adolescents becoming feminist on Twitter: New literacies practices, commitments, and identity work. *Journal of Adolescent & Adult Literacy*, *62*, 281–289. doi:10.1002/jaal.889.

Glesne, C. (2016). *Becoming qualitative researchers: An introduction* (5th ed.). Boston, MA: Pearson Education, Inc.

Golder, S., Ahmed, S., Norman, G., & Booth, A. (2017). Attitudes toward the ethics of research using social media: A systematic review. *Journal of Medical Internet Research*, *19*(6). doi:10.2196/jmir.7082.

Greenhalgh, S. P., Rosenberg, J. M., & Wolf, L. G. (2016). For all intents and purposes: Twitter as a foundational technology for teachers. *E-Learning and Digital Media*, *13*, 81–98. doi:10.1177/2042753016672131.

Greenhalgh, S. P., Staudt Willet, K. B., Rosenberg, J. M., & Koehler, M. J. (2018). Tweet, and we shall find: Using digital methods to locate participants in educational hashtags. *TechTrends*, *62*, 501–508. doi:10.1007/s11528-018-0313-6.

Greenhow, C., Li, J., & Mai, M. (2019). From tweeting to meeting: Expansive professional learning and the academic conference background. *British Journal of Educational Technology*, *50*, 1656–1672. doi:10.1111/bjet.12817.

Greenhow, C. M., Gleason, B., Marich, H., & Staudt Willet, K. B. (2017). Educating social scholars: Examining novice researchers' practices with social media. *Qwerty – Open and Interdisciplinary Journal of Technology, Culture and Education*, *12*(2), 30–45. Retrieved from www.ckbg.org/qwerty/index.php/qwerty/article/view/269/.

Greenhow, C. M., Gleason, B., & Staudt Willet, K. B. (2019). Social scholarship revisited: Changing scholarly practices in the age of social media. *British Journal of Educational Technology*, *50*, 987–1004. doi:10.1111/bjet.12772.

Gruzd, A., Mai, P., & Kampen, A. (2017). A how-to for using Netlytic to collect and analyze social media data: A case study of the use of Twitter during the 2014 Euromaidan revolution in Ukraine. In L. Sloan & A. Quan-Haase (Eds.), *The SAGE handbook of social media research methods* (pp. 513–529). Los Angeles, CA: SAGE.

Junco, R. (2013). Comparing actual and self-reported measures of Facebook use. *Computers in Human Behavior*, *29*, 626–631. doi:10.1016/j.chb.2012.11.007.

Kimmons, R. & Johnstun, K. (2019). Navigating paradigms in educational technology. *TechTrends*. doi:10.1007/s11528-019-00407-0.

Kimmons, R. & Veletsianos, G. (2018). Public Internet data mining methods in instructional design, educational technology, and online learning research. *TechTrends*, *62*, 492–500. doi:10.1007/s11528-018-0307-4.

Krutka, D. B., Asino, T. I., & Haselwood, S. (2018). Editorial: Eight lessons on networked teacher activism from #OklaEd and the #OklaEdWalkout. *Contemporary Issues in Technology and Teacher Education, 18*(2). Retrieved from www.citejournal.org/volume-18/issue-2-18/social-studies/editorial-oklaed-and-the-oklaed walkout-eight-lessons-on-networked-teacher-activism.

Krutka, D. G., Heath, M. K., & Staudt Willet, K. B. (in press). Foregrounding technoethics: Toward critical perspectives in technology and teacher education. *Journal of Technology and Teacher Education.*

Latzko-Toth, G., Bonneau, C., & Millette, M. (2017). Small data, thick data: Thickening strategies for trace-based social media research. In L. Sloan & A. Quan-Haase (Eds.), *The SAGE handbook of social media research methods* (pp. 199–214). Los Angeles, CA: SAGE.

Lee, R. M. (2015). *Unobtrusive measures.* doi:10.1093/OBO/9780199846740-0048.

Maxwell, J. A. (2013). *Qualitative research design: An interactive approach.* Thousand Oaks, CA: SAGE Publications, Inc.

Mishra, P., Koehler, M. J., & Greenhow, C. (2016). The work of educational psychologists in a digitally networked world. In L. Corno & E. M. Anderman (Eds.), *Handbook of educational psychology* (3rd ed., pp. 29–40). New York, NY: Routledge.

Moreno, M. A., Goniu, N., Moreno, P. S., & Diekema, D. (2013). Ethics of social media research: Common concerns and practical considerations. *Cyberpsychology, Behavior, and Social Networking, 16*, 708–713. doi:10.1089/cyber.2012.0334.

Nelson, L. K. (2017). Computational grounded theory: A methodological framework. *Sociological Methods & Research.* doi:10.1177/0049124117729703.

Ngai, E. W. T., Tao, S. S. C., & Moon, K. K. L. (2015). Social media research: Theories, constructs, and conceptual frameworks. *International Journal of Information Management, 35*(1), 33–44. doi:10.1016/j.ijinfomgt.2014.09.004.

Peng, R. & Matsui, E. (2017). *The art of data science.* Retrieved from https://bookdown.org/rdpeng/artofdatascience/.

Penuel, W. R. & Frank, K. A. (2016). Modes of inquiry in educational psychology and learning sciences research. In L. Corno & E. M. Anderman (Eds.), *Handbook of educational psychology* (3rd ed., pp. 30–42). New York, NY: Routledge.

Proferes, N. (2017). Information flow solipsism in an exploratory study of beliefs about Twitter. *Social Media + Society, 3*(1). doi:10.1177/2056305117698493.

Proferes, N. & Walker, S. (2020). Researcher views and practices around informing, getting consent, and sharing research outputs with social media users when using their public data. In *Proceedings of the 53rd Annual Hawai'i International Conference on System Sciences.* Los Alamitos, CA: IEEE Computer Society.

Remler, D. K. & Van Ryzin, G. G. (2015). *Research methods in practice: Strategies for description and causation* (2nd ed.). Thousand Oaks, CA: SAGE Publications Inc.

Rosenberg, J. M., Greenhalgh, S. P., Wolf, L. G., & Koehler, M. J. (2017). Strategies, use, and impact of social media for supporting teacher community within professional development: The case of one urban STEM program. *Journal of Computers in Mathematics and Science Teaching, 36*, 255–267.

Rosenberg, J. M., Reid, J. W., Dyer, E., Koehler, M. J., Fischer, C., & McKenna, T. J. (2019, August 21). Exploring the next generation science standards chat (#ngsschat) professional network on Twitter through social network analysis. *Open Science Framework Preprint.* doi: 10.31219/osf.io/uwza6

Selwyn, N. (2019). *What is digital sociology?* Medford, MA: Polity Press.

SIGCHI Ethics Committee. (2017, November 30). Do researchers need to follow TOS? [Medium post]. Retrieved from https://medium.com/p/f3bde1950d3c/.

Sloan, L. & Quan-Haase, A. (2017). *The SAGE handbook of social media research methods*. Thousand Oaks, CA: SAGE Publications Inc.

Sloan, L., Quan-Haase, A., Kitchin, R., & Beninger, K. (2017). *Social media research & ethics* [Streaming video]. doi:10.4135/9781526413642.

Staudt Willet, K. B., Koehler, M. J., & Greenhalgh, S. P. (2017). A tweet by any other frame: Comparing three theoretical frameworks for studying educator interactions on Twitter. In L. Liu & D. Gibson (Eds.), *Research highlights in technology and teacher education 2017* (pp. 63–70). Waynesville, NC: Association for the Advancement of Computing in Education (AACE). Retrieved from www.learntechlib.org/p/180960/.

Suomela, T., Chee, F., Berendt, B., & Rockwell, G. (2019). Applying an ethics of care to Internet research: Gamergate and digital humanities. *Digital Studies/Le Champ Numérique, 9*(1), 4. doi:10.16995/dscn.302.

Townsend, L. & Wallace, C. (2016). *Social media research: A guide to ethics*. Aberdeen, UK: University of Aberdeen. Retrieved from www2.port.ac.uk/research/ethics/CurrentDownloads/filetodownload,198032,en.pdf.

Tufekci, Z. (2014). Big questions for social media big data: Representativeness, validity, and other methodological pitfalls. In E. Adar & P. Resnick (Eds.), *Proceedings of the Eighth International AAAI Conference on Weblogs and Social Media*. Palo Alto, CA: The AAAI Press.

U.S. Department of Health and Human Services. (2018). *Revised common rule*. Retrieved from www.hhs.gov/ohrp/regulations-and-policy/regulations/finalized-revisions-common-rule/index.html.

van der Zee, T. & Reich, J. (2018). Open education science. *AERA Open, 4*(3), 1–15. doi:10.1177/2332858418787466.

Van Osch, W. & Coursaris, C. (2015). A meta-analysis of theories and topics in social media research. In T. X. Bui & R. H. Sprague (Eds.), *Proceedings of the 48th Annual Hawai'i International Conference on System Sciences* (pp. 1668–1675). Los Alamitos, CA: IEEE Computer Society.

Vitak, J., Proferes, N., Shilton, K., & Ashktorab, Z. (2017). Ethics regulation in social computing research: Examining the role of institutional review boards. *Journal of Empirical Research on Human Research Ethics, 12*, 372–382. doi:10.1177/1556264617725200.

Welser, H. T., Smith, M., Fisher, D., & Gleave, E. (2008). Distilling digital traces: Computational social science approaches to studying the Internet. In N. Fielding, R. M. Lee, & G. Blank (Eds.), *The SAGE handbook of online research methods* (pp. 116–141). Thousand Oaks, CA: SAGE Publications, Ltd.

Wenger, E. (1998). *Communities of practice: Learning, meaning, and identity*. New York, NY: Cambridge University Press.

Xing, W. & Gao, F. (2018). Exploring the relationship between online discourse and commitment in Twitter professional learning communities. *Computers & Education, 126*, 388–398. doi:10.1016/j.compedu.2018.08.010.

6 Becoming Action Researchers

Crafting the Curriculum and Learning Experiences for Scholarly Practitioners in Educational Technology

Ismahan Arslan-Ari, Fatih Ari, Michael M. Grant, Lucas Vasconcelos, Hengtao Tang, and William S. Morris

Introduction

The number of educational technology programs offering Ed.D. degrees has increased in recent years. With the inspiration of Carnegie Project on the Education Doctorate (CPED), an initiative established in 2007 to redesign the Ed.D. degree to prepare scholarly practitioners, our Ed.D. in Curriculum & Instruction—Educational Technology concentration program was initiated in 2016. Aligned with the CPED's goals, our program aims to prepare practitioners to research existing persistent issues within educational contexts, recommend actions, and improve teaching and learning and learning environments. In this sense, our curriculum is designed around the knowledge and skills a scholarly practitioner should possess to analyze a situation in his or her specific practice context, design, develop, and implement an appropriate innovation to address the problem; and evaluate the effectiveness and impact of the innovation. Therefore, an action research dissertation in practice is used as a signature pedagogy in our program. A signature pedagogy (Shulman, 2005) reflects the essential method of teaching and learning used to prepare students. Signature pedagogy provides the new knowledge, skills, and attitudes novices require to be enculturated into their new profession (Zambo, 2011).

Much has been written about the development of researchers within Ph.D. programs (e.g., Coryell, Wagner, Clark, & Stuessy, 2013; Hockey & Allen-Collinson, 2005; Kamler & Thomson, 2006, 2008). There is less literature, however, dedicated to the development of researchers as scholarly practitioners within Ed.D. programs (e.g., Buss & Zambo, 2016; Zambo, 2011). Even less, though, has been written about Ed.D. programs using an online delivery (e.g., Lasater, Bengtson, & Murphy-Lee, 2016; Mertler & Henriksen, 2018), and still less written about Ed.D. programs specializing in educational technology (Dawson, 2012; Dawson & Kumar, 2014; Kumar & Antonenko, 2014; Kumar & Dawson, 2012; Kumar, Johnson, & Hardemon,

2013) and using an online delivery (see e.g., Arslan-Ari, Ari, Grant, & Morris, 2018).

We have continued to critically examine and assess the strengths, weaknesses, and opportunities within our program and across our cohorts of students. At the time of this writing, we are enrolling our tenth cohort of students in just over three years. We also are attempting to fill a void in our educational technology field for reporting the process of supporting doctoral students' growth as action researchers within professional practice doctoral programs (cf. Dawson & Kumar, 2016; Kumar & Dawson, 2012, 2014). Therefore, in this chapter, we will present the process of preparing doctoral students in our Ed.D. program to become action researchers.

Throughout our program, we have incorporated an evaluative design in order to monitor the progress of our students and improve the program. In this chapter, we include surveys with both Likert-type items and open-ended items that were used two times during the program and across three cohorts of students (n = 15; n = 15; n = 9). Findings from these surveys are embedded throughout this chapter to document and describe our students' experiences with action research in the program. In addition, to describe the uses of action research in educational technology, this chapter presents examples of our students' dissertations in practice. In the next section, we will provide a brief overview of action research and some of its fundamental characteristics.

Action Research

Action research is generally described as a systematic inquiry toward one's practice to enhance his or her practice (Manfra & Bullock, 2014). Stringer (2007) defines action research as a collaborative inquiry process in which people take systematic actions "to 'get a handle' on their situations and formulate effective solutions to problems they face in their public and professional lives" (p. 8). In educational settings, action research is often referred to as the process where teachers address problems or issues related to their teaching practices using appropriate research-based solutions (Mills, 2017; Tripp, 2005). In the broadest interpretation and one that we reference in our program, Hine (2013) suggests "action research enables researchers to develop a systematic, inquiring approach toward their own practices ... oriented towards effecting positive change in this practice .. or within a broader community" (p. 152).

Although each reflects slightly different interpretations, these definitions indicate that action research happens in the professional practice context of a researcher. This key aspect distinguishes action research from traditional empirical research where the researcher is likely an outsider to the context (Herr & Anderson, 2005). In addition, action research, in its essence, is a *cyclical* inquiry process (Kemmis & Wilkinson, 1998; Stringer, 2007) involving some form of planning, action, and reflection. Mertler (2017) describes a cycle of action research using a four-stage model: planning, acting, developing, and reflecting. According to Mertler, researchers contextualize problems of practice within the established body of research literature and develop a research plan during the *planning* stage. In the *acting* stage, they implement the research plan and collect and analyze the research data. After data analysis and interpretation, action researchers develop an action plan, an innovative solution for the original problem of practice, in the *developing* stage. Finally, in the *reflecting* stage, researchers reflect on the action research process, which also informs the next cycle of their action research.

Stringer's (2007) description of a cycle of action research depicts a similar model: look, think, and act. According to Stringer, in the *look* stage, researchers gather information (e.g., observations, surveys, literature reviews) about the problem of practice to better understand the nature of the issue. In the *think* stage, researchers analyze the collected data that "provides the background information necessary for effective action to be taken" (Stringer, 2007, p. 239). In the *act* stage, researchers develop and implement solutions to address the problem of practice that they investigate. After each iteration of the action research cycle (i.e., look-think-act), researchers reflect on the effectiveness of the action or solution and make changes to their practice for the next iteration of the action research process until the problem under investigation is addressed.

Another characteristic of action research is that it reflects a collaborative process. Even though action research focuses on improving one's practice, it requires the practitioner-researcher to work with others "who have a stake in the problem under investigation" (Herr & Anderson, 2005, p. 4). In educational settings, for example, educators might need to work with their colleagues and administrators to improve a situation in their classrooms or institutions (Mertler, 2017). Moreover, the effects of an individual's practice in an organization, especially when there are positive outcomes, influence the practices of others who work in a similar capacity (Tripp, 2005).

Furthermore, action research is a participatory inquiry process. The positionality of the action researcher is one of an insider (Herr & Anderson, 2005). Action research, though usually facilitated by one practitioner-researcher, involves all stakeholders to the issue being investigated, including study participants (Stringer, 2007). Because of the action researcher's positionality and the participatory nature, there is an obligation of reciprocity, so that the participants benefit directly from the research (Robertson, 2000); current participants contribute and benefit—not just future ones. Moreover, an action researcher aims to improve his or her own practice, and thus intends to influence the lives of individuals in relation to his or her practice (Kemmis & Wilkinson, 1998; McNiff & Whitehead, 2002).

A final key characteristic of action research is critical reflection. In fact, the action research process starts with reflection (Coghlan & Brannick,

2005; Tripp, 2005). To identify what to improve, action researchers first need to reflect on their current practices (Tripp, 2005) and their contexts. According to Mertler (2017), action research is "developing critical reflection about one's teaching" (p. 17), and action research requires reflexivity during the research where researchers monitor their positionalities and biases (Robertson, 2000). Some researchers also argue that critical reflection should occur at every stage of an action research project, not solely as a separate stage after an action is implemented, to evaluate how the action research itself is going (Coghlan & Brannick, 2005; Tripp, 2005).

Action Research Experiences

These key characteristics suggest that action research is more than discrete research methods, and it has been "characterized as a strategic process or approach for investigation" (Buss & Zambo, 2016, p. 141). Throughout our curriculum, we have aligned students' research experiences concerning their (a) paradigms and positionalities, (b) quantitative methods, and (c) qualitative methods. Also, we have made changes to our curriculum to better prepare students for these research experiences. Each of these is discussed below.

In developing scholarly practitioners, we challenge our students to move away from a post-positivist research paradigm (Johnson & Onwuegbuzie, 2004). This, however, is the paradigm with which they have the most experience. They are most familiar with an objectivist epistemology that distances the researcher and what is researched. We ask students to eschew treatment-control experimental designs and adopt action research's iterative design with a purpose and lens toward improvement (Buss & Zambo, 2016). Moreover, we ask students to interrogate their positionalities within their research contexts, topics, and participants (Herr & Anderson, 2005). Through this process of reflexivity, students most often select a pragmatic, interpretive, or transformative paradigm. Our students consider their positionalities along Herr and Anderson's continuum, identifying their insider-outsider perspectives, and with Peshkin's (1988) *Is* of subjectivities. Within these paradigms, we have recorded 88% of our students design mixed-method studies while 12% design entirely qualitative studies. These proportions directly align with the types of studies designed, with the overwhelming majority being evaluations of existing or student-implemented innovations and a small number of descriptive studies.

Like traditional Ph.D. students, our Ed.D. students practice quantitative data analysis early in their programs. These assignments are reflective of typical students' proposed research methods of (a) surveys reporting descriptive statistics and (b) pretest-posttest design with instruments using a dependent t-test. Because our students are at a distance, they do not have easy access to traditional statistical software packages, such as SPSS and SAS, and our curriculum has been limited in the ability to offer more online statistics courses. So, we have recommended and used Statcrunch (www. statcrunch.com/), a web-based statistical package, with a reasonable subscription fee.

Our students have the least experience with qualitative research methods. Early in our program, students conduct informal observations and reflect on these. Students also write interview protocols, conduct interviews, and analyze these inductively. The steep learning curves and relatively high costs for professional qualitative data analysis software have prompted us to use a macro combining the commenting feature in Microsoft Word with sorting in Microsoft Excel (see Harold Peach's video at https://youtu.be/TbjfpEe4j5Y with additions from YouTube commenter "mgcains" to provide a more complete macro).

Examples of Action Research Methodologies in Educational Technology Research

In this section, we analyzed students' dissertation topics, literature, and methods to demonstrate the use of action research to answer a variety of research questions within educational technology. All of our students' dissertations emerged from a problem occurring in their practice contexts.

Using the Literature

In the first year of their program, our students begin reviewing research literature aligned with their topics. They amass a collection of annotations using a general template that we provide and a database of references using Mendeley (www.mendeley.com/). During the second year of their program, students survey and explore research literature in targeted ways. The use, evaluation, and synthesis of existing literature in dissertations have been used like Dawson and Kumar (2014) reported: (a) contextualizing and justifying the problem of practice, (b) providing a theoretical framework for the research, and (c) informing the innovation design. For example, in justifying the problem of practice, one student implementing a flipped classroom model with writing practices used literature on industry demands and insufficient national writing achievement to support the need for her study. In providing a theoretical frame, another student explored faculty experiences with active learning pedagogy using andragogy and principles of adult learning as the lens for teaching practices in higher education. Still, another study used social capital theory to frame culturally diverse students' experiences within an internship. To inform the innovation design, a student from our third cohort used special education evidence-based practices of constant-time delay, explicit vocabulary instruction, and active engagement with dual coding theory and Gagné's (Gagné, Wager, Golas, & Keller, 2005), nine events of instruction to inform her design of computer-assisted modules for students with intellectual disability and autism. Another student used situated learning and cognitive apprenticeship model to inform his design of individualized teacher technology integration professional development.

Types of Studies

Aligned with the Beltzer and Ryan's (2013) analysis, students in our Ed. D. program have studied three types of questions: (1) questions evaluating a policy or initiative that is already in place, (2) questions implementing and evaluating an intervention designed by the student, and (3) questions describing a current issue or problem to make appropriate and contextualized recommendations to address the problem in future cycles of action research. An example of action research under the umbrella of question Type 1 is from one of our students, also a member of the active learning initiative assessment team at his institution, who has been exploring an active learning initiative at a regional university where he worked as an instructional designer responsible for the design of the active learning classrooms, technology selection, and faculty training. More specifically, his action research study aimed to explore the experiences of and the professional development, classroom technology, and technical support needs of faculty who have taught in the active learning classrooms. To answer the research questions, he administered quantitative surveys to gather data about the experiences and needs of faculty who have previously taught or have been teaching in the active learning classrooms and conducted focus group interviews with a group of faculty.

For question Type 2, for instance, a student designed an action research study on evaluating the implementation of self-regulated learning strategies within an online homework platform for improving college students' self-regulated learning and mathematics self-efficacy skills within the context of his college Algebra course at a southeastern university. This particular student implemented several self-regulated learning strategies in an online homework platform to improve his students' low mathematics self-efficacy and self-regulated learning skills when learning new mathematical concepts. For instance, he strategically incorporated structured journals as part of assignments his students complete in his college algebra course. In addition to structured journals, data collection methods included pre- and post-surveys on mathematic self-efficacy and self-regulated learning, and focus group interviews with students.

Finally, for the question Type 3, a student, who is also a teacher and technology teacher leader at a high school, designed an action research study exploring teachers' needs and preferences, and the administrator perceptions of teachers' needs for educational technology-focused professional development at her high school to make recommendations for future professional development. Data collection methods included a quantitative survey gauging teachers' needs and preferences for educational technology-focused professional development, and focus group interviews with teachers and administrators. These example dissertations are indicative of how a practitioner-researcher might use action research with various research topics.

Gauging Success

To determine how well the curricular designs and action research experiences are impacting students, at the end of their first and second years in our program, our students completed program evaluation surveys. The descriptive findings presented here represent both quantitative and qualitative data. In the first-year survey, a large portion of the survey was focused on students' preparation with action research methods. In the second-year survey, the section with action research methods continued, and we also inquired about students' readiness for using theory and research literature plus academic writing.

On the first- and second-year surveys 17 items were common and addressed action research methods. The list of items is presented with the findings in Table 6.1. Seven additional items related to research were added as part of the second-year survey; they are shown in Table 6.2 with the findings. Nine items specific to using theory and literature are presented in Table 6.3. All of the items asked students to respond to the stem: "To what extent do you feel the Ed.D. program has impacted your knowledge and ability to ..." All items were scaled from (0) None at all, (1) To a small extent, (2) To a moderate extent, (3) To a large extent, (4) To a very large extent. According to the survey results, students rated their knowledge and ability about research methods between (3) To a large extent and (4) To a very large extent for most of the items after the first and second year. These ratings showed that students had gained some level of confidence in their knowledge of research methods during their first two years in the program. Mean scores for some items in the second year survey are slightly lower than the mean scores in the first year survey. While getting prepared for the doctoral comprehensive exam, which happens at the end of the second year, students might have realized the areas they still need to improve, and thus assessed their research methods, theory and ethics knowledge slightly lower.

For the additional research items that were part of the second-year survey, all of the cohorts' responses except two items (i.e., Item 2, Item 3) for Cohort 3 all ranged from (3) To a large extent to (4) To a very large extent with little variation in responses.

Similarly, the items from the second-year survey reflected the students' confidence in using theory and literature. All of these items ranged from (3) To a large extent to (4) To a very large extent. Cohort 3 recorded the lowest means on these items, and they also had the highest variation in responses for all of the second-year survey items.

Table 6.1 Means for Research Item Common in both First- and Second-year Surveys

To what extent do you feel the Ed. D. program has impacted your knowledge and ability to . . .	Cohort 1		Cohort 2		Cohort 3	
	Year 1 (n=13)	Year 2 (n=15)	Year 1 (n=15)	Year 2 (n=11)	Year 1 (n=7)	Year 2 (n=9)
1. Create instruction based on learning principles and research-based best practices.	2.77	2.40	2.87	2.55	2.14	2.00
2. Review the research of past and current theory of educational technology.	3.00	2.73	3.00	2.73	2.29	3.00
3. Review existing research literature to support research designs and methods.	3.62	2.67	3.33	2.73	3.29	2.33
4. Review existing research literature to support assessments or evaluation of learning and practice.	3.85	3.60	3.53	3.91	3.71	3.44
5. Conduct a literature search for research to enhance instructional practice.	3.54	3.53	3.33	3.45	2.43	3.22
6. Use research for decision-making.	3.77	3.13	3.53	3.55	3.57	2.78
7. Design research methods to solve problems and enhance practice.	3.62	3.13	3.47	3.73	3.71	3.22
8. Use quantitative and qualitative research methods.	3.69	2.93	3.53	3.73	3.57	3.00
9. Use quantitative and qualitative methods to assess and evaluate learning.	3.77	3.00	3.60	3.73	3.86	3.22
10. Use research methods to solve problems for learning and instruction.	3.85	3.13	3.60	3.73	2.71	3.11
11. Examine existing practices with research methods.	3.85	3.60	3.47	3.55	3.14	3.33
12. Use research methods in assessing and evaluating learning.	3.92	3.73	3.33	3.73	3.29	3.56

(*Continued*)

Table 6.1 (Cont.)

To what extent do you feel the Ed. D. program has impacted your knowledge and ability to ...	Cohort 1		Cohort 2		Cohort 3	
	Year 1 (n=13)	Year 2 (n=15)	Year 1 (n=15)	Year 2 (n=11)	Year 1 (n=7)	Year 2 (n=9)
13. Use methods of quality, rigor, and trustworthiness for sound academic research.	3.54	3.87	3.40	3.82	2.57	3.67
14. Use ethical practices in research.	3.85	3.47	3.60	3.82	3.86	2.89
15. Apply ethical research practices with human subjects.	3.85	3.47	3.40	3.82	3.86	2.67
16. Apply principles of the American Psychological Association for referencing.	3.92	3.60	3.53	3.82	3.71	3.56
17. Apply principles of the American Psychological Association to prevent plagiarism.	4.00	3.53	3.73	3.64	4.00	3.44

Students' research methods and data analysis experiences have worked with some successes. These successes are explained through the open-ended responses that were part of the second-year survey. Eleven open-ended items were included, asking questions such as:

Table 6.2 Additional Research Items from Second-year Survey

To what extent do you feel the Ed.D. program has impacted your knowledge and ability to ...	Cohort 1		Cohort 2		Cohort 3	
	Mean (n=15)	SD	Mean (n=11)	SD	Mean (n=9)	SD
1. Identify rigorous academic research.	3.87	0.35	3.82	0.40	3.67	0.71
2. Identify methodological flaws in academic research.	3.47	0.74	3.82	0.40	2.89	0.78
3. Identify theoretical assumptions in academic research.	3.47	0.64	3.82	0.40	2.67	0.50
4. Identify limitations of academic research.	3.60	0.63	3.82	0.40	3.56	0.53
5. Critique academic research.	3.53	0.64	3.64	0.50	3.44	0.53
6. Write academically.	3.73	0.46	3.73	0.47	3.56	0.53
7. Communicate research to others.	3.60	0.51	3.55	0.69	3.33	0.50

Table 6.3 Theory and Literature Items from Second-year Survey

To what extent do you feel the Ed.D. program has impacted your knowledge and ability to ...	Cohort 1		Cohort 2		Cohort 3	
	Mean (n=15)	SD	Mean (n=11)	SD	Mean (n=9)	SD
1. Use existing theory and research to support decision-making regarding practice.	3.53	0.64	3.64	0.50	3.11	0.78
2. Synthesize existing theory and research to frame research.	3.53	0.64	3.73	0.47	3.33	0.87
3. Synthesize existing theory and research to inform practice.	3.60	0.63	3.73	0.47	3.11	0.93
4. Associate leading authors with research and theories.	3.47	0.64	3.64	0.67	3.22	0.83
5. Identify and apply learning theory to inform practice.	3.47	0.64	3.73	0.47	3.56	0.53
6. Identify and apply learning theory to develop effective instruction.	3.47	0.64	3.73	0.47	3.44	0.53
7. Apply learning theory to achieve various instructional goals or purposes.	3.40	0.83	3.82	0.40	3.00	1.00
8. Distinguish between theory and research.	3.53	0.74	3.82	0.40	3.33	0.71
9. Distinguish between learning theories and instructional models.	3.53	0.64	3.73	0.47	3.22	0.97

- At the end of your second year in our program, what are some of your key takeaways?
- What are some of your personal areas for improvement?
- How confident do you feel about implementing action research? and
- What are your thoughts and feelings about literature review and writing academically?

These open-ended items were analyzed inductively (Liu, 2016; Thomas, 2006), beginning with open and *in vivo* coding in Microsoft Word using the Comment function, a macro, and then exporting the codes to Microsoft Excel for sorting (which is the same process our students have been practicing). The unit of analysis was a meaningful utterance/phrase. Two subsequent iterations through categorizing and organizing in Microsoft Word and sorting in Microsoft Excel occurred. In Round One, 162 codes were applied. In the second round, 94 relevant codes were categorized; in the final round, 83 relevant codes were carried forward into five themes.

Theme: Experiences with Research and Knowledge of Educational Theory Have Impacted Students' Instructional Design and Practice

The most prevalent theme in the open-ended comments addressed students' (a) experiences with research and (b) knowledge of education and how these two impacted their instructional design and their instructional practices. Twenty-seven of the 83 (33%) codes were associated with this theme. Because of students' experiences with research, they have become "better versed in research about educational technology," and they expressed "confidence" in "having the knowledge and the research that backs up why we should do some approaches and not do others."

The students also expressed their growth in knowledge of educational theory. This growth provided rationales "behind some district- and school-level initiatives" and how educational theories "impact the types of teaching and technologies that are appropriate in our local context."

The experiences in research and increased knowledge of educational learning theories impacted the students' instructional design. These affected students' "thinking ... before putting a training or policy together." Educational theories and models have prompted one student to reconsider her "lessons from the perspectives of various learning theories and making changes as a result." Theories have also changed the way she "think[s] about designing instructional units and professional development opportunities."

Similarly, experiences in research and increased knowledge of educational learning theories impacted students' practice. For example, one student stated, "As I prepare to teach, I cannot help but think through the ways that lessons and activities correlate with various learning theories." Another student wrote about changes in her practice by being "able to see several different strategies and solutions where before I would rely on traditional ways of thinking."

In summary, three students stated a common sentiment that experiences with research and their increased knowledge of learning theory "made me a better educator."

Theme: Students' Struggled with Becoming Academic Writers

The emphasis on reviews of related literature is a hallmark of the second year of the program. So, the struggle many students expressed with becoming better academic or scientific writers is expected. Eighteen out of 83 codes (22%) were reflective of this theme. Many students expressed a need to develop "a better ability to synthesize research" and "synthesizing [research literature] rather than summarizing." One student summed up the need for improvement as "my weaknesses in writing have definitely been exposed" while another student emphasized that learning to write academically is a skill that she will "continue to work on ... intently."

Theme: Students Expressed They Acquired More Knowledgeable about Research and Understanding the Scope and Depth of Research

In this theme, students said they had become more "critical researchers." Eleven of the 83 codes (13%) were associated with this theme. They offered examples of how their knowledge about research had provided the habit of mind for approaching an instructional problem developing "a research muscle." For example, one student wrote, "This program has given me a whole other level of thinking that enables me to engage in high-level conversations with academic administrators and deans. I view my environment through a different lens now, and it feels good."

Theme: Extant Theory and Research Literature Have Caused Students to be More Critical and Prompt the Need for More Study

Nine out of 93 (11%) codes were associated with this theme. Awareness of theory and research literature has caused students to be more critical of professional decisions and their practices. As scholarly practitioners, our students stated they had become more "reflective of [their] own teaching practices" and critical of "decisions and practices." This reflective practitioner stance was evident in their comments where they are "now more likely to question the effectiveness of different approaches" and stated they were now "able to look at situations and issues from many angles ... [and] identify poor and unfair practices that go on in my school and district."

Theme: Students Said They Needed More Experiences with Quantitative Research Methods and Statistical Analyses

When asked about their personal areas for improvement after their second year in the program, students focused most heavily on their needs for additional experiences and understanding with quantitative research methods and statistical analyses. Eight of 83 (10%) codes addressed this theme. One student wrote:

> There is no doubt that I also need to work on my understanding of how to analyze quantitative research. I feel I understand the basics, and that will probably be sufficient for my study, but when it comes to more complicated statistics, I have difficulty following studies that employ them, much less feeling equipped enough to utilize them.

Hence, this was an area that we have given significant attention to, and as a result, we made a few curriculum changes that are discussed below.

Conclusions and Reflections

In this chapter, we presented an overview of the process for preparing doctoral students as action researchers in our educational technology program. We described doctoral students' experiences with action research and other aspects of our program. Findings from surveys and open-ended questions indicated that our students have acknowledged the importance of (a) connecting research and theory into their practice; (b) practicing critical reflection through coursework and their interactions within the program and identified the areas for improvement in their practice as well as in their research skills and knowledge; and (c) becoming more knowledgeable about research and evaluation of professional decisions. In addition, our program faculty have critically reflected on our practices and the curriculum we designed, and we have started several initiatives to meet the needs of our students.

To better prepare our students as action researchers and to reduce their frustrations and barriers to analyzing data, we made two changes to our curriculum concerning research methods coursework. First, we replaced a theoretical introductory research methods course with a practice-oriented research design course because it (1) discusses mixed methods research designs in addition to quantitative and qualitative research methods, and (2) allows students to practice designing an action research study through writing a research proposal. Second, and most recently in Fall 2019, we exchanged an early assessment course for a new quantitative research and analysis course. It has been critical to work with our educational research faculty members to develop these online courses that supplement and complement our other research courses.

We have also observed the increased use of *R* for statistics, and we have chosen to use JASP, one of the promising software packages based on *R* (https://jasp-stats.org/). JASP has two advantages that meet our students' needs: It is open-source software, and the visual interface does not require programming, which would be a barrier for our students. We have also continued to look for alternatives to qualitative data analysis software that is reasonably priced, intuitive to use, and robust enough to handle moderate amounts of textual data from interviews, artifact descriptions, and memos. All of our students' studies include qualitative data, so we were concerned the macro approach described earlier would be too cumbersome and negatively affect students' analyses. We wanted to prevent the tool from becoming a barrier to analysis and findings. To date, we are piloting the use of Delve (https://delvetool.com/) with our first cohort of students to analyze their dissertation data. From our evaluation, Delve seems to fill the niche between the macro-based strategy our students have been using and the complex, sophisticated software packages that would require too much investment.

Besides these changes, based on student feedback as well as student performance assessments (e.g., comprehensive exam results), we are continuously reflecting on other aspects of our doctoral program (e.g., the sequence of coursework, course learning outcomes) and discussing viable actions that we can take to improve the quality of the program, and thus our students' experiences as action researchers.

Results presented in this chapter are limited to the data from three cohorts of students in our program who are still working on their dissertation in practice. The above-mentioned curriculum changes did not affect the courses these students have taken thus far. Therefore, to continue to evaluate and improve our program, we will need to examine the student feedback from cohorts, whose curriculum reflects these curriculum changes. Further, our assessment mostly relies on self-reported surveys at this point. To evaluate the long-term effects of a program, like ours, educational technology programs might consider sustaining the communication with their alumni after they complete their studies, and monitor their scholarly practices within their contexts.

References

Arslan-Ari, I., Ari, F., Grant, M. M., & Morris, W. S. (2018). Action research experiences for scholarly practitioners in an online education doctorate program: Design, reality, and lessons learned. *TechTrends*, *62*(5), 441–449.

Beltzer, A. & Ryan, S. (2013). Defining the problem of practice dissertation: Where's the practice, what's the problem? *Planning & Changing*, *44*(3), 195–207.

Buss, R. R. & Zambo, D. (2016). Using action research to develop educational leaders and researchers. In A. Perry (Ed.), *The EdD and the Scholarly Practitioner*, (pp. 137–152). Charlotte, NC: Information Age Publishing.

Coghlan, D. & Brannick, T. (2005). *Doing action research in your own organization* (2nd ed.). London: Sage.

Coryell, J. E., Wagner, S., Clark, M. C., & Stuessy, C. (2013). Becoming real: Adult student impressions of developing an educational researcher identity. *Journal of Further and Higher Education*, *37*(3), 367–383.

Dawson, K. (2012). Using action research projects to examine teacher technology integration practices. *Journal of Digital Learning in Teacher Education*, *28*(3), 117–123.

Dawson, K. & Kumar, S. (2014). An analysis of professional practice Ed. D. dissertations in educational technology. *TechTrends*, *58*(4), 62–72.

Dawson, K. & Kumar, S. (2016). Guiding principles for quality professional practice dissertations. In V. Storey & K. Hesbol (Eds.), *Contemporary approaches to dissertation development and research methods* (pp. 133–145). Hershey, PA: IGI Global. doi:10.4018/978-1-5225-0445-0.ch009.

Gagné, R. M., Wager, W. W., Golas, K. C., & Keller, J. M. (2005). *Principles of instructional design* (5th ed.). Belmont, CA: Wadsworth/Thomson Learning.

Herr, K. & Anderson, G. L. (2005). *The action research dissertation*. Thousand Oaks, CA: Sage.

Hine, G. S. C. (2013). The importance of action research in teacher education programs. *Issues in Educational Research*, *23*(2SPL), 151–163.

Hockey, J. & Allen-Collinson, J. (2005). Identity change: Doctoral students in art and design. *Arts and Humanities in Higher Education*, *4*(1), 77–93.

Johnson, R. B. & Onwuegbuzie, A. J. (2004). Mixed methods research: A research paradigm whose time has come. *Educational Researcher*, *33*(7), 14–26. doi:10.3102/0013189X033007014.

Kamler, B. & Thomson, P. (2006, April). Doctoral writing: Pedagogies for work with literatures. Paper presented at the American Educational Research Association Annual Meeting, San Francisco.

Kamler, B. & Thomson, P. (2008). The failure of dissertation advice books: Toward alternative pedagogies for doctoral writing. *Educational Researcher, 37*(8), 507–514.

Kemmis, S. & Wilkinson, M. (1998). Participatory action research and the study of practice. In B. Atweh, S. Kemmis, & P. Weeks (Ed.), *Action research in practice: Partnerships for social justice* (pp. 21–37). New York, NY: Routledge.

Kumar, S. & Antonenko, P. (2014). Connecting practice, theory and method: Supporting professional doctoral students in developing conceptual frameworks. *TechTrends, 58*(4), 54–61.

Kumar, S. & Dawson, K. (2012). Theory to practice: Implementation and initial impact of an online doctoral program. *Online Journal of Distance Learning Administration, 15*(1). Retrieved August 28, 2019 from www.learntechlib.org/p/76565/.

Kumar, S. & Dawson, K. (2014). The impact factor: Measuring student professional growth in an online doctoral program. *TechTrends, 58*(4), 89–97.

Kumar, S., Johnson, M., & Hardemon, T. (2013). Dissertations at a distance: Students' perceptions of online mentoring in a doctoral program. *International Journal of E-Learning & Distance Education/Revue Internationale Du E-learning Et La Formation À Distance, 27*(1). http://ijede.ca/index.php/jde/article/view/835/1481.

Lasater, K., Bengtson, E., & Murphy-Lee, M. (2016). An online CPED educational leadership program: Student perspectives on its value and influence on professional practice. *Impacting Education: Journal on Transforming Professional Practice, 1*(1). doi:10.5195/ie.2016.8.

Liu, L. (2016). Using generic inductive approach in qualitative educational research: A case study analysis. *Journal of Education and Learning, 5*(2), 129–135.

Manfra, M. M. & Bullock, D. K. (2014). Action research for educational communications and technology. In J. M. Spector, M. D. Merrill, J. Elen, & M. J. Bishop (Eds.), *Handbook of research on educational communications and technology* (pp. 161–172). New York, NY: Springer.

McNiff, J. & Whitehead, J. (2002). *Action research: Principles and practice*. London: Routledge Falmer.

Mertler, C. A. (2017). *Action research: Improving schools and empowering educators* (5th ed.). Los Angeles: Sage.

Mertler, C. A. & Henriksen, D. (2018). Creative and innovative solutions to accommodate the growth of a professional practice doctoral program. *Impacting Education: Journal on Transforming Professional Practice, 3*(1), 36–44. doi:10.5195/ie.2018.55.

Mills, G. E. (2017). *Action research: A guide for the teacher researcher* (6th ed. ed.). Boston, MA: Pearson.

Peshkin, A. (1988). In search of subjectivity—One's own. *Educational Researcher, 17* (7), 17–21. doi:10.2307/1174381.

Robertson, J. (2000). The three Rs of action research methodology: Reciprocity, reflexivity and reflection-on-reality. *Educational Action Research, 8*(2), 307–326. doi:10.1080/09650790000200124.

Shulman, L. S. (2005). Signature pedagogies in the professions. *Daedalus, 134*(3), 52–59. doi:10.1162/0011526054622015.

Stringer, E. T. (2007). *Action research* (3rd ed.). London: Sage.

Thomas, D. R. (2006). A general inductive approach for analyzing qualitative evaluation data. *American Journal of Evaluation, 27*(2), 237–246.

Tripp, D. (2005). Action research: A methodological introduction. *Educação E Pesquisa, 31*(3), 443–466.

Zambo, D. (2011). Action research as signature pedagogy in an education doctorate program: The reality and hope. *Innovative Higher Education, 36*(4), 261–271.

7 Making Data Science Count In and For Education

Joshua M. Rosenberg, Michael Lawson, Daniel J. Anderson, Ryan Seth Jones, and Teomara Rutherford

Introduction

Today, data analysts and programmers leverage data to inform and even transform many aspects of contemporary life, from policing and insurance to media and advertising (O'Neil, 2016). In education, teachers, administrators, and policymakers use data to understand educational processes and outcomes, such as student learning (Buckingham Shum et al., 2013; Datnow & Hubbard, 2015; Moore & Shaw, 2017) and the presence of inequities (Reardon, Fahle, Kalogrides, Podolsky, & Zárate, 2019). Parents, too, use data to guide decisions about where to live and send their children to school (Hasan & Kumar, 2019). Students use data in their classes to learn about their communities (Wilkerson & Laina, 2018), social issues (Gutstein, 2016), and scientific phenomena (Lehrer & Schauble, 2004). With all of this in mind, it is evident that the availability of data impacts both contemporary life and teaching and learning in educational systems.

The role of data is especially germane to those studying learning design and technology (LDT) and related fields, such as the learning sciences (e.g., Wilkerson & Polman, 2019) and educational technology (e.g., Hillman & Säljö, 2016). LDT scholars have been at the forefront of efforts to identify ways to address new and long-standing questions using novel data sources. For example, LDT researchers have found ways to utilize novel data sets from social media to understand the role of social media in teaching and learning (Coughlan, 2019; Greenhalgh, Rosenberg, Staudt Willet, Koehler, & Akcaoglu, 2020; Kimmons & Smith, 2019; Romero-Hall, Kimmons, & Veletsianos, 2018), use telemetric data collected as students interact with educational technology to gain insight into students' motivation and learning (e.g., Bernacki, Nokes-Malach, & Aleven, 2015; Peddycord-Liu et al., 2018; Rodriguez et al., 2019), and use data sets from wearable devices to engage and understand the learning of K-12 students about data analysis and interpretation (Lee, Drake, & Williamson, 2015).

However, the LDT field's creative integration of novel data sets also brings with it new challenges. For instance, issues related to student privacy and the length of time data can be stored are essential concerns to be raised, especially as new and expansive forms of data tracking are becoming commonplace (Leibowitz, 2018). Some issues are social, such as how widely accessible data should be, and how data are used by educational stakeholders as part of improvement processes, rather than merely for evaluation (American Educational Research Association, 2015). Furthermore, when it comes to state-of-the-art uses of educational data, scholars who apply data science as a methodology often carry out their work in isolation from those who study how to help students learn to analyze new data sources. As a consequence, scholars who work on one of these different topics may talk past the other—to the detriment of both and this growing area of work.

This chapter, then, is intended to articulate one view of the role of data in LDT and the broader field of education. We do this through the lens of *data science*, because data science, which we define in the next section, aligns with the types of research involving digital technologies that are already being carried out in LDT, and because data science can distinguish newer ways in which data is used in education from those that are commonplace. The specific aims of this chapter, then, are twofold:

- To convey a view of data science and the state of educational data science. Doing so involves being precise about what data science is—and also what it is not. We do this in the *Defining Data Science* section of this chapter.
- To articulate what we view as two common, but commonly confused, perspectives for how data science can be applied in education. The first is as a research method—what we refer to as data science in education. The second is as a context for teaching and learning—data science for education. We do this in the *Intersections of Data Science and Education* section.

Defining Data Science in Education and Data Science for Education

For our purposes, we adopt a similar definition of data science that has been used in computer science and engineering, which defines *data science* as the intersection of a) the application of mathematics and statistics, b) computer science and programming techniques, and c) knowledge about a particular discipline (Conway, 2010; VanderPlas, 2016). Here, each dimension of data science is of the same importance—the combination of any two without the third defines a related activity (such as machine learning or educational technology) that is not directly representative of data science.

Applying the above definition of data science to education can illustrate how data science is similar to and different from other types of work, as represented in Figure 7.1.

In this description, quantitative methods are represented by the combination of disciplinary knowledge and math and statistics; machine learning

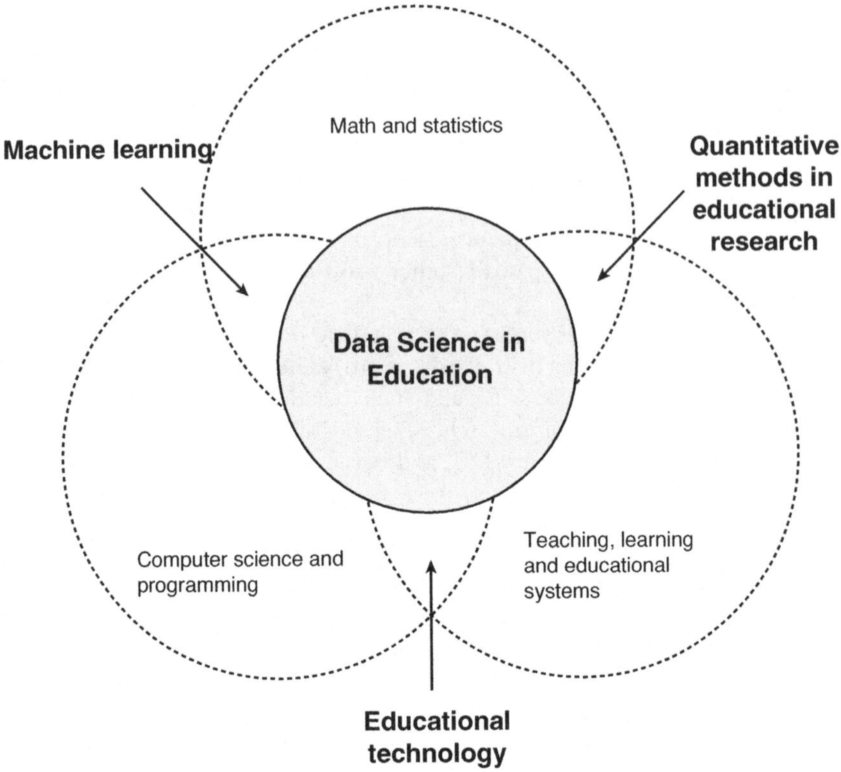

Figure 7.1 A definition of data science as the intersection of capabilities related to math and statistics, computer science programming and knowledge about teaching, learning, and educational systems

is represented by the combination of computer science and math and statistics; and, educational technology is represented by the combination of disciplinary knowledge and computer science and programming. Thus, this definition lays out what data science is, as well as what it is not: From this view, machine learning is not a synonym for data science, but, instead, a part of it. In the field of educational data science, the substantive knowledge that is brought to bear upon questions and topics is specific to knowledge about teaching, learning, and educational systems. In other words, educational data science involves the application of mathematics and statistics, computer science and programming skills, and knowledge about teaching, learning, and educational systems to ask (and answer) questions and pose (and work to solve) problems.

Although we argue that these three core dimensions define educational data science, others have defined data science by the scale of the data, rather than the domains marshaled to work with data (Schutt & O'Neil, 2014). We believe this is a cause of the many data science practices arising as solutions to dealing with large and complex data sets (e.g., audio-visual data). However, the practice of data science does not necessarily involve large and complex data sets. Although many of the data science methodologies may have developed in response to *Big Data* (Gandomi & Haider, 2015), the application of data science methodologies can also extend to data of a much smaller scale—with similar benefits. Programming, for instance, is central to the practice of data science, and researchers who can use programming in the course of analyzing data are better prepared to tackle data-related challenges that emerge in their work no matter the scale. As two examples, programming and the application of computer science-related capabilities can facilitate the organization and coding of survey-based data, or make it easy to explore textual data through the use of Natural Language Processing techniques. This emphasis away from the scale of the data used (and focus toward programming) has implications for the community of data scientists. For example, there is a vast and rapidly growing network of individuals supporting open source work in data science (Augur, 2016; Gutierrez, 2015), for which programming is helpful—or even necessary to ensure the trustworthiness and the reproducibility of analyses at any scale (Lowndes et al., 2017). Engaging in a more programmatic approach to analyzing data, regardless of its scale, can broaden participation in this community, which can contribute to a more open, transparent, and reproducible research practice (Lowndes et al., 2017). In summary, we use this definition to argue that data science can be seen as a field that extends beyond the analysis of Big Data—and includes, but is broader than, machine learning, quantitative methods in educational research, and educational technology.

The Intersections of Data Science and Education

In the previous section, we defined data science as the intersection of capabilities in three domains—mathematics and statistics, computer science and programming, and teaching, learning, and educational systems—with the disciplinary expertise being focused around knowledge about teaching, learning, and educational systems. In this section, we distinguish between two perspectives on how data science intersects with education.

The first perspective concerns the application of data science to answer educational questions or to solve educational problems, data science as a research methodology. This is what we refer to as *data science in education*. The second perspective relates to data science as a context for teaching and learning; data science as a domain, akin to science or mathematics education. We refer to this as *data science for education*. Both perspectives are described below.

Data Science in Education: Data Science as a Methodology

Data science in education, then, is specifically oriented around researching teaching, learning, and educational systems through the lens and techniques of data science. For those using data science in education as a methodology, a distinctive consideration is how the research process typically proceeds. In non-data science research, the researcher begins with a question, framed in a theoretical or conceptual framework (Booth, Colomb, & Williams, 2003). However, in the application of data science in education, scholars may begin with a theory-driven question, but allow the data to guide their inquiry through exploratory data analysis; moreover, a data set can be new enough that its description alone can serve as a novel contribution. For example, Kimmons and Smith (2019) reported descriptive data on the accessibility of the websites of K-12 schools in the United States. There is also another way that the data can guide research activity: A compelling data set can serve as a context for the generation of new questions. For instance, data generated as students interact with educational games highlight questions about the nature of student decision-making in a context different than in a typical face-to-face classroom (e.g., Liu, Cody, Barnes, Lynch, & Rutherford, 2017). Thus, one consideration for those doing data science in education has to do with considering which data sources are best to answer specific questions (in a top-down manner) and what questions can be answered with preexisting data (in a more bottom-up manner). Regardless of the data science methods used, a sound educational theory must inform either the *questions* asked in top-down approaches or the *interpretation* of data-driven insights gained from bottom-up approaches.

Related to the usefulness of new data sets, a common way that researchers have carried out data science in education is by *combining disparate sources of data* to explore novel research questions. As examples, Kelchen, Rosinger, and Ortagus (2019) demonstrated how data on state-level educational policies in the United States could be joined to data on student outcomes to compare the effects of different policies between states, and Rosenberg, Terry, Bell, Hiltz, and Russo (2016) combined data on how many public school teachers were employed in each state in the United States with social media data to understand the activity of participants in one of 47 state-based educational Twitter hashtags. These new combined data sets can give rise to exploratory bottom-up analyses as well; differences between states in participants' activity sparked a study of the activity of regularly occurring Twitter chats (Greenhalgh et al., 2020). Such data set combinations may require new types of skills from the dimensions of computer science and statistics to integrate and analyze the data correctly, and will likely also require the addition of researchers with more diverse knowledge bases relating to teaching, learning, and educational systems than are needed by single-data-type studies.

Using new data sources presents opportunities but also challenges, and these challenges may necessitate the development of new methods to suit the data at hand. For example, Anderson, Rowley, Stegenga, Irvin, and Rosenberg (2020) used Natural Language Processing techniques on the text of state-wide science standards to provide content-related validity evidence for science education assessment items. The development of these types of new methods is especially relevant for data sources that have traditionally been analyzed using qualitative methods: Analyzing audio and visual data, for instance, requires deciding not only what data to model and how to model it, but also to decide what the unit of analysis in audio-visual data is and how to create variables (Bosch, Mills, Wammes, & Smilek, 2018; D'Angelo et al., 2019). Further, such methods present challenges regarding the nature of how algorithms to process language data, especially of those from marginalized groups—care must be taken in specifying training data and creating algorithms that do not themselves reproduce existing inequities (Mayfield et al., 2019; Zou & Schiebinger, 2018).

In addition to the aforementioned methodological challenges, there are more foundational challenges presented by ready access to data. Social media provides an example of this tension. Although social media can meet the professional learning-related needs of educators (Greenhalgh & Koehler, 2017; Trust, Krutka, & Carpenter, 2016), teach students to write (Galvin & Greenhow, 2020), and facilitate communication between those enrolled in graduate programs (Romero-Hall, 2017; Rosenberg et al., 2016), it also can represent the exploitation of users' data. These issues are not distinct to social media platforms; Morris and Stommel (2017) describe how the terms of service for the popular plagiarism-detection service TurnItIn allows the company to own the license for all of the student papers submitted to it, and Rubel and Jones (2016) raise key questions for researchers and analysts using administrative (e.g., student grades, test scores) and learning management system data in light of increasingly ubiquitous applications of learning analytics in post-secondary educational institutions that may bely students' reasonable expectations of privacy. These questions are pressing, and scholars are working to address them through, for instance, developing values-driven learning analytics approaches (Chen & Zhu, 2019), ethical uses of artificial intelligence and machine learning that recognize the potential for ingrained biases (Greene, Hoffmann, & Stark, 2019), and examining how teachers can prepare students to protect themselves online (Krutka et al., 2019); those using data science methodologies in education should consider these issues and nascent solutions to them in the course of carrying out their work.

In summary, data science in education is the perspective of educational data science that concerns applying the dimensions of data science to educational research: studies about teaching, learning, and educational systems. This area of work is relatively new, but can be characterized by describing compelling data sets, combining different data sources to create new (and useful) sources of data, and developing new research methods that are suited to the kinds of data—such as text and audiovisual data—increasingly brought to bear upon educational questions and problems.

Although we are optimistic about this growing application of data science, we also describe how the use of large, often unobtrusively collected data sources highlights the importance of considering privacy of those from whom the data is collected as well as broader ethical and equity questions about how new methods are developed and applied.

Data Science for Education: Data Science as a Teaching and Learning Context

Data science for education pertains to the teaching and learning of data science and the concepts, people, and resources that support it. The use of the word "education" here might instill visions of K-12 classrooms, but we take the view that data science education is not restricted to any particular educational context, but, instead, is defined by the development of an individual's work with data (Wise, 2019). From this perspective, data science education is an expansive domain that includes teaching and learning data science in different contexts (e.g., K-12, post-secondary, industry, online, and informal settings), and examples of data science education include graduate seminars on data science methods (Schneider, Reilly, & Radu, 2020), workshops and training (Anderson & Rosenberg, 2019), and K-12 courses that engage students in working with data. These K-12 courses are often situated in mathematics and science content or classes (e.g., Hancock, Kaput, & Goldsmith, 1992; Lee et al., 2015; Lehrer & Schauble, 2004), but occasionally in other content areas (e.g., social studies; Drier & Lee, 1999; Lehrer & Romberg, 1996).

Data science for education spans not only a diverse set of contexts but also a different set of ideas and practices. Supporting students in growing their understanding and competency in what professional data scientists know and do is a complicated endeavor; this endeavor is further complicated by the need to consider the developmental trajectories for learners along and across each of the dimensions that make up data science. There is past research that is focused on one or more of the components of data science education—especially quantitative methods (the intersection of math and statistics education)—but there is less research that recognizes and encompasses the intersection of all three components.

As an example of the complexity of data science for education, consider two extreme ends of a hypothetical learning progression (Alonzo & Gotwals, 2012) for creating models of data: learning about algorithms as step-by-step instructions to carry out a classroom task in the elementary grades, and building a machine learning-based classification model to predict water quality in an undergraduate-level class. To progress along this path, the student's knowledge of algorithms in early grades needs to grow into ideas about statistics, probability, and modeling (Lehrer & English, 2018). These ideas will need to be coordinated with those about computer hardware and software, and proficiency within particular technologies and even programming languages to leverage the power of computing for analyzing large data sets and with domain knowledge specific to the study of water quality.

What is more, students' engagement with these topics needs to productively resemble the ways professionals engage with them (e.g., Jones, Lehrer, & Kim, 2017). Other fields, such as mathematics, have applied ideas regarding professional socialization and mathematics practices to the development of standards for learners (Cuoco, Goldenberg, & Mark, 1996; National Council for Teachers of Mathematics, 2000). Disciplinary identity is a necessary prerequisite to such a practice. This is why data science education must be conceived as a meta-discipline with a disciplinary identity beyond its component parts. This will involve coordinating research at the K-12 and undergraduate levels and between mathematics education, statistics education, science education, and computer science education. This will also include creating (and researching) opportunities for data science learners to use statistical and data science-related tools that are designed not only for learning but also for professional data science practice (McNamara, 2019; Rosenberg, Edwards, & Chen, 2020), even if, at first, learners must use tools designed for professionals in a more constrained way. Learners must also be socialized into the conventions of data scientists that go beyond tools: conventions such as dispositions toward open science and privacy and ethical issues.

This socialization can start early—even young children can learn to work with data in ways that engage the synergies between the three dimensions of data science and that reflect the professional dispositions of data scientists. Lehrer and Schauble (2004) describe an instance in which late elementary students investigate plant growth through *data modeling* as a way to understand the statistical concepts of variation and distribution. In such situations, data modeling can serve as an organizing set of practices for engaging in inquiry in science and mathematics learning (Lehrer & Schauble, 2015). As learners encounter and generate data, they can be supported to see and use data visualization, statistics, and models as tools to create new knowledge about the natural world (e.g., Arnold, Confrey, Jones, Lee, & Pfannkuch, 2018; Konold & Pollatsek, 2002; Lehrer & Romberg, 1996). In these examples, students' work with data is used to support the learning of domain-specific content; however, meaningful engagements with data can themselves be their own end, operating as part of a data science education that can be applied beyond specific disciplinary content. This goal aligns with and complements the increasingly relevant constructs undergirding computational thinking, a set of competencies and dispositions that leverage the affordances of computational processes to solve problems and express ideas (Papert, 1996; Wing, 2006). Becoming proficient in working with data can provide learners with an increasingly in-demand capability, as the number of occupations, from education to entrepreneurship, that demand or involve taking action based on data skyrocket (Wilkerson & Fenwick, 2017). Additionally, becoming data fluent can be personally empowering, because of the parts of our lives—from paying energy bills to interpreting news articles—that use data. Although these examples suggest fruitful points of coordination for integrating developmental trajectories related to data science education, much more work is needed to envision what a productive data science education might look like.

In summary, data science for education is a perspective focused on teaching (and learning) how to analyze data in ways akin to how data scientists make sense of data. Teaching and learning data science is challenging, in part because there are three distinct sets of capabilities comprising data science: math and statistics, computer science and programming, and knowledge of a specific domain. Moreover, although there are examples of data science-related research at the K-12 and post-secondary levels, much of the existing research is grounded in other disciplines (e.g., statistics or science education). Establishing data science education as a scholarly discipline in and unto itself will be necessary for the practices and dispositions of data scientists to proliferate. This need presents both challenges and opportunities for those researching this area. Given their disciplinary knowledge of teaching, learning, and educational systems, those actively engaged in *data science in education* may be uniquely positioned to communicate how their research practices can be applied to *data science education*.

Discussion: Three Synergies and Future Directions for Educational Data Science

In this chapter, we have sought to address two aims, defining educational data science through its focus on capabilities related to computer science and programming, math and statistics, and teaching, learning, and educational systems, and articulating two perspectives on data science within the field of education, data science in education and data science for education. As we conclude this chapter, we would like to consider how these two perspectives on data science within the field of education may work better together than in isolation. In particular, we believe three synergies that propel educational data science forward.

Our first synergy comes from considering together the software tools for conducting data science research and those for teaching and learning data science. Historically, scholars have found these to be separate (Gould et al., 2018). For example, tools for professionals, such as R, have emphasized their performance (R Core Team, 2020). In contrast, those for learners, such as the Common Online Data Analysis Platform (CODAP), have emphasized their ease-of-use (Common Online Data Analysis Platform, 2014). This delineation contributes to an issue: Learners eventually require functionality that the tool they have used does not provide, whereas the tools used by professionals remain challenging to begin to use. McNamara (2019) recommends that developers of statistical tools recognize that individuals analyzing data are likely to use different tools over time. So it is necessary to "build (either technically or pedagogically) an onramp toward the next tool" (p. 382). In this way, those designing (and studying the impacts of) tools for learners can be informed by the high-performing software used by professional statisticians and data scientists. Also, those developing (or improving) tools such as R can expand their user base by considering how tools for learners make use of their lower barriers to entry. The tidyverse set of R packages is an example of a statistical software tool that is both accessible and performant (Wickham et al., 2019). In the realm of programming and computer science, Scratch (Resnick et al., 2009) is another example of a low-barrier, but high-ceiling, tool. Although tidyverse and Scratch are promising examples, more work is needed to develop a smooth pathway of learning from entry-level to sophisticated, professional tools; such a path is necessary to support the consistent identity of data scientists across the learning trajectory.

The second synergy concerns a focus on representation, inclusivity, and access. Issues of equity are deeply entwined with issues of education. Similarly, the use of data and the practice of data science is inherently a political one (Green, 2018). As such, the community of educational data science must be representative of the students it serves. As an emerging field, data science has the opportunity to build a culture that emphasizes representation from the start; indeed, there have been calls to prioritize diversity within data science more broadly (e.g., Berman & Bourne, 2015). However, as data science draws heavily on its component dimensions, starting "from scratch" is mostly an illusion—the fields of math and statistics and computers and programming are already overwhelmingly male and white (Fisher, Margolis, & Miller, 1997; Lewis, Shah, & Falkner, 2019), and this likely spills over into data science. As a response, members of marginalized groups have organized to improve diversity in specific data science platforms (e.g., R-Ladies Global[1] and pyladies[2]) and the use of data for racial justice (e.g., Data for Black Lives[3]). Data science cannot rest on its status as a new field to absolve itself of marginalizing individuals from non-dominant groups. In essence, steps are needed to increase representation for a robust data science community.

To build an inclusive and representative data science, there must be broad access to developing expertise in data science and its component domains. Within educational data science, the idea of access includes enabling those with a deep grounding in educational disciplinary knowledge to develop expertise within the other data science components. Some educational graduate students have strong statistics-related capabilities. Still, there is substantial variability across sub-fields: Students in curriculum and instruction and teacher education, for example, may have fewer requirements and expectations related to statistics and quantitative methods than those in education policy or educational psychology. Educational graduate students may also have had limited experience with (and formal educational experiences in) programming. For educational researchers and others using data science methods in education—including data analysts, administrators, and educators—access to data science requires opportunities to learn how to program and apply programming skills in the context of using quantitative methods to ask education-related questions and solve education-related problems. Learning to program may be most fruitful if learning opportunities are created either by those with experience and expertise in education (e.g., Anderson, 2020 courses; Bovee et al.'s [2020] book, *Data Science in Education Using R*), or through collaboration and joint training opportunities (e.g., university Data Science centers, such as that at the University of Delaware,[4] Nosek et al.'s [2019] proposed *STEM Education Research Hub* focusing on building the capacity of educational researchers to use new research practices, many of which involve programming). In sum, for educational data science to successfully expand as a discipline, those already involved in it must think carefully about who is welcomed into it, and how to recognize and invite the expertise of all of those who wish to be involved.

A final synergy concerns the application of data science to itself as a discipline to understand how data science is taught and learned. For example, the tidycode R package (McGowan, 2019) is a data science tool that can be used to analyze the R code of those learning about data science: It could be used to understand, for example, how the breadth of the code someone writes (e.g., code not only for creating visualizations but also to prepare data and to use statistical models) expands over the semester for a data science class. As another example, much of the research on how data science is taught and learned uses qualitative research methods (Lehrer & Schauble, 2015); audio and visual data from data science education classes or workshops could also be analyzed using Natural Language Processing techniques to better understand the experiences of teachers and learners and to improve how data science is taught and learned. As with all data science research, and as we have argued above, such bottom-up and novel methods should be interpreted in light of theory and insights gleaned from prior and concurrent research using more traditional methods.

Conclusion

In this chapter, we sought to elucidate the importance of educational data science (how it counts) by defining it in terms of the intersection of math and statistics, programming and computer science, and teaching, learning, and educational systems, and articulating two (related) perspectives, data science in education (data science as a distinctive research methodology characterized by considering top-down and bottom-up research approaches and new sources of data and methods), and data science for education (data science as complex teaching and learning context characterized by a diverse set of ideas and practices and the need to establish a new field of study).

As being able to understand and work with data continues to grow as a source of power (and empowerment) in our society, researchers in LDT and the broader field of education have a responsibility and great potential to advance the field of data science. Accordingly, we described synergies concerning the creation of tools that can be used by both learners and professionals, representation, inclusivity, and access as first-order concerns for those involved in educational data science, and turning data science as a methodology upon itself to study teaching and learning about data science.

Inquiring about and using data is not only something done by researchers or data analysts, but also comprises a set of practices being taken up more broadly by citizens to inform decision making (O'Neil, 2016). Increasingly, those who hold the data hold power; data scientists are key players in social and educational change. Researchers in LDT and the broader field of education, we believe, have a unique role in applying data to compelling social issues and in understanding and molding the knowledge of future data scientists.

Notes

1 https://rladies.org/
2 www.pyladies.com/
3 http://d4bl.org/
4 https://dsi.udel.edu/

References

Alonzo, A. C. & Gotwals, A. W. (Eds.). (2012). *Learning progressions in science: Current challenges and future directions*. Rotterdam: Sense Publishing.

American Educational Research Association. (2015). AERA statement on use of value-added models (VAM) for the evaluation of educators and educator preparation programs. *Educational Researcher, 44*(8), 448–452.

Anderson, D. (2020). *Data science specialization for UO COE*. Retrieved from https://github.com/uo-datasci-specialization.

Anderson, D. J. & Rosenberg, J. M. (2019). *Transparent and reproducible research with R*. Workshop carried out at the Annual Meeting of the American Educational Research Association. Toronto, Canada.

Anderson, D. J., Rowley, B., Stegenga, S., Irvin, P. S., & Rosenberg, J. M. (2020). Evaluating content-related validity evidence using a text-based, machine learning procedure. Learning Procedure. Educational Measurement: Issues and Practice, pp. 1–12. doi:10.1111/emip.12314.

Arnold, P., Confrey, J., Jones, R. S., Lee, H. S., & Pfannkuch, M. (2018). Statistics learning trajectories. In D. Ben-Zvi, K. Makar, J. Garfield, (Eds.) *International handbook of research in statistics education* (pp. 295–326). Cham: Springer.

Augur, H. (2016). *The future of big data is open source*. Retrieved from https://dataconomy.com/2016/06/the-future-of-big-data-is-open-source/.

Berman, F. D. & Bourne, P. E. (2015). Let's make gender diversity in data science a priority right from the start. *PLoS Biology, 13*(7). https://journals.plos.org/plosbiology/article?id=10.1371/journal.pbio.1002206

Bernacki, M. L., Nokes-Malach, T. J., & Aleven, V. (2015). Examining self-efficacy during learning: Variability and relations to behavior, performance, and learning. *Metacognition and Learning, 10*(1), 99–117.

Booth, W., Colomb, G., & Williams, J. (2003). *The craft of research.* Chicago, IL: University of Chicago Press.

Bosch, N., Mills, C., Wammes, J. D., & Smilek, D. (2018). Quantifying classroom instructor dynamics with computer vision. In C. Penstein Rosé, R. Martínez-Maldonado, U. Hoppe, R. Luckin, M. Mavrikis, K. Porayska-Pomsta, B. McLaren, and B. du Boulay, (Eds.) *International Conference on Artificial Intelligence in Education* (pp. 30–42). Springer, Cham.

Bovee, E. A., Estrellado, R. A., Motsipak, J., Rosenberg, J. M., & Velásquez, I. C. (2020). *Data science in education using R.* London, UK: Routledge.

Buckingham Shum, S., Hawksey, M., Baker, R. S., Jeffery, N., Behrens, J. T., & Pea, R. (2013). Educational data scientists: A scarce breed. In *Proceedings of the Third International Conference on Learning Analytics and Knowledge* (pp. 278–281). Leuven, Belgium.

Chen, B. & Zhu, H. (2019). Towards value-sensitive learning analytics design. In *Proceedings of the 9th International Conference on Learning Analytics & Knowledge* (pp. 343–352). Tempe, AZ.

Common Online Data Analysis Platform [CODAP Computer software]. (2014). The Concord Consortium. Concord, MA. Retrieved from https://codap.con cord.org/.

Conway, D. (2010). *The data science Venn diagram.* Retrieved from http://drewcon way.com/zia/2013/3/26/the-data-science-venn-diagram.

Coughlan, T. (2019). The use of open data as a material for learning. *Educational Technology Research and Development.* doi:10.1007/s11423-019-09706-y.

Cuoco, A., Goldenberg, E. P., & Mark, J. (1996). Habits of mind: An organizing principle for mathematics curricula. *The Journal of Mathematical Behavior, 15*(4), 375–402.

D'Angelo, C. M., Smith, J., Alozie, N., Tsiartas, A., Richey, C., & Bratt, H. (2019). Mapping individual to group level collaboration indicators using speech data. In *Proceedings of the Computer-Support Collaborative Learning Conference.* Lyon, France.

Datnow, A. & Hubbard, L. (2015). Teachers' use of assessment data to inform instruction: Lessons from the past and prospects for the future. *Teachers College Record, 117*(4), 1–26.

Drier, H. S. & Lee, J. K. (1999). Learning about climate: An exploration in geography and mathematics. *Social Studies and the Young Learner, 12*(1), 6–10.

Fisher, A., Margolis, J., & Miller, F. (1997). Undergraduate women in computer science: Experience, motivation and culture. In *Proceedings of the 28th SIG-CSE Technical Symposium on Computer Science Education* (pp. 106–110). ACM Press: San Jose, CA.

Galvin, S. & Greenhow, C. (2020). Writing on social media: A review of research in the high school classroom. *TechTrends, 64*, 57–69.

Gandomi, A. & Haider, M. (2015). Beyond the hype: Big data concepts, methods, and analytics. *International Journal of Information Management, 35*(2), 137–144.

Gould, R., Wild, C. J., Baglin, J., McNamara, A., Ridgway, J., & McConway, K. (2018). Revolutions in teaching and learning statistics: A collection of reflections. In D. Ben-Zvi, K. Makar, J. Garfield, (Eds.) *International handbook of research in statistics education* (pp. 457–472). Cham: Springer.

Green, B. (2018). *Data science as political action: Grounding data science in a politics of justice.* arXiv preprint arXiv:1811.03435.

Greene, D., Hoffmann, A. L., & Stark, L. (2019). Better, nicer, clearer, fairer: A critical assessment of the movement for ethical artificial intelligence and machine learning. In *Proceedings of the 52nd Hawaii International Conference on System Sciences.*

Greenhalgh, S. P. & Koehler, M. J. (2017). 28 days later: Twitter hashtags as "just in time" teacher professional development. *TechTrends, 61*(3), 273–281.

Greenhalgh, S. P., Koehler, M. J., Rosenberg, J. M., & Staudt Willet, B. (in press). Considerations for using social media data in learning design and technology research. In E. Romero-Hall (Ed.), *Research methods in learning design & technology.* London, UK: Routledge.

Greenhalgh, S. P., Rosenberg, J. M., Staudt Willet, K. B., Koehler, M. J., & Akcaoglu, M. (2020). Identifying multiple learning spaces within a single teacher-focused Twitter hashtag. *Computers and Education.* doi:10.1016/j.compedu.2020.103809.

Gutierrez, D. (2015). *Open source software fuels a revolution in data science.* Retrieved from https://insidebigdata.com/2015/03/16/open-source-software-fuels-a-revolution-in-data-science/.

Gutstein, E. (2016). "Our Issues, Our People—Math as Our Weapon": Critical Mathematics in a Chicago Neighborhood High School. *Journal for Research in Mathematics Education, 47*(5), 454–504. doi:10.5951/jresematheduc.47.5.0454

Hancock, C., Kaput, J. J., & Goldsmith, L. T. (1992). Authentic inquiry with data: Critical barriers to classroom implementation. *Educational Psychologist, 27*(3), 337–364.

Hasan, S. & Kumar, A. (2019). *Digitization and divergence: Online school ratings and segregation in America.* SSRN. Retrieved from https://papers.ssrn.com/sol3/papers.cfm?abstract_id=3265316.

Hillman, T. & Säljö, R. (2016). Learning, knowing and opportunities for participation: Technologies and communicative practices. *Learning, Media and Technology, 41*(2), 306–309.

Jones, R. S., Lehrer, R., & Kim, M. J. (2017). Critiquing statistics in student and professional worlds. *Cognition and Instruction, 35*(4), 317–336.

Kelchen, R., Rosinger, K. O., & Ortagus, J. C. (2019). How to create and use state-level policy data sets in education research. *AERA Open.* doi:10.1177/2332858419873619.

Kimmons, R. & Smith, J. (2019). Accessibility in mind? A nationwide study of K-12 web sites in the United States. *First Monday, 24*, 2. doi:10.5210/fm.v24i2.9183

Konold, C., & Pollatsek, A. (2002). Data analysis as the search for signals in noisy processes. *Journal for Research in Mathematics Education, 33*(4), 259–289.

Krutka, D., Manca, S., Galvin, S., Greenhow, C., Koehler, M., & Askari, E. (2019). Teaching "against" social media: Confronting problems of profit in the curriculum. *Teachers College Record, 121*(14): pp. 1–19.

Lee, V. R., Drake, J., & Williamson, K. (2015). Let's get physical: K-12 students using wearable devices to obtain and learn about data from physical activities. *TechTrends, 59*(4), 46–53.

Lehrer, R. & English, L. (2018). Introducing children to modeling variability. In D. Ben-Zvi, K. Makar, J. Garfield, (Eds.) *International handbook of research in statistics education* (pp. 229–260). Cham: Springer.

Lehrer, R. & Romberg, T. (1996). Exploring children's data modeling. *Cognition and Instruction, 14*(1), 69–108.

Lehrer, R. & Schauble, L. (2004). Modeling natural variation through distribution. *American Education Research Journal, 41*(3), 635–679.

Lehrer, R. & Schauble, L. (2015). Developing scientific thinking. In L. S. Liben & U. Müller (Eds.), *Handbook of child psychology and developmental science: Cognitive processes* (Vol. 2, 7th ed. ed., pp. 671–714). Hoboken, NJ: Wiley.

Leibowitz, A. (2018, September 6). *Could monitoring students on social media stop the next school shooting?* New York Times. Retrieved from www.nytimes.com/2018/09/06/us/social-media-monitoring-school-shootings.html

Lewis, C., Shah, N., & Falkner, K. (2019). Equity and diversity. In S. Fincher & A. Robins (Eds.), *The Cambridge handbook of computing education research* (pp. 481–510). Cambridge, UK: Cambridge University Press.

Liu, Z., Cody, C., Barnes, T., Lynch, C., & Rutherford, T. (2017). The antecedents of and associations with elective replay in an educational game: Is replay worth it? In *Proceedings of the 10th International Conference on Educational Data Mining.* Wuhan, China.

Lowndes, J., Best, B., Scarborough, C., Afflerbach, J., Frazier, M., O'Hara, C., . . . Halpern, B. (2017). Our path to better science in less time using open data science tools. *Nature Ecology & Evolution, 1*(6), 160–167.

Mayfield, E., Madaio, M., Prabhumoye, S., Gerritsen, D., McLaughlin, B., Dixon-Román, E., & Black, A. W. (2019). Equity beyond bias in language technologies for education. In *Proceedings of the Fourteenth Workshop on Innovative Use of NLP for Building Educational Applications* (pp. 444–460).

McGowan, L. D. (2019). *tidycode: Analyze lines of R code the tidy way* (R package version 0.1.0). Retrieved from: https://CRAN.R-project.org/package=tidycode.

McNamara, A. (2019). Key attributes of a modern statistical computing tool. *The American Statistician, 73*(4), 375–384.

Moore, R. & Shaw, T. (2017). *Teachers' use of data: An executive summary.* ACT. Retrieved from www.act.org/content/dam/act/unsecured/documents/R1661-teachers-use-of-data-2017-12.pdf.

Morris, S. M. & Stommel, J. (2017). *A guide for resisting EdTech: The case against TurnItIn.* Hybrid Pedagogy. Retrieved from http://hybridpedagogy.org/resisting-edtech/.

National Council for Teachers of Mathematics. (2000). *Principles and standards for school mathematics.* Reston, VA: NCTM.

Nosek, B. A., Ofiesh, L., Grasty, F. L., Pfeiffer, N., Mellor, D. T., Brooks, R. E., III, . . . Baraniuk, R. (2019). Proposal to NSF 19-565 to create a STEM education research hub. doi:10.31222/osf.io/4mpuc.

O'Neil, C. (2016). *Weapons of math destruction: How big data increases inequality and threatens democracy.* New York, NY: Crown.

Papert, S. (1996). An exploration in the space of mathematics educations. *International Journal of Computers for Mathematical Learning, 1*(1), 95–123.

Peddycord-Liu, Z., Harred, R., Karamarkovich, S. M., Barnes, T., Lynch, C., & Rutherford, T. (2018). Learning curve analysis in a large-scale, drill-and-practice serious math game: Where is learning supported? In *Proceedings of the 19th International Conference on Artificial Intelligence in Education.* London, UK.

R Core Team (2020). *R: A language and environment for statistical computing.* R Foundation for Statistical Computing: Vienna, Austria. Retrieved from www. R-project.org/.

Reardon, S. F., Fahle, E. M., Kalogrides, D., Podolsky, A., & Zárate, R. C. (2019). Gender achievement gaps in US school districts. *American Educational Research Journal, 56*(6), 2474–2508.

Resnick, M., Maloney, J., Monroy-Hernández, A., Rusk, N., Eastmond, E., Brennan, K., . . . Kafai, Y. B. (2009). Scratch: Programming for all. *Communications of the ACM, 52*(11), 60–67.

Rodriguez, F., Yu, R., Park, J., Rivas, M. J., Warschauer, M., & Sato, B. K. (2019). Utilizing learning analytics to map students' self-reported study strategies to click behaviors in STEM courses. In *Proceedings of the 9th international conference on learning analytics & knowledge* (pp. 456–460).

Romero-Hall, E. (2017). Posting, sharing, networking, and connecting: Use of social media content by graduate students. *TechTrends, 61*(6), 580–588.

Romero-Hall, E., Kimmons, R., & Veletsianos, G. (2018). Social media use by instructional design departments. *Australasian Journal of Educational Technology, 34*(5), 86–98.

Rosenberg, J. M., Edwards, A., & Chen, B. (2020). Getting messy with data: Tools and strategies to help students analyze and interpret complex data sources. *The Science Teacher, 87*(5), 30–34.

Rosenberg, J. M., Terry, C. A., Bell, J., Hiltz, V., & Russo, T. E. (2016). Design guidelines for graduate program social media use. *TechTrends, 60*(2), 167–175.

Rubel, A. & Jones, K. M. (2016). Student privacy in learning analytics: An information ethics perspective. *The Information Society, 32*(2), 143–159.

Schneider, B., Reilly, J., & Radu, I. (2020). Lowering barriers for accessing sensor data in education: Lessons learned from teaching multimodal learning analytics to educators. *Journal for STEM Education Research.* Retrieved from https://link. springer.com/article/10.1007/s41979-020-00027-x.

Schutt, R. & O'Neil, C. (2014). *Doing data science: Straight talk from the frontlines.* Sebastopol, CA: O'Reilly Media.

Trust, T., Krutka, D. G., & Carpenter, J. P. (2016). "Together we are better": Professional learning networks for teachers. *Computers & Education, 102*, 15–34.

VanderPlas, J. (2016). *Python data science handbook: Essential tools for working with data.* Sebastopol, CA: O'Reilly Media.

Wickham, H., Averick, M., Bryan, J., Chang, W., McGowan, D., Francois, R., . . . Yutani, H. (2019). Welcome to tidyverse. *The Journal of Open Source Software, 4*(43), 1686.

Wilkerson, M. & Fenwick, M. (2017). Using mathematics and computational thinking. In C. Schwarz, C. Passmore, & B. Reiser (Eds.), *Helping students make sense of the world using next generation science and engineering practices* (pp. 181–204). Arlington, VA: NSTA Press.

Wilkerson, M. & Polman, J. (2019). Situating data science: Exploring how relationships to data shape learning. *Journal of the Learning Sciences.* doi:10.1080/10508406.2019.1705664.

Wilkerson, M. H. & Laina, V. (2018). Middle school students' reasoning about data and context through storytelling with repurposed local data. *ZDM, 50*(7), 1223–1235.

Wing, J. M. (2006). Computational thinking. *Communications of the ACM, 49*(3), 33–35.

Wise, A. F. (2019). Educating data scientists and data literate citizens for a new generation of data. *Journal of the Learning Sciences.* doi:10.1080/10508406.2019.1705678.

Zou, J. & Schiebinger, L. (2018). AI can be sexist and racist—it's time to make it fair. *Nature, 559*, 324–326.

8 Ethnographic Consideration Within Instructional Design Research Practices

Jill E. Stefaniak

Introduction

One of the most exciting aspects of instructional design is that it does not assume a one-size-fits-all approach. With a goal of instructional design being to facilitate learning and improve performance (Richey, Klein, & Tracey, 2011), solutions that are designed must be customized to meet the unique needs of the learning environment and audience. For an instructional designer to be successful at truly understanding their learning audiences' needs, they must understand the contextual factors that may promote or hinder learning and performance in these environments (Tessmer & Richey, 1997; Tessmer & Wedman, 1995). This can be accomplished by the instructional designer fully immersing himself or herself in the environment to understand better the unique factors that impact the learning environment being studied. Ethnography provides a mechanism for an instructional designer to research their instructional design experiences and solutions by gathering artifacts that provide a rich layer of insight into the learning environment (Barab, Thomas, Dodge, Squire, & Newell, 2004; Thomas, 2003; Yanchar, South, Williams, Allen, & Wilson, 2010).

Ethnography is a qualitative research method used to deeply understand "the social and cultural life of communities, institutions, and other settings" (LeCompte & Schensul, 1999). This method uses the researcher as a primary data collection source to gain a perspective of individuals belonging to a particular group or environment. According to LeCompte and Schensul (1999), an ethnographic inquiry is comprised of the following characteristics: studies are carried out in a natural setting, studies present an accurate reflection of participants' perspectives, studies involve interactions with the participants, and studies use the concept of culture as the lens for interpreting the results.

These ethnographic considerations align nicely with instructional design principles in that the instructional designer needs to consider the unique culture of the setting (i.e., organization or school) when designing learning and performance interventions. Gathering data from a natural setting, presenting an accurate portrayal of participants' experiences, and interacting with the participants can help the instructional designer leverage their goals during a contextual analysis where they are tasked with gathering as much insight as they can on their learning audience, the instructional setting, and how the learners will be transferring knowledge in a real-world environment.

The purpose of this chapter is to provide instructional designers with an overview of the various types of ethnographic methodologies used in instructional design research and explain how ethnographic methodologies align with instructional design practices, particularly taking into account the influence that contextual factors may have on a design intervention or study. Furthermore, this chapter will provide strategies for how an instructional designer can infuse ethnographic approaches into their instructional design research practices. A conceptual framework will also be presented to demonstrate how an instructional design researcher may use aspects of ethnographic inquiry to understand their learning and research environments better.

Types of Ethnographic Methodologies Used in Educational Research

Many instructional design studies include elements of ethnography as researchers are often interacting with their learning and research audience. Instructional design researchers engaged in ethnographic practices are further integrated into their field since they have experience as designers and learners (Gordon, Holland, & Lahelma, 2011). Ethnography requires the researcher to immerse themselves in the environment and gather data through direct observations, interactions with participants, and recordings of everyday life (Delamont & Atkinson, 1995; Spindler, 1982). Participant-observation (Spradley, 1980) is often used to serve two purposes for a study: (1) to engage in activities appropriate to the situation and (2) to observe the activities, people, and physical aspects of the situation (p. 54). Techniques such as participant-observation are useful to instructional design research studies by providing the instructional design researcher with the first-hand experience with the individual(s) for whom they are typically designing interventions.

There are several approaches that an instructional researcher may employ when conducting an ethnographic study. Ethnographic methods that have been predominantly used in instructional design include realist ethnography, critical ethnography, rapid ethnography, netnography, duoethnography, autoethnography, and feminist ethnography. It should be noted that these approaches are not always mutually exclusive, as one or two approaches may be overlapped. Table 8.1 provides an overview of these methods as well as examples of ethnographic studies that have been conducted with instructional design foci.

A realist ethnographic approach is synonymously referred to a traditional ethnography. In this approach, the researcher provides an objective account of a situation and the experiences of the individuals comprising a group

Table 8.1 Overview of Ethnographic Approaches Used in Instructional Design Research

Type	Description	Examples of Ethnography in Instructional Design	Reference
Realist Ethnography	An objective account of a situation where the researcher reports of experiences from individuals in a group (Barron, 2013). The researcher often writes in third-person and avoids using personal reflections to present an objective interpretation of the situation.	Using ethnographic methods to infuse culture into instructional designs	Young (2008)
		An instructional designer's journey to becoming a civic-minded professional	Yusop and Correia (2014)
Critical Ethnography	An ethnographic approach that uses ethnographic analysis to better understand the broader social implications and power dynamics related to a particular group of individuals. (Anderson, 1989; Carspecken, 2013)	Understanding the impact of learning technologies through stakeholders' complex digital learning experiences	Gratch and Warren (2018)
		An exploration of how teachers are promoting literacy in the classroom	Williams (2012)
Rapid Ethnography	An ethnography approach where the observation of a group is conducted in real-time to inject insights into the functionality of objects members of the group use regularly (Baines & Cunningham, 2013; Isaacs, 2016).	Contextual influences on the use of handheld learning technologies	Penuel, Tatar, and Roschelle (2004)
		Use of personas to inform instructional design practices	Maier and Thalmann (2010)
Netnography	An online research method for studying social interactions that occur in digital contexts (Costello, McDermott, & Wallace, 2017; Kozinets, 2010)	Designing instruction for students with special needs	Adam, Rigoni, and Tatnall (2006)
		Teachers learning to teach with technology in an online environment	Kulavuz-Onal (2013)
		Critical examination of learning that occurs within a MOOC	Wasson (2013)
Duoethnography	An ethnographic approach where two or more individuals engage in dialogue on their experiences	Use of virtual environments to teach research methods	Snelson, Wertz, Onstott, and

(Continued)

Table 8.1 (Cont.)

Type	Description	Examples of Ethnography in Instructional Design	Reference
	within a particular group or context (Norris & Sawyer, 2016)		Bader (2017)
		Reflecting on K-12 students' experiences in an online learning environment	Barbour, Siko, and Simuel-Everage (2012)
Autoethnography	A form of ethnography where the researcher self-reflects on their experiences related to understanding cultural, political, and social meanings of an environment or context (Adams, Jones, & Ellis, 2015; Ellis, Adams, & Bochner, 2011).	Exploring feminism in instructional design practices	Campbell (2015)
		An autoethnography exploring instructional strategies used to teach adult learners research methods	Suzanne (2019)
		A recount of a classroom teacher teaching in an online environment for the first time	Lewis (2018)
		A collaborative autoethnography of international students' experiences learning in an online environment	Rasi, Jantunen, Curcher, and Teras (2018)
Feminist Ethnography	An exploration of the relationship between social dynamics, politics, power, and privilege and gender (Buch & Staller, 2014).	Exploring how women with learning disabilities learn in secure wards	(Fish, 2017)
		Examination of race-based professional development on performance outcomes	Adams (2013)
		Exploring women's perspectives and experiences in the field of educational technology	Donaldson (2016)

(Barron, 2013). Studies that utilize this approach are often written in the third person, where the researcher (ethnographer) collects artifacts and provides their interpretation of the situation. A commonality among these types of studies is that the researcher is describing the unique culture of the group being studied and factoring how that culture influences the learning experience.

Examples of instructional design studies that utilized a realist ethnographic approach to providing an objective account of their study participants is evident in Young (2008)'s study that described how ethnography strategies were used to infuse culture into instructional design practices. A second example is Yusop and Correia's (2014) depiction of instructional designers' experiences that contributed to a civic-minded professional mindset.

A study is classified as being a critical ethnography when the central focus of the study is to explore social implications and power dynamics experienced by a group of individuals (Anderson, 1989; Carspecken, 2013). Often, the goal of these studies is to better understand the environment to help liberate a marginalized group of individuals.

Williams' (2012) study explored how teachers were promoting literacy in the classroom. Her study emphasized how a sociocultural theoretical approach could address the diverse literacy needs of students. Through ethnographic analysis, she explained how students were more apt to engage in literacy education if they were presented with culturally relevant examples throughout the coursework (Lehner, Thomas, Shaddai, & Hernen, 2017). Critical ethnography also served as the primary framework for Gratch and Warren's (2018) study, where they explored how learning technologies impacted students' digital learning experiences. Their research presents an overview of how they used video, screen images, and artifacts to capture the unique experiences of their learning audience.

Rapid ethnography is an approach used in real-time where the researcher is gathering data to use to inform decisions that will impact members of the group (Baines & Cunningham, 2013). This technique is becoming more widely recognized in human–computer interaction research (Millen, 2000) and user-design practices (Dourish, 2007). Examples of ethnographic studies that are grounded in instructional design practices include the use of data to develop personas as an extension of learner analysis. These techniques are beneficial to instructional design research on the impact that persona development has on instructional design practices as well as studies exploring researchers' depictions of a particular group of individuals that comprise a learning audience (Baylor, Ryu, & Shen, 2003; Pulsinelli & Roubie, 2001; Tempelman-Kluit & Pearce, 2014).

With the growth of distance education over the past few decades, netnography has emerged as the most recent ethnographic approach for research. This approach focuses solely on studying social interactions that occur in digital contexts (Costello et al., 2017; Kozinets, 2010). This has become a method of choice for instructional design researchers who are interested in exploring social media and distance learning environments (Adam et al., 2006; Wasson, 2013). Examples of studies utilizing a netnographic approach include Kulavuz-Onal's (2013) study that explored how teachers were learning *how* to teach with technology in an online environment. Another example is Wasson's (2013) study that examined *how* learning occurs in MOOC environments. A commonality among most netnographic studies is that emphasis is placed on studying the interactions and discourse among members of the learning environment (Kozinets, 2010).

Duoethnography is an approach used when two or more individuals collaborate to offer a dialogue on their experiences within a particular setting (Norris & Sawyer, 2016). These studies typically involve the researchers providing their individual recounts of an experience. These experiences are combined and shared to identify themes that may be used to understand better the customs and social dynamics of a particular group. While this approach has not been used too often in instructional design research, it certainly is a viable method to promote reflection-in-action, a concept Schön (1983) developed where designers frequently pause and recount what they are feeling, experiencing, or have observed while they are engaged in design work. Similarly, autoethnography is a form of ethnography where the researcher self-reflects and provides a first-person portrayal or interpretation of their experiences in a particular setting (Adams et al., 2015; Ellis et al., 2011).

Few instructional design studies have been published that have utilized a duoethnographic approach. Two studies that appear when searching instructional design and duoethnography. One of these is Barbour et al.'s study, where three researchers shared their reflections as a professor, designer, and graduate student participant in a study teaching to a K-12 audience in an online learning environment. A second study utilizing this technique is Snelson et al.'s (2017) study, where the researchers shared recounts of what it was like to teach a research methods course in an online format.

Feminist ethnography is an approach where the goal of the study is to explore the relationship between social dynamics, political power, and privilege as they relate to gender (Buch & Staller, 2014). These studies are grounded in exploring experiences encountered by women in a particular group or environment (Skeggs, 2001). One scholarly example of feminist ethnography in the instructional design is the compilation of female instructional design practitioners and researchers who share stories of the impact being a woman had on their career trajectories and various design projects (Donaldson, 2016).

Benefits of Using Ethnography in Instructional Design Practices

There are a lot of synergies between strategies used to collect data for ethnographic studies and principles of instructional design. Depending on the situation, techniques for gathering ethnographic data include, but are not limited to, direct observations, document analysis, interviews with members in a particular group or setting, field notes, and researcher reflections. Most ethnographic studies utilize multiple data sources to triangulate themes and support the objectivity of the researcher's interpretation of the environment (Spradley, 1980).

While several instructional design models have been designed to guide instructional practices, the majority of these models identify five typical phases found in the instructional design process: analysis, design, development, implementation, and evaluation (Branch, 2017). Some models go into greater depth, breaking down each of these phases into multiple steps, where others take a more general approach (Branch & Dousay, 2015).

One of the first steps common to all instructional design models is conducting a needs assessment. A needs assessment provides the means for understanding the specific needs relevant to a project. Unfortunately, instructional designers are not always privy to conducting a needs assessment. They must rely on information provided to them by their employer or client when they are beginning a new instructional design project. This results in the instructional designer having to design instruction for needs that have been presented at face value. Employing ethnographic strategies during a needs assessment could help enhance the ways instructional designers collect data to identify and verify needs pertinent to their projects and learning audiences (Johns & Makalela, 2011; Leighter, Rudnick, & Edmonds, 2013; Savage, 2006). By encouraging the instructional designer to take on a more active role by experiencing the environment first-hand, they can better understand their learners in a much different light than they would be presented with demographic data.

One of the first tasks in most instructional design projects is to conduct a learner analysis. During this phase of a project, the instructional designer is provided with details to help them better understand their learning audience. The client sometimes presents this information to the instructional designer, or the instructional designer is responsible for gathering their data to provide an accurate portrayal of the learners. Data collection techniques used to collect data for a learner analysis often involve surveys, interviews, document analysis, and focus groups (Stefaniak & Baaki, 2013). Ethnographic inquiry such as direct observations, field notes, and researcher reflections align with methods being recognized for developing learner personas in our field (Baaki, Maddrell, & Stauffer, 2017; Baylor & Kim, 2005; van Rooij, 2012).

In addition to learner analysis, contextual analysis involves developing an understanding of the instructional environment and the application setting where learners will apply what they learn during instruction (Dick, Carey, & Carey, 2009). Tessmer and Richey (1997) have broken down contextual analysis into three lenses: orienting, instructional, and transfer. The orienting context comprises the learner analysis. This lens explores learner perceptions, dispositions, experiences, and prerequisite skills that the learners are bringing to the instructional experience that is going to be designed for them. The more information that an instructional designer has regarding their learning audience, the more apt they will be in designing effective instructional materials.

The instructional lens involves gathering data on factors that will influence the delivery of instruction. This includes gathering information on the learning platform to be used (face-to-face instruction, online, mobile, blended), technological supports needed during training, content to be delivered, and instructional activities needed to foster the learners' acquisition of knowledge (Dick et al., 2009). The selection of instructional strategies and platforms should be influenced by information gathered about the orienting and transfer contexts.

The transfer lens consumes the environment where learners will apply their learning in a real-world setting. The instructional designer must understand what is expected of the learners after training, any challenges that may impact their ability to apply new knowledge the way it was intended or presented, and the desired performance outcomes for the real-world environment (Dick et al., 2009). While each of these three lenses has individual factors that need to be considered by the instructional designer, they are not mutually exclusive of one another.

Use of Ethnography in Instructional Design Research

While not all learner analyses require instructional designers to fully immerse themselves in the learning environment, we have begun to see a shift in instructional design scholarship that requires a more in-depth look at the learner experience and how new knowledge acquired through instructional design practices can be used in real-world settings. This is evident in the increased focus that is being directed towards empathetic design practices, design thinking, and user design (Avgerinou & Andersson, 2007; Martin, 2007; van Rooij, 2012).

There is a call for instructional design researchers to explore ways in which instructional design can be leveraged to address social issues on a larger platform. Reeves and Reeves (2015) criticized the lack of impact of educational technology research due to our field's focus on researching *things* rather than the *problems* that should concern us as educators. They suggest the value of educational technology research would be enhanced if our research efforts focused on problems such as "ineffective teaching, inadequate high order learning, poor learner motivation, failure to engage, little preparation for the real world, lack of intellectual curiosity, under-developed creativity, insufficient time-on-task, and the declining value of degrees" (p. 27). If we are to seriously consider the recommendations made by instructional researchers (Reeves & Reeves, 2015; Yusop and Correia, 2012) to shift our educational technology practices and research foci to complex real-world problems, we should also be focusing on research efforts which explore and develop an understanding for *how* we, as a field, solve these problems (Jonassen, 2000). To approach this, we must examine our field through a systemic lens that addresses the competing interests inherent in complex social issues and their interrelationships.

Ethnographic practices provide an opportunity for instructional design research to provide a more objective and rich understanding of factors that promote and inhibit learning and design practices (Nelson, 2013). As a result, this will not only inform future research. It will also provide the necessary information needed by instructional design practitioners to align learners' needs and instructional affordances as the demands for instruction and training in real-world contexts continues to grow (Antonenko, Dawson, & Sahay, 2017; Howard & Das, 2019; Niederhauser et al., 2018).

In recent years, there has been a growing movement in instructional design research to promote empathetic design. Empathetic design involves recognizing and resonating with members of a learning audience and customizing instruction to support their efficacy, motivation, and abilities throughout education. Ethnographic techniques can provide researchers with the necessary data they need to conduct further research on their learners and design practices (Baaki et al., 2017; Matthews, Williams, Yanchar, & McDonald, 2017; Scully & Montilus, 2018; Tracey & Hutchinson, 2019; Vann, 2017; Williams, 2016).

A Framework Demonstrating the Use of Ethnographic Inquiry to Better Understand Instructional Design Environments

An ethnographic approach to understanding a learning environment can significantly benefit instructional designers by providing them the opportunity to take a more visible role in the actual environment to better understand and design for it. A framework is offered (Figure 8.1) to emphasize the benefits and affordances that ethnographic inquiry can contribute to instructional design research.

This framework demonstrates the close relationship needed between the instructional designer and their learning audience to be fully aware of the unique customs, social interactions, and power dynamics influencing the learning environment. The instructional designer is an active participant in the environment who interacts with members, gathers data from multiple sources, and practices reflection-in-action throughout the entire instructional design process often entailing analysis of the situation, designing and developing instructional and non-instructional solutions, implementing these solutions, and evaluating learning and performance outcomes as a result of the implemented solutions.

The analysis is intentionally emphasized in two parts of the framework. A needs assessment has been highlighted as a separate event from the instructional design process. This has been done in part because, in many instructional designer projects, analysis is limited solely to learner analysis. By emphasizing needs assessment as an exclusive event in this framework, it highlights the need for the instructional designer to be actively engaged in

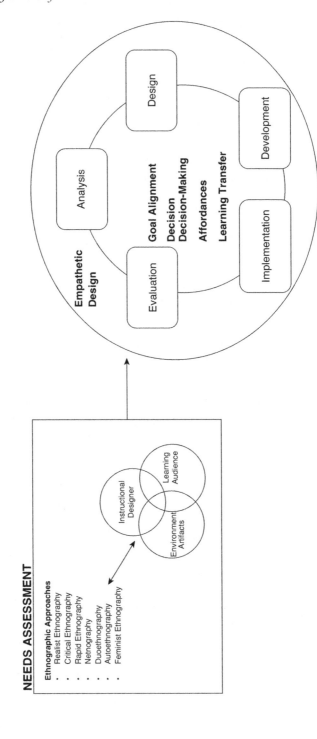

Figure 8.1 Overview of ethnographic approaches used in instructional design research

determining learner needs, verifying those needs, and understanding how they must align with other instructional design activities. Data gathered from the needs assessment should be used to inform all aspects of the instructional design project. The use of ethnographic inquiry provides a mechanism for the instructional designer to be immersed in the environment, experience, and observe first-hand the relationship between contextual factors that will significantly influence the results of a learning intervention that is designed.

As previously mentioned in this chapter, utilizing an ethnographic approach strengthens an instructional designer's ability to adequately ensure goal alignment, inform sound design decision-making, accurately account for affordances in the learning environment, and facilitate a successful transfer of learning. Ethnography helps draw attention to contextual factors that significantly influence the environment, either positively or negatively. This can help inform instructional design research that is either qualitative or quantitative by identifying specific areas and issues where further research is needed.

Conclusion

Ethnography is a qualitative research method that can significantly benefit instructional design research by emphasizing the role of the instructional designer (and researcher) in the environment they are working within and exploring. The goal of this chapter is to provide an overview of a variety of ethnographic approaches and demonstrate how they have been utilized in instructional design research to date. Also, this chapter offers a framework to assist instructional design researchers and practitioners with considering how ethnographic characteristics can be used to enhance their research agendas.

References

Adam, T., Rigoni, A., & Tatnall, A. (2006). Designing and implementing curriculum for students with special needs: A case study of a thinking curriculum. *Journal of Business Systems Governance and Ethics*, *1*(1), 49–63.

Adams, S. R. (2013). The meaning of race-based professional development: A critical feminist ethnography. (Doctoral Dissertation). Retrieved from ProQuest Dissertations and Theses Indiana University, Bloomington, IN.

Adams, T. E., Jones, S. L. H., & Ellis, C. (2015). *Autoethnography: Understanding qualitative research*. New York, NY: Oxford University Press.

Anderson, G. L. (1989). Critical ethnography in education: Origins, current status, and new directions. *Review of Educational Research*, *59*(3), 249–270.

Antonenko, P. D., Dawson, K., & Sahay, S. (2017). A framework for aligning needs, abilities and affordances to inform design and practice of educational technologies. *British Journal of Educational Technology*, *48*(4), 916–927.

Avgerinou, M. D. & Andersson, C. (2007). E-moderating personas. *The Quarterly Review of Distance Education*, *8*(4), 353–364.

Baaki, J., Maddrell, J., & Stauffer, E. (2017). Designing authentic and engaging personas for open education resources. Designers. *International Journal of Designs for Learning, 8*(2), 110–122.

Baines, D. & Cunningham, I. (2013). Using comparative perspective rapid ethnography in international case studies: Strengths and challenges. *Qualitative Social Work, 12*(1), 73–88.

Barab, S. A., Thomas, M. K., Dodge, T., Squire, K., & Newell, M. (2004). Critical design ethnography: Designing for change. *Anthropology & Education Quarterly, 35* (2), 254–268.

Barbour, M., Siko, J., & Simuel-Everage, K. (2012). Narratives from the online frontier: A K-12 student's experience in an online environment. *The Qualitative Report, 17,* 1–19.

Barron, I. (2013). The potential and challenges of critical realist ethnography. *International Journal of Research & Method in Education, 36*(2), 117–130.

Baylor, A., Ryu, J., & Shen, E. (2003). The effects of pedagogical agent voice and animation on learning, motivation and perceived persona. In D. Lassner & C. McNaught (Eds.), *Proceedings of ED-MEDIA 2003–World Conference on Educational Multimedia, Hypermedia & Telecommunications* (pp. 452–458). Honolulu, Hawaii, USA: Association for the Advancement of Computing in Education (AACE). Retrieved June 23, 2020 from https://www.learntechlib.org/primary/ p/13800/

Baylor, A. L. & Kim, Y. (2005). Simulating instructional roles through pedagogical agents. *International Journal of Artificial Intelligence in Education, 15*(2), 95–115.

Branch, R. M. (2017). Characteristics of foundational instructional design models. In R. A. Reiser & J. V. Dempsey (Eds.), *Trends and issues in instructional design and technology* (4th ed., pp. 23–30). New York, NY: Pearson.

Branch, R. M. & Dousay, T. A. (2015). *Survey of instructional design models* (5th ed.). Bloomington, IN: Association for Educational Communications and Technology.

Buch, E. & Staller, K. (2014). What is feminist ethnography? In S. N. Hesse-Biber (Ed.), *Feminist research practice: A primer* (pp. 107–144). Thousand Oaks, CA: Sage Publications, Inc.

Campbell, K. (2015). The feminist instructional designer: An autoethnography. In B. Hokanson, G. Clinton, & M. W. Tracey (Eds.), *The design of learning experience* (pp. 231–249). New York, NY: Springer.

Carspecken, F. P. (2013). *Critical ethnography in educational research: A theoretical and practical guide.* New York, NY: Routledge.

Costello, L., McDermott, M. L., & Wallace, R. (2017). Netnography: Range of practices, misperceptions, and missed opportunities. *International Journal of Qualitative Methods, 16*(1), 1–12.

Delamont, S. & Atkinson, P. (1995). *Fighting familiarity: Essays in education and ethnography.* Cresskill, NJ: Hampton Press.

Dick, W., Carey, L., & Carey, L. O. (2009). *The systematic design of instruction* (8th ed.). New York, NY: Pearson.

Donaldson, J.A. (2016). *Women's voices in the field of educational technology.* New York, NY: Springer.

Dourish, P. (2007). Responsibilities and implications: Further thoughts on ethnography and design. In *Proceedings of the 2007 conference on Designing for User eXperiences* (pp. 2–16). New York: ACM.

Ellis, C., Adams, T. E., & Bochner, A. P. (2011). Autoethnography: An overview. *Qualitative Social Research, 12*(1), 273–290.

Fish, R. (2017). *A feminist ethnography of secure wards for women with learning disabilities locked away.* New York, NY: Routledge.

Gordon, T., Holland, J., & Lahelma, E. (2011). Ethnographic research in educational settings. In P. Atkinson, A. Coffey, S. Delamont, J. Lofland, & L. Lofland (Eds.), *Handbook of ethnography* (pp. 188–203). Washington, DC: Sage.

Gratch, J. & Warren, S. J. (2018). Critical CinéEthnographic Methods: a New Dimension for Capturing the Experience of Learning in Twenty-First Century Qualitative Research. *TechTrends, 62*(5), 473–482.

Howard, C. D. & Das, A. (2019). Designing competitive discussions for equity and inclusion. *International Journal of Designs for Learning, 10*(1), 1–13.

Isaacs, E. (2016). The value of rapid ethnography. In B. Jordan (Ed.), *Advancing ethnography in corporate environments* (pp. 92–107). New York, NY: Routledge.

Johns, A. M. & Makalela, L. (2011). Needs analysis, critical ethnography, and context: Perspectives from the client and the consultant. In D. Belcher, A. M. Johns, & B. Paltridge (Eds.), *New directions in English for specific purposes research* (pp. 197–221). Ann Arbor. MI: University of Michigan Press.

Jonassen, D. H. (2000). Toward a design theory of problem solving. *Educational Technology Research and Development, 48*(4), 63–85.

Kozinets, R. V. (2010). *Netnography: Doing ethnographic research online.* Thousand Oaks, CA: Sage.

Kulavuz-Onal, D. (2013). English language teachers' learning to teach with technology through participation in an online community of practice: A netnography of webheads in action. (Doctoral Dissertation). Retrieved from ProQuest Dissertations and Theses. University of South Florida, Tampa, FL.

LeCompte, M. D. & Schensul, J. J. (1999). *Designing and conducting ethnographic research.* New York, NY: Altamira Press.

Lehner, E., Thomas, K., Shaddai, J., & Hernen, T. (2017). Measuring the effectiveness of critical literacy as an instructional method. *Journal of College Literacy and Learning, 43*, 36–53.

Leighter, J. L., Rudnick, L., & Edmonds, T. J. (2013). How the ethnography of communication provides resources for design. *Journal of Applied Communication Research, 41*(2), 209–215.

Lewis, K. A. (2018). A digital immigrant venture into teaching online: An auto-ethnographic account of a classroom teacher transformed. *The Qualitative Report, 23*(7), 1752–1772.

Maier, R. & Thalmann, S. (2010). Using personas for designing knowledge and learning services: Results of an ethnographically informed study. *International Journal of Technology Enhanced Learning, 2*(1–2), 58–74.

Martin, J. (2007). Design-personae: Matching students' learning profiles in web-based education. In E. McKay (Ed.), *Enhancing Learning Through Human Computer Interaction* (pp. 110–131). Heshey, PA: IGI Global.

Matthews, M. T., Williams, G. S., Yanchar, S. C., & McDonald, J. K. (2017). Empathy in distance learning design practice. *TechTrends, 61*(5), 486–493.

Millen, D. R. (2000). Rapid ethnography: Time deepening strategies for HCI field research. In *Proceedings of the 3rd conference on Designing interactive systems: processes, practices, methods, and techniques* (pp. 280–286). New York: ACM.

Nelson, W. A. (2013). Design, research, and design research: Synergies and contradictions. *Educational Technology, 53*(1), 3–11.

Niederhauser, D. S., Howard, S. K., Voogt, J., Agyei, D. D., Laferriere, T., Tondeur, J., & Cox, M. J. (2018). Sustainability and scalability in educational technology initiatives: Research-informed practice. *Technology, Knowledge and Learning, 23*(3), 507–523.

Norris, J. & Sawyer, R. D. (2016). Toward a dialogic methodology. In R. D. Sawyer & J. Norris (Eds.), *Duoethnography* (pp. 9–40). New York, NY: Routledge.

Penuel, W. R., Tatar, D. G., & Roschelle, J. (2004). The role of research on contexts of teaching practice in informing the design of handheld learning technologies. *Journal of Educational Computing Research, 30*(4), 353–370.

Pulsinelli, A. & Roubie, C. (2001). Using diversity modeling for instructional design. *Performance Improvement, 40*(7), 20–27.

Rasi, M., Jantunen, A., Curcher, M., & Teras, H. (2018). Unexpected insights: A collaborative autoethnography of the experiences of international students on an authentic e-learning distance educational leadership program. In T. Bastiaens, J. Van Braak, M. Brown, L. Cantoni, M. Castro, R. Christensen, G. Davidson-Shivers, K. DePryck, M. Ebner, M. Fominykh, C. Fulford, S. Hatzipanagos, G. Knezek, K. Kreijns, G. Marks, E. Sointu, E. Korsgaard Sorensen, J. Viteli, J. Voogt, P. Weber, E. Weippl & O. Zawacki-Richter (Eds.), *Proceedings of EdMedia: World Conference on Educational Media and Technology* (pp. 2023–2028). Amsterdam, Netherlands: Association for the Advancement of Computing in Education (AACE). Retrieved June 24, 2020 from https://www.learntechlib.org/primary/p/184443/.

Reeves, T. C. & Reeves, P. M. (2015). Educational technology research in a VUCA world. *Educational Technology, 55*(2), 26–30.

Richey, R. C., Klein, J. D., & Tracey, M. W. (2011). *The instructional design knowledge base: Theory, research, and practice.* New York, NY: Routledge.

Savage, J. (2006). Ethnographic evidence: The value of applied ethnography in healthcare. *Journal of Research in Nursing, 11*(5), 383–393.

Schön, D. A. (1983). *The reflective practitioner: How professionals think in action.* New York, NY: Basic Books, Inc.

Scully, E. & Montilus, K. D. (2018). Empathetic design thinking to fuel your learning experience design. *The Emerging Learning Design Journal, 5*(2), 4, 18–20.

Skeggs, B. (2001). Feminist ethnography. In P. Atkinson, A. Coffey, S. Delamont, J. Lofland, & L. Lofland (Eds.), *Handbook of ethnography* (pp. 426–442). Thousand Oaks, CA: Sage.

Snelson, C., Wertz, C. I., Onstott, K., & Bader, J. (2017). Using World of Warcraft to teach research methods in online doctoral education: A student-instructor duoethnography. *The Qualitative Report, 22*(5), 1439–1456.

Spindler, G. (1982). *Doing the ethnography of schooling: Educational anthropology in action.* New York: NY: Holt, Rinehart, and Winston.

Spradley, J. D. (1980). *Participant Observation.* New York, NY: Holt, Rinehart, and Winston.

Stefaniak, J. E. & Baaki, J. (2013). A layered approach to understanding your audience. *Performance Improvement, 52*(6), 5–10.

Suzanne, M. (2019). Instructional strategies and adult learning theories: An auto-ethnographic study about teaching research methods in a doctoral program. *Education, 139*(3), 178–186.

Tempelman-Kluit, N. & Pearce, A. (2014). Invoking the user from data to design. *College & Research Libraries*, *75*(5), 616–640.

Tessmer, M. & Richey, R. C. (1997). The role of context in learning and instructional design. *Educational Technology Research and Development*, *45*(2), 85–115.

Tessmer, M. & Wedman, J. (1995). Context-sensitive instructional design models: A response to design research, studies, and criticism. *Performance Improvement Quarterly*, *8*(3), 38–54.

Thomas, M. K. (2003). Designers' dilemmas: The tripartheid responsibility of the instructional designer. *TechTrends*, *47*(6), 34–39.

Tracey, M. W. & Hutchinson, A. (2019). Empathic design: Imagining the cognitive and emotional learner experience. *Educational Technology Research and Development*, *67*, 1–14.

van Rooij, S. W. (2012). Based personas: Teaching empathy in professional education. *Journal of Effective Teaching*, *12*(3), 77–86.

Vann, L. S. (2017). Demonstrating empathy: A phenomenological study of instructional designers making instructional strategy decisions for adult learners. *International Journal of Teaching and Learning in Higher Education*, *29*(2), 233–244.

Wasson, C. (2013). "It was like a little community": An ethnographic study of online learning and its implications for MOOCs. In *Ethnographic praxis in industry conference proceedings, 2013 (1)*, 186–199.

Williams, G. S. (2016). *Empathy and the instructional designer*. Unpublished master's thesis. Provo, UT: Brigham Young University.

Williams, J. (2012). Using a critical literacy model to foster critical reflections on race, social class, and education among developmental readers. *Affective Reading Education Journal*, *27*(2), 36–44.

Yanchar, S. C., South, J. B., Williams, D. D., Allen, S., & Wilson, B. G. (2010). Struggling with theory? A qualitative investigation of conceptual tool use in instructional design. *Educational Technology Research and Development*, *58*(1), 39–60.

Young, P. A. (2008). Integrating culture in the design of ICTs. *British Journal of Educational Technology*, *39*(1), 6–17.

Yusop, F. D. & Correia, A. P. (2012). The civic-minded instructional designers framework: An alternative approach to contemporary instructional designers' education in higher education. *British Journal of Educational Technology*, *43*(2), 180–190.

Yusop, F. D. & Correia, A. P. (2014). On becoming a civic-minded instructional designer: An ethnographic study of an instructional design experience. *British Journal of Educational Technology*, *45*(5), 782–792.

9 Complex, Multiple, Interdependent Layers (C-MIL)

A Conceptual Model For Usability Studies in 3-Dimensional Virtual Worlds

Sarah Espinosa and Peter Leong

Introduction

With technology enhancing today's classrooms, many educators are opting to utilize 3-Dimensional Virtual Worlds (3D VW) to showcase material and provide students with alternative learning methods within immersive online environments. While educators are creating content and developing simulations, often overlooked is the testing of the usability of the simulation.

Usability testing is a research method for collecting detailed and direct user feedback about a website, system, or mobile application. In a usability test, researchers collect qualitative data such as participant observations and feedback, and quantitative data such as task completion times and success rates while users perform typical tasks with a website, system, or any other product with a user interface. Researchers then analyze the data to identify usability problems with the product or system and recommend improvements to address these problems.

Usability studies of simulations within 3D VW have features that are unique compared to a traditional usability study of a website or mobile application. The purpose of this chapter is to describe a proposed conceptual model developed for usability studies of 3D VW simulations that is based on previous literature and a study to evaluate the usability of the Crafter's Ear simulation in Minecraft (Espinosa, 2019).

The Crafter's Ear Simulation

To address a lack of aural music theory training for beginning music students in the 10–13-year-old age range, a simulation was created in Minecraft for teacher use in the music classroom (see Figure 9.1). This potential solution aimed to improve upon the typical "drill and practice" methods utilized for aural music theory skill development. The sandbox game Minecraft was chosen as the simulation platform due to its ability to construct "redstone-

Figure 9.1 The Crafter's Ear aural music theory simulation in Minecraft

powered" musical note blocks that can "show" what the musician already aurally perceives. Individual note block pitch can be selected from a two-octave range that varies in starting pitch from the material it is built upon. These blocks can be utilized individually or strung together to create melodies, intervals, and chords. "Primitives" (single or multi-part virtual objects) were provided for pitch identification and used as a template for constructing personal, interactive aural theory aids not dependent upon formal music notation or playing/singing ability.

Lacking a specific methodology to test the usability of a 3D VW simulation, a literature review was conducted to determine strategies to effectively measure navigation, effectiveness, and user satisfaction of a 3D VW simulation. Three iterations of the usability testing were performed, and data were collected using several evaluation instruments that were modified from traditional usability testing of websites or mobile applications to meet the needs of a 3D VW simulation. The Crafter's Ear iterations helped identify components integral to the usability studies of 3D VW simulations that have been integrated into this proposed conceptual model.

Challenges and Features of Usability Testing of 3D VW Simulations

This section discusses the challenges and features that are unique to 3D VW simulations. Figure 9.2 shows the differences between a traditional usability study of a website and a virtual world usability study.

Usability testing of 3D VW simulations are quite different from a traditional website or mobile application usability test. Usability testing

	Web 1.0	Virtual Worlds
Usability Testing	• Web design • Navigation • User Friendliness • Functionality	• Virtual content design • Navigation • User Friendliness • Functionality • User appeal
User Feedback	• User profile • Demographics • Satisfaction • Use and Impact	• Demographics • Satisfaction • Use and Impact

Figure 9.2 Chwen, Yung, Man, and Siong (2013) Usability comparison

can be done directly on the 3D VW platform and is primarily focused on single-user interaction. When educators build interactive content within the 3D VW, the result is a simulation. The simulation is then the locus of control of usability testing.

Traditional Usability Vs. 3D VW Simulation Usability

There are four major differences between the usability testing of a website or mobile application and that of a 3D VW simulation. These include task performance, interaction with virtual world objects, non-linear user action, and user ability level. These differences create a complex layering relationship between the operating system and its input/output devices and user interface, user experience variables, and the 3D VW simulation.

Usability testing in the 3D VW is further complicated by the need to distinguish between the locus of control (LOC)—the simulation created in the VW, and non-locus of control (nLOC)—the virtual world platform itself. Current research designs are often ill-equipped to differentiate the role of VR from confounding factors (Garrett et al., 2018). There continues to be a strong need for novel approaches in virtual reality usability testing.

Task Performance

According to Nielsen (1993), traditional usability has five quality components: learnability, efficiency, memorability, error recovery, and satisfaction. Chwen et al. (2013) created a modified approach for usability testing within a virtual world learning environment (VWLE) that explored areas effective for creating usability tasks. These included effectiveness, safety, efficiency, universality, satisfaction, usefulness, learnability, and navigation. Usability instruments in virtual reality also vary depending on user interaction within the virtual environment. Research by Zilles Borba, Corrêa, de Deus Lopes, and Zuffo (2019) indicates that realism, interaction, and engagement form the container in which immersion and sense of presence within the virtual simulation reside. To test a virtual simulation's usability, tools must be chosen that correspond to these pillars of immersion (Zilles Borba et al., 2019). There continues to be debate around the efficacy of the tools used to evaluate efficiency, efficacy and satisfaction measures. The most frequently used tools, including Nielsen's heuristic evaluation, Slater-Usoh-Steed Questionnaire, and Simulator Sickness Questionnaire (Zilles Borba et al., 2019) may not always provide accurate results for specific physiological responses and vulnerabilities (Lin, Wang, Wang, & Wang, 2018). Because of this, other instruments, such as the perceived physiological vulnerability to IT usage, have been developed to provide alternative options (Lin et al., 2018).

None of the existing approaches appear to provide a clear methodology for which tools to use under which circumstances in virtual reality usability studies. There is, therefore, the need for comparison and analysis on a broad scale to provide usability testers with a clear way to determine which usability measures and tasks make the most sense for a particular 3D VW simulation. Understanding the complexities and layers involved will aid in this determination.

Interaction with Virtual World Objects

Sutcliffe and Alrayes (2010) conducted usability testing in Second Life, focusing on user experience and performance. Task completion through object interaction was utilized successfully in the 3D VW. While traditional user tasks often involve clicking on embedded information, 3D VW user tasks are multifaceted. Examples include users manipulating virtual world objects or creating within the virtual world setting. Gabbard (1997) said, "the focus of most existing methods, while properly user-task-based, is on a single user performing isolated, low-level user tasks—very different than the typical VE in which one or more users are performing integrated, shared, multi-threaded tasks" (p. 3). This interaction becomes increasingly complicated when multiple users manipulate objects at the same time.

Non-linear User Action

In a 3D VW, the nature of the virtual world allows users to interact in the environment non-linearly. While a website's design has a distinct narrative (with specific information to digest), a virtual world sandbox (i.e., Minecraft) does not inherently provide this. Without specific guidance, the user has complete freedom to interact within the environment with or without purpose. If particular outcomes or goals are desired, specific guidelines must be provided to gauge the usability of the simulation.

User Ability Level

Unlike web usability, 3D VWs require more than a point-and-click method to interact within the simulation. TREG's (Training in Requirements Engineering Game) usability tests provided valuable material for the 3D VW usability methodology, particularly their discussion on interface, mechanisms, and gameplay (Vega, Pereira Soares, Robichez, & Fuks, 2010). The TREG study strongly emphasized leveling the playing field for usability participants by ensuring that they are familiar with the features of the 3D VW required for the simulation (Vega et al., 2010). This led to the development of a separate beginner participant tutorial to help usability participants start at similar ability levels in Minecraft for the Crafter's Ear simulation.

Because of these four areas, a traditional 3D VW usability study protocol was deemed inadequate, hence the need to develop a method for testing the usability of simulations within 3D VWs.

C-MIL: A Conceptual Model for Usability Testing in 3D VW Simulations

We proposed a conceptual model consisting of Complex, Multiple, and Interdependent Layers (referred to as the C-MIL model) for usability testing in 3D VW simulations. The following section summarizes the salient points of the C-MIL model:

- Locus of control.
- Complex, multiple, interdependent layering, namely the interdependence of input/output (I/O) devices and the interdependence of user interface (UI).
- User experience of the actual 3D VW simulation or content created.

Locus of Control

Performing a usability study assumes that the researcher has the authority and ability, or locus of control, to revise the tested product. Sandbox virtual worlds allow for content development on an already established platform. Moreover, layers are added to the established platform that interacts, enhances, and impedes participation on the platform. Usually, the researcher will not have access or the authority to change the mechanics of the virtual world (drop-down bars, navigation, etc.). Within the virtual world, any content created that can be tested and revised by the researcher, i.e., the simulation itself is in the researcher's locus of control.

Complex, Multiple, Interdependent Layering

3D virtual worlds have complex, multiple, interdependent layers that must be taken into consideration when understanding and developing tasks for usability testing. Before designing tasks and creating usability protocol, the research designer must take into consideration items outside of the locus of control and attempt to minimize and plan for these variables. Figure 9.3 shows possible variables affecting a 3D VW simulation usability study.

The usability study involves the simulation, the evaluation instruments chosen, and the tasks being evaluated. In simple or compound layers (for websites and mobile applications usability), data is collected from each usability iteration, issues are identified, and changes are made at the completion of each iteration. In complex layering, the researcher should consider removing as many variables as possible before testing while keeping them in mind during data analysis as possible influencing factors in the study. Maintaining the primary focus on the simulation rather than the microlayers will aid in data collection and analysis. In the Crafter's Ear simulation, multiple issues from these complex layers provided insight into future practices. Each of these layers is discussed in the conceptual model presented (see Figure 9.3).

Unless the simulation is only available on one operating system, it is important to ensure compatibility across platforms. The 3D VW may behave differently across platforms (Apple, Microsoft, Linux), as well as interact differently with the software, input/output devices, and user interface utilized by participants.

Interdependence of Input/Output (I/O) Device

When considering the simulation platform, input and output devices interact positively or negatively within the simulation (see Figure 9.4). Input and output devices send and receive information. They include headphones, microphone, webcam, mouse, keyboard, joystick, monitors, etc. While the simulation content may have been designed for use with a mouse, participants may utilize a joystick, keyboard, or trackpad if no input device has been specified, potentially affecting the intended purpose. In the Crafter's Ear, participants were required to use a keyboard and mouse rather than a trackpad or joystick to navigate and build more effectively and efficiently. Input and output devices should be predetermined before the usability testing. This also includes I/O devices used to gather usability testing during the research phase. Ensuring functional and compliant I/O devices is key to successful data gathering.

The recommendation for I/O device usability is to:

1. Identify the I/O devices possible on the desired platform.
2. Test the I/O devices to determine the best fit for the simulation.

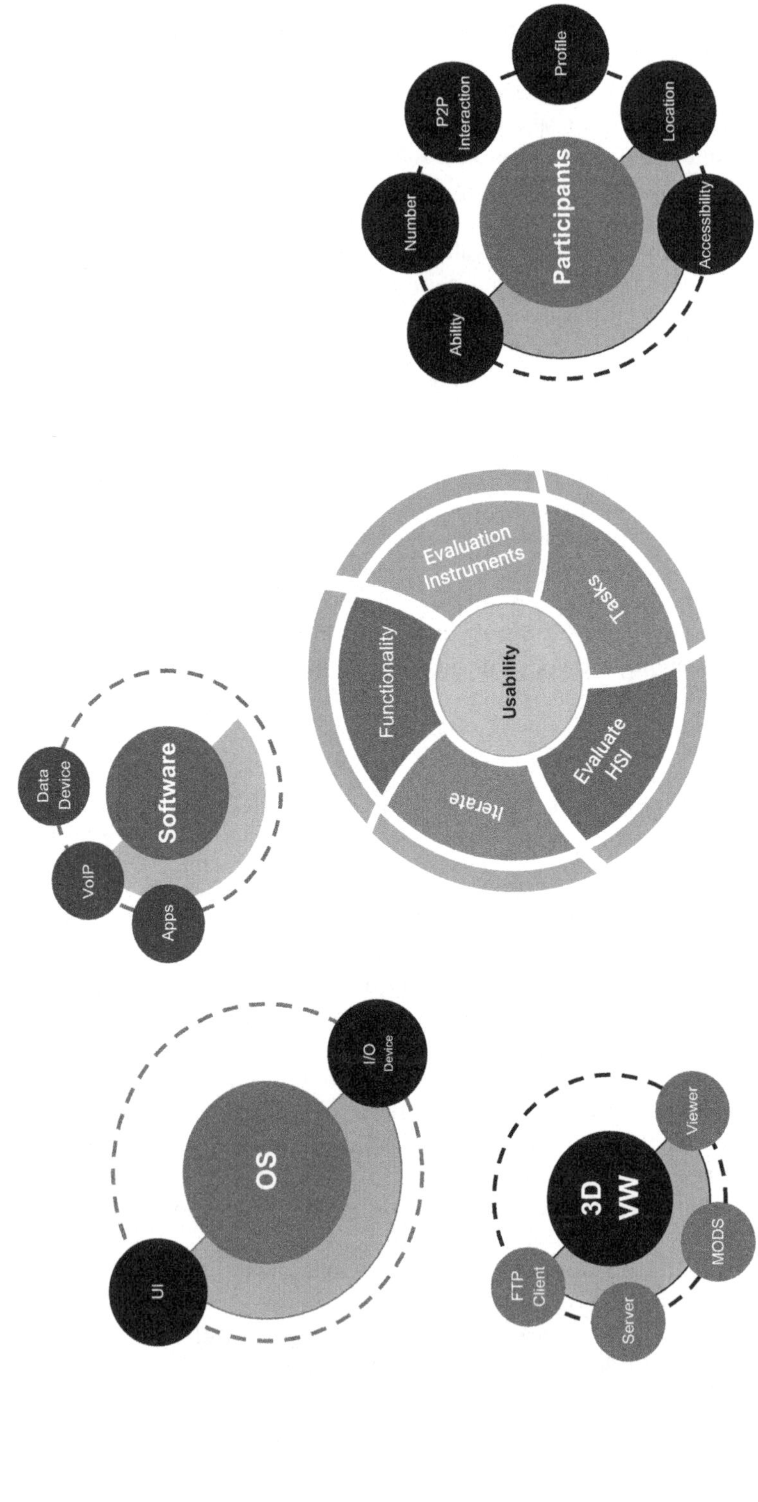

Figure 9.3 Example of complex "layering"

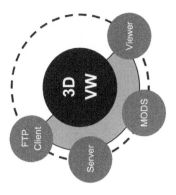

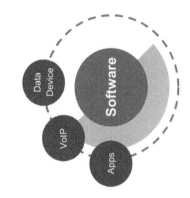

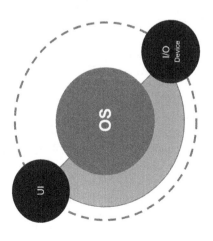

Figure 9.4 Example of Interdependence

3. Develop the simulation with the I/O devices in mind.
4. Specify the I/O devices to participants.
5. Identify the input and output devices being utilized on the tested simulation through survey or interview if allowing for multiple options.Because the I/O devices are interdependent with the simulation, they will still need to be identified and accounted for during the usability testing. This can be done through pre-survey questionnaires or interviews.

Interdependence of User Interface (UI)

The user interface is defined as the ways by which the user interacts with a computer system and refers specifically to the use of input devices and software (see Figure 9.5). The user interface combines ergonomics, aesthetics, and interface technology for human–computer interaction (Lo, 2014). The graphic in Figure 9.5 highlights how the participant interacts with the hardware and software through sensing and learning.

The user interface includes the interaction with all of the non-locus of control (nLOC) elements, as well as the simulation's (LOC) structural design, attractiveness/appeal, ease of use, and virtual manipulatives and primitives. The researcher should identify and label the simulation's user interface elements into two groups, nLOC, and LOC, making note of any overlap.

The recommendation for UI:

1. Identify when the user interface occurs.
2. Separate user interface nLOC from LOC, noting any overlap.
3. Minimize the use of external mods, applications, and software if possible.
4. When necessary, choose external mods, applications, and software that provide the greatest flexibility to the simulation designer.

Examples of nLOC elements include the system itself, the input/output device, and the user interface between the VW and the user. The LOC includes a user interface within the VW to which the simulation designer has direct access and revision ability. An example of an overlap of nLOC and LOC is a primitive created by an external party that has been locked and is not modifiable. The simulation designer can include or not include the item in the simulation, but changes to the item are not possible without permission.

In the Crafter's Ear, modifications were implemented to enhance Minecraft's gameplay. An FTP client and a server were utilized. While these elements are not in the researcher's direct control, coding, and game functions being used in the created virtual world should be tested to determine effectiveness and functionality. Primitives can also be enhanced with code and should be tested for functionality. While the virtual world gaming functions should not be included in a usability test, it will have an impact on the outcome of the success of the created content. The usability

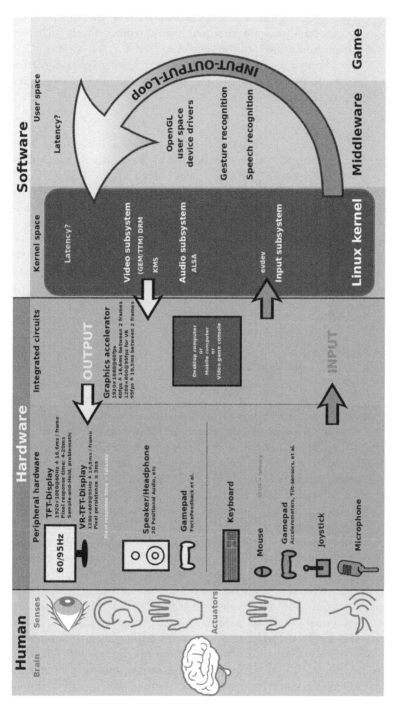

Figure 9.5 User interface graphic by Shmuel Csaba Otto Traian CC BY-SA 3.0 (http://creativecommons.org/licenses/by-sa/3.0) or GFDL (www.gnu. org/copyleft/fdl.html), via Wikimedia Commons

participants of the Crafter's Ear had expected and desired a simulation on Minecraft Education Edition; however, Minecraft Java was the platform utilized, creating both positive and negative outcomes in the usability study. Minecraft Education Edition was not used for the Crafter's Ear because it has a limited ability to utilize multiplayer for participants across different servers. Minecraft Java has a multiplayer function, allowing for remote testing of the simulation.

User Experience

Usability testing affords the product or simulation designer with information on the user's experience with user interface and design aspects. The researcher must determine the focus of the usability test. While Chwen et al. (2013) offer effectiveness, navigation, efficiency, safety, satisfaction, universality, learnability, and usefulness as areas for usability testing, limiting the scope of testing is recommended. The Crafter's Ear simulation tested navigation, effectiveness, and user satisfaction to gauge the ability of the user to function within the 3D VW environment, as well as ensure the tasks within the environment served a clear purpose within the intended design.

Navigation

Because of the environment's non-linear, user interaction ability, testing navigation in the simulation is a necessity. Navigational testing in the simulation does not refer to nLOC elements such as pre-programmed navigational functions of the game or the input devices. Navigation within a virtual simulation is primarily concerned with the user's ability to wayfind and mimics real-world navigation and movement. While a website's design has a distinct narrative (with specific information to digest), a virtual world sandbox (i.e., Minecraft) does not inherently provide this. Without specific guidance, the user has complete freedom to interact within the environment with or without purpose. If particular outcomes or goals are desired, specific guidelines must be provided to gauge the usability of the simulation. Within the Crafter's Ear, simulation content was designed to be visited in a particular order, but also with flexibility for the participant to navigate between sections based upon user preference or interest. It was imperative in the usability study to ensure that the navigational directions were clear and that there were measures built into place to help the participant avoid becoming lost. If the virtual world environment can use navigational portals to jump from one location to another, these must be tested for both correct end location (functionality before usability testing) and cause and reaction from the jump (navigation and effectiveness). When using add-ons or modifications (mods), interface interaction should be tested. As with traditional usability testing, the navigation should be intuitive, functional, and consistent throughout the simulation, providing environmental information to aid the user in wayfinding (Minocha & Hardy, 2016).

Effectiveness

Ideally, a simulation developed in a 3D VW will have a distinct purpose that lends itself particularly well to the virtual world environment. While the effectiveness of a website might be in its task success, the 3D VW simulation's effectiveness will also be in its ability to be immersive and purposeful. An effective design will incorporate the same consistency, intuitiveness, and function expected from well-designed navigational cues, as well as through its task success and usefulness in a virtual space. Testing for effectiveness allows the researcher to gauge whether or not the simulation was successful in its design purpose through "the accuracy and completeness with which users achieve specified goals" (ISO 9241–11, 1998). While task completion may have similar elements between the web and 3D VW simulation, a key difference is in the user's ability to function within the virtual world to participate in the task. In Figure 9.6 is a portion of the tasks asked in the Crafter's Ear

Tasks can include interaction and manipulation of created elements *and* participant creation of elements if the simulation's purpose calls for user builds. This ties back to participant experience and ability within virtual worlds prior to usability testing. Pre-screening may be required depending on the simulation's target audience. Ability level or experience should be taken into consideration during data analysis and can be identified by a beginner, intermediate, or advanced ability through a user survey/interview. Offering participants a virtual world tutorial before usability (not of the created simulation) may also assist in providing more consistent user experience data.

User Satisfaction

Incorporating user satisfaction into the usability testing takes the successful design and navigation and asks whether the users found the simulation engaging and relevant. Aesthetics, overall feel, content merit are all items that can be qualitatively measured through an informal or formal interview process. The Crafter's Ear utilized an informal interview with leading questions to gauge the simulation's use potential, design aesthetics, functions, and concerns.

Recommendations for user experience:

1. Determine the focus of the usability test.
2. Limit testing to one to three areas.
3. Test navigation within the simulation utilizing the "think-aloud" method (Krug, 2010).
4. Flexibility between researcher and participant tasks.

Scenarios for Usability Study aligned with Research Question #2
How effective was the virtual content design of the musical mechanisms in the sandbox environment for aural theory training for use with teachers of beginner music students age 10-13?

11. We are now at the composition simulation. I'd like you to use your avatar to walk around and interact with various objects.	
12. Can you open the material dispenser and read the instructions?	
13. Please find and play the song, "Row, Row, Row Your Boat."	

See the principles and scale below. For each principle, indicate choice for how the design performed according to the scale. In addition, provide specific feedback if any usability issues are identified (anything scoring 2 or higher should be provided comments about specific items to be addressed).

Severity Rating Scale
0: No specific usability problem identified
1: Cosmetic problem only – need not be fixed unless extra time is available on project
2: Minor usability problem – fixing this should be given low priority
3: Major usability problem – important to fix, so should be given high priority
4: Usability catastrophe – imperative to fix this before product can be released

Principles (Heuristics)	Scale				
1. Speak the users' language. Use words, phrases, and concepts familiar to the user. Present information in a natural and logical order.	0	1	2	3	4
1.1. Various kinds of communication between avatar and simulated material	0	1	2	3	4
1.2. Interaction between avatars is analogous to people interaction in the real world	0	1	2	3	4
2. Consistency. Indicate similar concepts through identical terminology and graphics. Adhere to uniform conventions for layout, formatting, typefaces, labeling, etc.	0	1	2	3	4
2.1. Prediction of the result of performed actions	0	1	2	3	4
2.2. Ability to the influence of past actions to present state	0	1	2	3	4
2.3. Ability to apply an experience from other systems	0	1	2	3	4
2.4. Ability to perform several tasks at the same time	0	1	2	3	4

Figure 9.6 Evaluation protocol and scale

Adapted from Levi and Conrad (1996) "A heuristic evaluation of a world wide web prototype," *Interactions magazine,* July/August, Vol.III.4, pp. 50–61 and from Butkute and Lapin (2010) "Usability Heuristics for Online Virtual Worlds," www.researchgate.net/publication/228826733_Usability_heuristics_for_online_virtual_worlds.

The C-MIL Conceptual Model Explained

Based upon the complex layering of a 3D VW simulation and results from the Crafter's Ear, usability testing should be kept as simple as possible and separated into stages if multiplayer usability is an end goal. The functionality of the simulation must be thoroughly tested before each usability round. Because the simulation is built in a continually changing virtual environment, the researcher must be aware of any updates to the system, the viewer, modifications used, and how any changes interact with the simulation elements. Before the usability test, functional testing, cognitive walkthrough of the simulation, and a heuristic evaluation should take place.

Through the design and testing of usability protocol for the Crafter's Ear usability study, three areas emerged as beneficial for 3D VW usability testing: navigation, effectiveness, and user experience. The primary concern of the research designer is that of identifying the locus of control and staying within the purview of the simulation. As shown in Figure 9.7, the locus of control consists of all the content created within the virtual world simulation. Additionally, the generated content is filtered through software that the designer has partial control over and should be tested in a usability study to ensure proper functioning.

The usability participant will follow task prompts from the research designer all within the locus of control; however, as shown in Figure 9.7, the intricate layers have an impact on the locus of control.

The conceptual model for a 3D VW simulation usability study incorporates the complex layering of I/O and UI with human–simulation interaction (HSI). Human–simulation interaction incorporates both human–computer interaction and human–human interaction. This is one of the key differences between web and 3D VW usability. The latter can involve multi-user variables rather than testing single participant interaction. Because of the complications human–human interaction causes within the simulation, phases of usability testing are recommended (see Figure 9.8) beginning with simple and building in complexity only as necessary based upon the target audience of the simulation. Large-scale groups should coalesce into smaller groups with focused interaction, and then remixed overtime to maximize possible interaction in manageable and observable chunks (Erickson, Shami, Kellogg, & Levine, 2011).

The Crafter's Ear usability study modeled Phase One. Phase One has three rounds of usability testing, utilizing predetermined evaluation instruments based upon the needs of the simulation. These may include task protocol script and evaluation forms, surveys, and interview questions. Each round of testing is modeled after the web approach and contains a minimum of three participants in each round. Because of the scope of data collection, the recommendation is to keep the participants between three to five per round. Because the Crafter's Ear focused on single-user, Krug's (2010) recommendation of three subjects for each round of testing was determined to be sufficient.

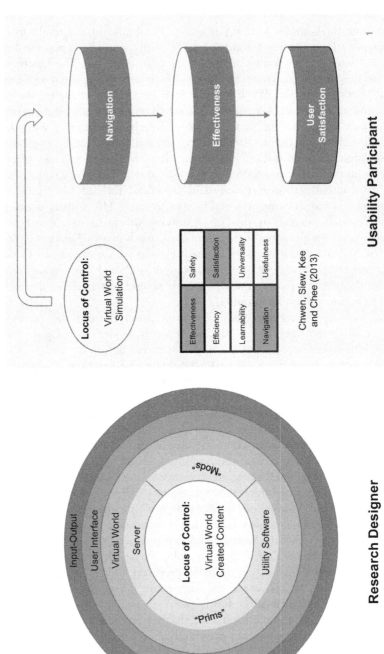

Figure 9.7 Locus of control usability categories

Both qualitative and quantitative data from the usability tests, including any pre- and post-survey data, should be included in the evaluation phase with recommendations for improvement. Each issue was rated by the researcher based on its severity using Nielsen's (1994) five-level scale (catastrophic, major, minor, cosmetic, and none) for usability problem severity. Using this scale alongside the tasks enables quick identification of usability issues. Along with Phase One, micro iterations should take place between participants in one round to address any catastrophic matters that hinder the function of the simulation. All other changes should take place between rounds based upon participant feedback.

Phase Two and Phase Three are based upon a literature review and provide a theoretical framework for scaffolding a usability study towards a more substantial, multiplayer usability test. Phase Two would include two rounds, testing the same tasks as Phase One, but with multiple players at once.

According to Chwen et al. (2013), participant richness in multiplayer usability recommendation is 36. In their study on group usability testing in virtual reality environments, a comparison was made from Downey (2007) on "several-to-many" approach to performing tasks at the same time. Two rounds were done in both the Downey and Chwen et al. group usability testing and could be modified for varying sized groups of multiplayer. The evaluation materials were similar to the ones utilized in the Crafter's Ear: user profile survey, task protocol, and post-interview/survey. Unlike the single-player usability test in Phase One, the group testing required more

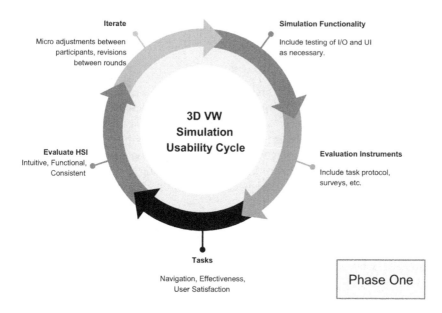

Figure 9.8 Phase One: Three single users in three rounds, nine total

moderators/observers. To minimize lost data, Chwen et al.'s study involved the participants in the recording of usability issues. Having multiple observers and participants recording data provides more reliable data in a way that is faster and more cost-effective. This study also recommended screen and video recording for data analysis. The Crafter's Ear implemented this recommendation in single-player usability and found it beneficial for copying transcripts and analyzing qualitative data.

Iteration Considerations

The purpose of usability is to improve the product. Iteration in usability testing typically involves a series of researcher-prompted tasks completed by individuals grouped in several phases. Usability issues are identified in each stage, and modifications are made to the product based upon the severity of the issue. The amendments are usually done after each phase. In a 3D VW, we recommend making adjustments to the simulation within each phase for catastrophic and severe issues that impede the function of the simulation. In the Crafter's Ear, several catastrophic issues were created by server updates, which prevented the coding function of several of the primitives. Because the function of the primitives was vital to the navigational testing, adjustments were made between participants in order to collect more usable data.

Evaluation Instruments

Using Slone's (2009) methodology for measuring usability skills through heuristic evaluation, instruments were designed for evaluating the Crafter's Ear and utilized throughout the iterative process.

User Profile Survey

Downey (2007) proposed using a simple user profile survey with participants to classify them based on predetermined characteristics. The purpose of the user profile survey used in the Crafter's Ear was to ensure the homogeneity of participants who underwent the usability testing process later. The user profile survey was created from a Google Form containing a simple survey of music theory knowledge (including recorded aural theory examples), prior musical experience, and computer/gaming literacy.

Usability Task Protocol

In the Crafter's Ear, the task protocol was the core of the usability testing process. Selected basic tasks were given to the participants using a set of verbal instructions. For the purpose of the study, the basic functions given in this testing were to identify objects and to interact with the created simulation and objects. The participants were allowed to ask questions

Navigation Task Segment Transcribed: (__minutes)

Scenarios for Usability Study aligned with Research Question #1
How easy or difficult was it to locate the virtual content design areas within the virtual learning environment?

1. Please find the teleportation portals.	
2. Please take your Avatar to the interval location.	

See the principles and scale below. For each principle, indicate your choice for how the design performed according to the scale. In addition, provide specific feedback if any usability issues are identified (anything scoring 2 or higher should be provided comments about specific items to be addressed).

Severity Rating Scale
0: No specific usability problem identified
1: Cosmetic problem only – need not be fixed unless extra time is available on project
2: Minor usability problem – fixing this should be given low priority
3: Major usability problem – important to fix, so should be given high priority
4: Usability catastrophe – imperative to fix this before product can be released

Principles (Heuristics)	Scale				
6. Navigational feedback.	0	1	2	3	4
6.1. Navigation is intuitive and memorable	0	1	2	3	4
6.2. Minimal use of additional instructions	0	1	2	3	4
6.3. Minimal use of deep hierarchical structure	0	1	2	3	4
6.4. The system ensures the consistency between navigation information	0	1	2	3	4
6.5 Search for all kinds of content.	0	1	2	3	4
6.6 Navigation achieved with no outside influence.	0	1	2	3	4

Figure 9.9 Evaluation protocol and scale

Adapted from: Levi and Conrad (1996) "A heuristic evaluation of a world wide web Prototype," *Interactions magazine,* July/August, Vol.III.4, pp. 50–61 and from Butkute and Lapin (Butkute & Lapin, 2010) "Usability Heuristics for Online Virtual Worlds," www.researchgate.net/publication/ 228826733_Usability_heuristics_for_online_virtual_ worlds during the testing. Participants performed the basic tasks given to them individually. The facilitator interacted with participants, answered questions, and also minimally prompted them to think aloud. Usability tasks were recorded in Zoom with the participants' consent using the screen share function and stored in a secure location.

Observation Transcript Form

In conjunction with the usability task protocol, Butkute and Lapin's (2010) Heuristics for Online Virtual Worlds was adapted to make quick assessments of the tasks during the usability test. The recordings could also be transcribed later. Figure 9.9 is an example chart.

Usability Issue Discussion and Informal Interview

An informal interview was also conducted with each participant following the usability study to gain further insight and clarify issues to improve each iteration of testing.

Conclusion

The Crafter's Ear usability study of a virtual world simulation in Minecraft validated the need for a conceptual usability model by integrating existing elements of usability theories and models from the web and 3D VW usability. The development of this conceptual model began with a literature review and drew from the experiences and results from the Crafter's Ear usability study. Because of the complex layering and multiple variables possible across devices, platforms, simulation purposes, and participants, concepts were provided with examples for developing personalized evaluation instruments as well as discussion on three phases of usability testing scaffolded from simple to complex. We hope the proposed conceptual model will address the challenges and needs that are unique to 3D VW simulations compared to a traditional usability study.

References

Butkute, V. & Lapin, K. (2010). *Usability heuristics for online virtual worlds* [PowerPoint slides]. Retrieved from https://klevas.mif.vu.lt/~moroz/papers/VU_Usability_heuristics_slides_IT2010.pdf.

Chwen, J., Siew, Y., Kee, M., & Chee, S. (2013). Group usability testing of virtual reality-based learning environments: A modified approach. *Procedia: Learning and Behavioral Sciences, 97,* 691–699.

Downey, L. (2007). Group usability testing: Evolution in usability techniques. *Journal of Usability Studies, 2*(3), 133–144.

Erickson, T., Shami, N. S., Kellogg, W. A., & Levine, D. W. (2011). Synchronous interaction among hundreds: An evaluation of a conference in an avatar-based virtual environment. *Proceedings of the 2011 Annual Conference on Human Factors in Computing Systems – CHI '11, 503.* 10.1145/1978942.1979013.

Espinosa, S. (2019). The Crafter's Ear evaluating an aural theory simulation in Minecraft. *Technology, Community & Colleges 2019 International Conference.* Retrieved from https://scholarspace.manoa.hawaii.edu/bitstream/10125/61881/1/Espinosa%20Final%20Project%20Paper.pdf.

Gabbard, J. (1997). A taxonomy of usability characteristics in virtual environments. (Master's Thesis). Retrieved from http://citeseerx.ist.psu.edu/viewdoc/download?doi=10.1.1.99.6728&rep=rep1&type=pdf.

Garrett, B., Taverner, T., Gromala, D., Tao, G., Cordingley, E., & Sun, C. (2018). Virtual reality clinical research: Promises and challenges. *JMIR Serious Games, 6*(4), e10839. doi:10.2196/10839.

ISO 9241–11. (1998). Ergonomic requirements for office work with visual display terminals (VDTs) – Part 11 Guidance on usability.

Krug, S. (2010). *Rocket surgery made easy: The do-it-yourself guide to finding and fixing usability problems.* Berkeley, CA: New Riders.

Levi, M. and Conrad, F. (1996). A heuristic evaluation of a World Wide Web prototype. *Interactions, 3*(4), 50–61.

Lin, H., Wang, Y., Wang, Y., & Wang, Y. (2018). Measuring perceived physiological vulnerability to IT usage: An initial test in a virtual reality-based learning environment. *Interactive Learning Environments,* 1–16. doi:10.1080/10494820.2018.1545672.

Lo, P. (2014). *User interface, input output design.* [PowerPoint Slides]. Retrieved from www.peter-lo.com/Teaching/CS211/L07.pdf.

Minocha, S. & Hardy, C. (2016). Navigation and wayfinding in learning spaces in 3D worlds. In M. Lee, B. Tynan, B. Dalgarno, & S. Gregory (Eds.), *Learning in virtual worlds: Research and applications* (pp. 3–41). Edmonton, Alberta, Canada: AU Press.

Nielsen, J. (1993). *Usability engineering.* Cambridge, MA: Academic Press.

Nielsen, J. (1994, November 1). *Severity ratings for usability problems.* Retrieved from https://www.nngroup.com/articles/how-to-rate-the-severity-of-usability-problems/

Slone, D. (2009). A methodology for measuring usability evaluation skills using the constructivist theory and the Second Life virtual world. *Journal of Usability Studies, 4*(4), 178–188.

Sutcliffe, A. & Alrayes, A. (2010). Comparing user experience and performance in Second Life and Blackboard. In Campos, P., Graham, N., Jorge, J. & Nunes, N., Palanque, P., & Winckler, M. (2011). *Human-Computer Interaction-INTERACT 2011, Part 3: 13th IFIP TC 13 International Conference, Lisbon, Portugal, September 5–9, 2011, Proceedings.*

Vega, K., Pereira Soares, A. Robichez, G., & Fuks, H. (2010). *TREG usability tests: Evaluating a training game in Second Life.* 2010 VII Brazilian Symposium on Collaborative Systems (SBSC 2010)(SBSC), Belo Horizonte, 2010, 63–70. doi:10.1109/SBSC.2010.17.

Zilles Borba, E., Corrêa, A. G., de Deus Lopes, R., & Zuffo, M. (2019). *Usability in virtual reality: Evaluating user experience with interactive archaeometry tools in digital simulations. Multimedia tools and applications.* doi:10.1007/s11042-019-07924-3.

10 Learning User Experience Design (LUX)

Adding the "L" to UX Research Using Biometric Sensors

Quincy Conley

Introduction

Learners' affective state is considered to be strongly correlated with their learning process (Astleitner & Wiesner, 2004; Oaksford, Morris, Grainger, & Williams, 1996; Park, Flowerday, & Brünken, 2015). The term affective state refers to the underlying emotional disposition. From the literature, there is a relationship between the design of educational experiences with learners' affective state (attention, emotion, motivation, and cognition). A learner's emotional disposition, either positive, negative, or neutral, may lead to task-irrelevant thoughts (attention) that impair learning performance (Seibert & Ellis, 1991). Learners' emotional disposition can be a strong predictor of learning outcomes when the task requires executive function (i.e., mental control and self-regulation) (Oaksford et al., 1996). Additionally, a learner's emotional disposition impacts intrinsic and extrinsic motivation levels (Isen & Reeve, 2005). Positive activating emotions such as engagement and excitement towards learning can increase student interest and thereby their motivation to study (Pekrun, Frenzel, Goetz, & Perry, 2007). At the same time, positive emotions can increase cognitive processing capacity by broadening a learner's ability to focus (Fredrickson & Branigan, 2005), improving valued learning processes such as creative problem solving (Isen, Daubman, & Nowicki, 1987) and memory encoding and retrieval (Nasby & Yando, 1982). Schachter-Singer theory offers another explanation of the connection between affect and learning (Berkowitz, 2014; Reisenzein, 2017). This theory suggests that the physiological stimulation occurs first. Then the learner identifies the reason for the stimulation to experience and label it as an emotion before taking any actions that could lead to learning. Given this explanation, affective elements such as emotion, attention, motivation, and cognition are influential factors for the learning process.

While taking significant measures to reveal these invisible learning operations, learning designers and researchers routinely design studies to identify and predict how learners act, make decisions, plan, and memorize during a learning experience using surveys, subjective observations, and archival data. However, as Makeig, Gramann, Jung, Sejnowski, and Poizner (2009) emphasize, these traditional research methodologies are particularly challenged in the systematic and objective observation and interpretation of emotions. Even more challenging, researchers struggle to witness and assess the connection between those affective components and the learning process to design efficacious learning experiences. Therefore, the purpose of this chapter is to provide a comprehensive explanation of the emerging research method, biometrics, that is specifically geared towards the systematic and objective observation and interpretation of learners' affective states. This chapter defines the field of biometrics as a formal research method, but also when to use it, and how to use it for investigating the impacts of learning experiences with learners.

What Is Biometric Research?

Born from advancements in the study of psychological theory and assistive technology, *biometrics* is the growing research approach of analyzing non-conscious physiological signals from humans recorded by sensors that can help deepen the understanding of human behavior. Physiological signals include eye movements, facial expressions, skin temperature and perspiration, brain wave activity, heart rate, muscle response, mouse movements and clicks, and speech inflection. Such signals are recorded using one or more biosensor technologies such as eye-tracking, facial expression recognition (FER), galvanic skin conductance, electroencephalogram (EEG) technology, and others. Beyond traditional educational research methods, these tools can provide an extra layer of data for identifying relevant human learning behavior during a learning experience, such as (Farnsworth, 2017; Mirza-Babaei, Long, Foley, & McAllister, 2011):

- Attention—what aspects are engaging or distracting?
- Emotion—when are learners excited or frustrated?
- Motivation—when are learners the most or least motivated?
- Cognition—are learners focused on germane or extraneous information?

Previous non-biometric research has regularly attempted to collect affective state data to inform and unlock the efficacy of digital experiences (Yubo Chen, Wang, & Xie, 2011; Mayer & Estrella, 2014; Park, Knörzer, Plass, & Brünken, 2015; Plass, Heidig, Hayward, Homer, & Um, 2014; Um, Plass, Hayward, & Homer, 2012). However, some studies of this nature have created more questions than answers due to the subjective nature of the results. By contrast, recent biometric research has already shown the potential to inform the design of digital learning experiences in a way that guides a user's affective state on the way to desirable outcomes (Alemdag & Cagiltay, 2018; Azevedo & Gašević, 2019; Chen, 2018; D'Mello, Dieterle,

& Duckworth, 2017; Eckstein, Guerra-Carrillo, Miller Singley, & Bunge, 2017; Park et al., 2015). Nevertheless, it is clear that learning designers and researchers are in search of empirical methods to gain insights into how to design and develop efficacious learning experiences.

How Can Biometrics Enhance Educational Research?

Although biometrics research is not new, given the recent technological advances, it is gaining momentum as a more conventional research method in areas such as marketing, psychology, medical, and computer science fields. The emergence of biometrics as a reliable research tool is especially true in user experience research (UXR), where it is commonly used to enhance the design of products such as websites, games, and mobile apps. In such explorations, biometrics has been shown to help answer difficult questions such as what aspects of an experience attract users' attention, as well as what impact the experience has on them emotionally and physiologically (Jain, Nandakumar, & Ross, 2016). For these reasons, it is timely to consider biometrics more centrally as a research approach in the educational sector, given the proliferation of new instructional technologies entering the market every day and the demand for them to be learner-focused. Based on previous scientific inquiries, it is clear that there is an untapped opportunity for using biometrics to deepen our knowledge about how to design the next generation of instructional technologies.

Four main points support the compelling argument for how biometrics can enhance educational research explorations. First, biometrics can help uncover what learners have difficulty telling us about a learning experience (D'Mello & Graesser, 2012; Jarodzka, Holmqvist, & Gruber, 2017; Mirza-Babaei et al., 2011; Scharinger, Soutschek, Schubert, & Gerjets, 2015), such as:

- What elements capture their attention?
- What are the roadblocks to their learning?
- Are they prepared emotionally for learning?
- When are learners the most motivated during a learning experience?
- What are their decision-making cues?
- Are their learning behaviors changing over time?

Second, another area where biometrics excels is at answering questions about human behavior related to learners' affective states. From neuroscience research, a person's affective state can be measured in terms of three foundational constructs (Balconi, Grippa, & Vanutelli, 2015):

- Actions—what activities do learners perform?
- Emotions—how do learners feel?
- Cognitions—what are learners thinking about?

Understanding how these constructs are impacted by the design and context of learning experiences impact is relatively unknown or under-diagnosed (Chu, Rosenfield, & Portello, 2014; Mayer, 2014; Nasby & Yando, 1982; Oaksford et al., 1996; Park et al., 2015). However, based on established learning science, learners' affective states are omnipresent during anything they do as a reaction to and an interaction with certain stimuli (Park et al., 2015). Expressly, learners' actions, emotions, and cognitions are tightly connected to help them either persist or resist during a learning experience (Astleitner & Wiesner, 2004; Berkowitz, 2014; Fredrickson & Branigan, 2005; Isen et al., 1987; Makeig et al., 2009; Pekrun et al., 2007; Reisenzein, 2017; Seibert & Ellis, 1991). For instance, while completing homework (action), if a learner is sad (emotion) and ruminating on relationship issues (cognition), they could go for a walk to clear their head (action) to increase their ability to focus on the assignment potentially. This behavior could determine if they return to complete the assignment to the best of their ability, or muddle through it, or walk away and not complete the assignment at all.

The third reason to consider biometrics is due to its innate ability to help minimize common biases that are known to detract from the findings of educational design research. The physiological signals recorded by biometric sensors are difficult to control for humans. Besides faking one's face during facial expression recognition, most physiological signals are difficult for people to falsify. Therefore, the signals are generally accepted as valid and reliable for scientific research explorations (Debener, Emkes, De Vos, & Bleichner, 2015; Kasneci, Kübler, Broelemann, & Kasneci, 2017; Majaranta & Bulling, 2014). Conversely, traditional research methods typically rely heavily on subjective data collected from such as surveys, interviews, and observations (Marshall & Rossman, 2014). There is a multitude of respon-dent biases that researchers have to accept regardless of scientific rigor when using these approved educational research instruments (Podsakoff, MacK-enzie, & Podsakoff, 2012). Respondent biases include participants in the study responding in ways that are always in agreement with others, or wanting to be more liked by the researcher, or experiencing response fatigue and no longer are being truthful in their answers. Although these research issues are widely known, they are particularly problematic when testing instructional interventions or learning experiences. To help reduce the impact of these kinds of biases, educational researchers are often required to work with large data sets with overly strict protocols, sometimes creating non-authentic environments to compensate for these types of issues.

Lastly, by nature, biometrics is a complement to other research methods. To conduct educational research, biometrics works well with other vital instru-ments commonly used, such as surveys, observation checklists, knowledge tests, learning activities, and perception questionnaires. The data produced by all of these instruments work well for data triangulation, which leads to better generalizability, validity, and reliability of research results.

Prominent Biosensors for Educational Research

New biometric sensors available today are practical, reasonably priced, and suitable for learning designers and researchers (Gonzalez-Sanchez, Baydogan, Chavez-Echeagaray, Atkinson, & Burleson, 2017). Furthermore, the latest generation of biometric hardware and software make it easier to use for research purposes by providing built-in research design templates and quicker data analysis.

Eye-tracking

In the form of either display or head-mounted systems, eye-tracking is used to record eye movement data during a user experience. To the participant, the display-mounted setup looks like a standard monitor; the only difference is a small near-infrared light-emitting diode (attached or detached) positioned on the frame of the monitor. This design aspect helps promote more natural user behavior by not placing unnatural restrictions on participants to cause distraction (e.g., helmets, headrests, etc.). The head-mounted setup looks like a typical pair of glasses that monitor eye movements. This design is effective during experiences that require the user to be more mobile in a larger setting with more than one stimuli like a classroom with multiple sources of instructional content (i.e., whiteboard, class presentation, individual computer, etc.). Given today's advancements in eye-tracking technology, both form factors are capable of collecting accurate eye-tracking data.

Beginning in the 1970s, eye movement research has flourished due to advances in both types of eye-tracking technologies. Steadily, eye-tracking has become useful as a means of studying the usability of human–computer interfaces and as a means of designing software (Jacob & Karn, 2003; Krafka et al., 2016; Majaranta & Bulling, 2014; Poole & Ball, 2005). Through eye-tracking, researchers can collect more precise information about how attention-grabbing visual elements, such as text, graphics, links, videos, or navigational tools, impact learners' focus and awareness (Duchowski, 2007; Lu, Okabe, Sugano, & Sato, 2014; Veneri et al., 2012).

Facial Expression Recognition (FER)

Facial expression recognition (FER) software is currently one of the most active areas of biometric research, particularly among software design researchers. Recent advances open up the possibility of automatic detection and classification of emotional facial signals to design an ideal user experience. Current interest in this area stems from FER being considered as a critical component in the development of affective computing technologies such as intelligent tutoring software. Another driver is that the technology behind facial expression recognition is to the point where simple low-resolution web cameras can identify faces almost immediately even under poor environmental circumstances (i.e., low light, obstructions, etc.).

Using a webcam placed near the top of a monitor (or wherever the participant will view the stimuli for the study), the software identifies the face and then locates the main feature points on the face, such as eyes and mouth, in real-time and create a digital map of those features. Then it assesses movement, shape, and texture of the face at a pixel level from that map as a user progresses through an experience. The software analyzes each frame of video (live or recorded) from the camera and generates an interpretation of the changes in the learner's facial expressions into emotions.

Galvanic Skin Response (GSR)

A long-time established technology developed in the 1950s, the galvanic skin response (GSR) is designed to sense and record the autonomic activation of sweat glands at the skin level in humans. Not to be confused with a polygraph machine, a GSR sensor monitors skin conductivity between two reusable electrodes attached to a part of the body—usually placed on the hands or feet—where the largest concentration of sweat glands is located. When the sweat glands become active (due to an emotional response to a stimulus), moisture on the skin is produced, allowing the current to be transferred between the electrodes (increasing skin conductance). Due to their detection sensitivity and accuracy, GSR sensors are considered a powerful biometric tool for gauging a user's affective state. GSR is particularly helpful for people who are less expressive in their facial expressions. It provides an additional data point for learners whose facial behaviors may be hard to assess. As such, the GSR is typically affiliated with the measurement of a user's engagement and stress levels (Lin, Omata, Hu, & Imamiya, 2005). As a powerful way to measure the usability of software, GSR sensors are useful for assessing the optimal performance when designing digital learning experiences. Unwanted spikes can identify trouble spots during the experience in GSR data. Similarly, GSR spikes can help determine when and where learners are the least motivated in need of prompts to complete a particular task.

EEG Brain-computer Interface

Electroencephalogram (EEG) sensors are used to record electrical signals produced by the brain that take place during cognitive and psychomotor activities. Electrodes placed at the surface of the scalp record electrical activity in the form of brain waves signals (alpha, beta, delta, theta, and others), which are then analyzed and interpreted. Compared with other brain imaging techniques (i.e., computed tomography (CT), functional magnetic resonance imaging (fMRI), magnetoencephalography (MEG), and positron emission tomography (PET), etc.), EEG is considered a developing yet encouraging method for "understanding how the human brain functions in real-world, operational settings while individuals move freely in perceptually-rich environments" (Hairston et al., 2014, p. 1). Due to the portability and affordability of the current generation of EEG sensors, they are an unobtrusive method of producing excellent insight into human behavior from measuring brain activity.

Brain activity ultimately drives behavior; however, beyond self-reported data and exam scores, without additional technology, it is difficult to assess cognitive activities. Furthermore, when interested in mental processes such as response workload, creativity, or critical thinking, explicit behavioral actions might be very subtle. The importance of these kinds of mental processes makes EEG an ideal biometric technology for exploring learner behavior during a learning experience (Balconi et al., 2015). With EEG, the electrical brain activation patterns are discernible, in which brain areas are active and how they interact during a learning experience. In tandem with other biometric sensors, EEG can help provide more in-depth insights about learners' cognitive behavior beyond the spectrum of emotions (Hairston et al., 2014; Lukanov, Maior, & Wilson, 2016).

Common Affective State Measures for Biometric Research

Typically, biometric testing works well in conjunction with other qualitative or quantitative research techniques. Data collection for biometric research can take place in laboratory or field environments. The idea behind some research efforts is to conduct data collection more authentically. Biometrics excels at allowing for data collection more naturally than typical scientifically contrived settings. In the case of educational research, these locations are usually classroom environments or study areas. For biometric research, all that is generally needed is a comfortable workspace (with or without) internet connectivity to hook up the research equipment. Given the improved robustness of the technology, biometric data collection sessions can even take place on-the-go in places like a busy coffee shop as long as external distractions are limited. Depending on the design of the study, standard measures currently associated with biometrics are attention, emotional state, motivation levels, and cognitive activity, as shown in Table 10.1.

Attention

Attention is measured by the action of the eyes as recorded by an eye-tracking sensor. Think of attention as where the learner looks and for how long as a predictor of other variables; what they visually focus on. Eye-tracking data can be easily aggregated across several learners to produce

Table 10.1 Biometric Research Variables, Measures, and Instruments

Learning Behavior	Variable	Measure	Instrument
Attention	Areas of Interest Navigation Paths	• TTFF • Fixation Count • Ratio • F-Pattern • Gaze Point • Saccade Pattern	Eye-tracking
Emotion	Emotional Valence	• Positive • Negative • Neutral	Facial Recognition Software

Motivation	Emotional Arousal	• Number of Peaks:
		  ○ Per Minute
		  ○ Per Event
			Galvanic Skin Conductance

Cognition	Mental Effort	• Engagement • Excitement • Frustration • Boredom • Blink Rate* • Pupil Dilation* • Head Alignment	EEG & Eye-tracking

* As measured in conjunction with eye-tracking data, increased cognitive load associated with reduced blink rate (Chu et al., 2014) and increased pupil dilation (Scharinger et al., 2015).

visuals such as heat maps and saccade patterns, which show the gaze distribution and indicate which locations on-screen attracted the most attention (concentration of attention).

Areas of interest (AOIs) are researcher-defined subregions of a displayed stimulus. Extracting metrics for separate AOIs is practical when comparing learners' performance between multiple stimuli, such as different designs of an interface, learning object locations, or navigational tools. This approach can also be used to compare groups of learners with varying attributes within the same stimuli to determine if the stimuli meets their learning needs.

Additionally, time to first fixation (TTFF) is the amount of time it takes a user to look at a specific AOI. TTFF can help identify a learning flow and show where an intervention is needed to direct (or redirect) the learner's attention. For example, a goal may be for the learner to first focus on the instructions for a learning activity before starting a problem-solving task. Therefore, it is desirable to design the experience where the instructions are more attractive to the student's eye. TTFF is a simple yet very valuable metric in diagnosing the optimal flow during a learning experience.

Respondent count (or ratio) is how many of a group of learners guided their gaze towards a given AOI. A higher count shows that the stimulus is widely attended to, while a low count shows something different may be needed to gain the learners' attention if it is deemed necessary to the learning experience.

Time spent (TS) quantifies the amount of time that students spent on an AOI. Time spent quantifies the amount of time that respondents spent looking at an AOI. As learners have to blend out other stimuli in the visual periphery that could be equally interesting, the amount of time spent often indicates motivation and conscious attention. Prolonged visual attention at a specific region points to a high level of interest. At the same time, shorter times suggest that other areas on the screen or in the environment might be more attractive.

Gaze points constitute the basic unit of measure for the point on the screen where a learner looked. Related, a saccade pattern describes the collection (and sequence) of eye movements. Other advanced attention-related metrics include F-pattern, E-pattern, and revisits that are helpful to measure learners' performance during a learning experience.

Emotion

As one of the most indicative aspects of the learning process, emotional valence (e.g., anger, contempt, disgust, fear, joy, sadness, surprise), is measured from learners' faces as either positive, negative, or neutral events. In conjunction with other measures, this measure is effective at identifying sticking points of a learning experience. It could also be a precursor for other activities such as an action or cognition. When a learner expresses frustration, it could be a predictor that they need help and need assistance completing the task such as a math problem. When this happens, it could be a reliable indicator of the need for performance support, or instructional prompt, during the learning experience designed to help the learner become unstuck.

Motivation

While facial expressions provide insights into the general direction of an emotional response (positive-negative), they cannot be used to determine the strength of the emotion alone. As depicted in Figure 10.1, emotional arousal levels (magnitude or intensity) as measured by GSR along with emotional direction (valence) as measured by FER can be used together to inform a learner's motivation. A learner's emotional arousal level is

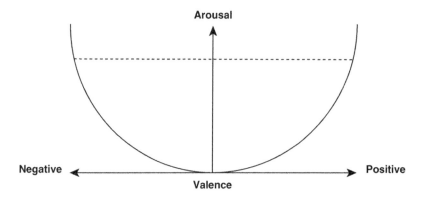

Figure 10.1 Depiction of how emotional valence and magnitude combine to inform a learner's motivational state—copyright 2017 by iMotions

Figure adapted with permission from *Human Behavior: The Complete Pocket Guide* by Bryn Farnsworth, 2019, iMotions Blog, Retrieved from https://imotions.com/blog/human-behavior/

a precursor of regulation of consciousness, attention, and information processing.

Cognition

There are various types of EEG equipment to record and analyze a learner's cognitive responses to prescribed learning experiences. Borrowing from cognitive and data sciences, the cognitive signals are recorded by brain wave type, location, and signal strength. Each brand of equipment usually offers its methodology to translate the signals into useful meaning. When attempting to assess affective status, descriptors such as engagement, excitement, boredom, meditative, frustration, are considered some of the most relevant translations of brain wave signals for learning outcomes that educational researchers can use to understand learning behavior better.

Essential Considerations of Biometric Research

Biometric Research Is Complicated

With only a few exceptions, conducting biometric research requires similar undertakings as traditional educational research methods (study design, participant recruitment, data collection, results analysis, etc.); however, it also usually involves using multiple computers, hardware, and software tools. Because testing with biometric equipment is by nature more technologically challenging, it is vital to have members of the research team who are well-versed in using the technology. Although modern biometric technology is becoming more stable and reliable than ever, this added complexity will require having someone on the team who can attend to and troubleshoot the equipment. To lessen the impact of technical issues, most vendors who offer biometric equipment offer training and technical support for researchers.

Data Collection and Analysis Is Time-consuming

Conducting biometric research generates a vast amount of data, quantitative and qualitative. As a result, data collection and analysis can be time-consuming. Therefore, it is prudent to consider extra help with extrapolating the data. It requires researchers not only to be skilled at sophisticated statistical analysis but also in working with large sets of data. To lessen this issue, there is an increasing number of software platforms available designed to simplify and speed up the data analysis process. As the popularity and collective wisdom continue to grow, the data will become easier to extrapolate and synthesize, making it a worthwhile endeavor. The compelling visualizations and concrete insights produced from biometrics make for a persuasive reason to use the promising research approach.

Conclusions

Biometrics is an emerging research methodology well suited for investigating learning behavior during a learning experience. In situations where researchers and designers want to compare content or features across multiple learning experiences, biometrics can generate observable data that can be analyzed for insights about learning behavior that other research methodologies currently cannot provide. Through physiological signal processing, learning designers and researchers can explore the connection between learners' actions, emotions, and cognitions with their behavior during a learning experience. Albeit more technically complicated and of higher cost, biometrics excels at bringing to light the invisible affective drivers of the learning process. For example, thinking about foundational learning theories such as self-regulation, motivation, and growth mindset, biometrics can allow us to more easily pinpoint if a learner is even prepared emotionally or cognitively to absorb the information presented during a learning experience. Since cognitive theory tells us that too little or too much arousal can adversely affect a learner's learning performance, biometrics can help us find the ideal levels for learning (Sweller, 1994).

Concurrently, even if it is only a modicum improvement, biometrics also helps to reduce the level of bias in educational research. Biometrics records signals produced by the human-automation system, which are difficult to consciously manipulate for reasons that are known to bias research results when working with human subjects. By having more objective learning data, it is foreseeable how learning experiences could potentially be designed and developed in a way that more closely mirrors efficient learning. When the learning process can be mapped out, there is a higher chance to create a learning experience that aligns with it, saving time and money in the long run. More so than traditional educational research methods alone, biometrics can help improve the design and development of learning experiences that are more efficacious, making it a worthwhile investment for learning designers and researchers.

References

Alemdag, E. & Cagiltay, K. (2018). A systematic review of eye tracking research on multimedia learning. *Computers & Education, 125,* 413–428.

Astleitner, H. & Wiesner, C. (2004). An integrated model of multimedia learning and motivation. *Journal of Educational Multimedia and Hypermedia, 13*(1), 3–21.

Azevedo, R. & Gašević, D. (2019). Analyzing multimodal multichannel data about self-regulated learning with advanced learning technologies: Issues and challenges. *Computers in Human Behavior, 96,* 207–210.

Balconi, M., Grippa, E., & Vanutelli, M. E. (2015). What hemodynamic (fNIRS), electrophysiological (EEG) and autonomic integrated measures can tell us about emotional processing. *Brain and Cognition, 95,* 67–76.

Berkowitz, L. (2014). Towards a general theory of anger and emotional aggression: Implications. In R. S. Wyer, Jr. & T. K. Srull (Eds.), *Perspectives on anger and emotion: Advances in social cognition* (Vol. 6, pp. 1–46). Hove: Psychology Press.

Chen, Y. (2018). Reducing language speaking anxiety among adult EFL learners with interactive holographic learning support system. In T. T. Wu, Y. M. Huang, R. Shadiev, L. Lin, & A. Starčič (Eds.), *Innovative Technologies and Learning* (Vol. 11003, pp. 101–110). New York: Springer.

Chen, Y., Wang, Q., & Xie, J. (2011). Online social interactions: A natural experiment on word of mouth versus observational learning. *Journal of Marketing Research, 48*(2), 238–254.

Chu, C. A., Rosenfield, M., & Portello, J. K. (2014). Blink patterns: Reading from a computer screen versus hard copy. *Optometry and Vision Science, 91*(3), 297–302.

D'Mello, S., Dieterle, E., & Duckworth, A. (2017). Advanced, analytic, automated (AAA) measurement of engagement during learning. *Educational Psychologist, 52*(2), 104–123.

D'Mello, S. & Graesser, A. (2012). Dynamics of affective states during complex learning. *Learning and Instruction, 22*(2), 145–157.

Debener, S., Emkes, R., De Vos, M., & Bleichner, M. (2015). Unobtrusive ambulatory EEG using a smartphone and flexible printed electrodes around the ear. *Scientific Reports, 5,* 16743.

Duchowski, A. T. (2007). *Eye tracking methodology: Theory and practice.* Berlin: Springer-Verlag.

Eckstein, M. K., Guerra-Carrillo, B., Miller Singley, A. T., & Bunge, S. A. (2017). Beyond eye gaze: What else can eyetracking reveal about cognition and cognitive development? *Developmental Cognitive Neuroscience, 25,* 69–91.

Farnsworth, B. (2017, April 4). *What is biometric research?* iMotions. Retrieved from https://imotions.com/blog/what-is-biometric-research/.

Fredrickson, B. L. & Branigan, C. (2005). Positive emotions broaden the scope of attention and thought-action repertoires. *Cognition & Emotion, 19*(3), 313–332.

Gonzalez-Sanchez, J., Baydogan, M., Chavez-Echeagaray, M. E., Atkinson, R. K., & Burleson, W. (2017). Affect measurement: A roadmap through approaches, technologies, and data analysis. In M. Jeon (Ed.), *Emotions and affect in human factors and human-computer interaction* (pp. 255–288). Cambridge, MA: Academic Press.

Hairston, W. D., Whitaker, K. W., Ries, A. J., Vettel, J. M., Bradford, J. C., Kerick, S. E., & McDowell, K. (2014). Usability of four commercially-oriented EEG systems. *Journal of Neural Engineering, 11*(4), 046018.

Isen, A. M., Daubman, K. A., & Nowicki, G. P. (1987). Positive affect facilitates creative problem solving. *Journal of Personality and Social Psychology, 52*(6), 1122–1131.

Isen, A. M. & Reeve, J. (2005). The Influence of positive affect on intrinsic and extrinsic motivation: Facilitating enjoyment of play, responsible work behavior, and self-control. *Motivation and Emotion, 29*(4), 295–323.

Jacob, R. J. K., & Karn, K. S. (2003). Eye tracking in human–computer interaction and usability research: Ready to deliver the promises. In J. Hyönä, R. Radach, & H. Deubel (Eds.), *The mind's eyes: Cognitive and applied aspects of eye movements* (Vol. 2, pp. 573–605). New York, NY: Elsevier Science.

Jain, A. K., Nandakumar, K., & Ross, A. (2016). 50 years of biometric research: Accomplishments, challenges, and opportunities. *Pattern Recognition Letters, 79*, 80–105.

Jarodzka, H., Holmqvist, K., & Gruber, H. (2017). Eye tracking in educational science: Theoretical frameworks and research agendas. *Journal of Eye Movement Research, 10*, 1. doi:10.16910/jemr.10.1.3.

Kasneci, E., Kübler, T., Broelemann, K., & Kasneci, G. (2017). Aggregating physiological and eye tracking signals to predict perception in the absence of ground truth. *Computers in Human Behavior, 68*, 450–455.

Krafka, K., Khosla, A., Kellnhofer, P., Kannan, H., Bhandarkar, S., Matusik, W., & Torralba, A. (2016). Eye tracking for everyone. In T. Tuytelaars, F.F. Li, & R. Bajcsy (Eds.), *Proceedings of the IEEE conference on computer vision and pattern recognition* (pp. 2176–2184). IEEE.

Lin, T., Omata, M., Hu, W., & Imamiya, A. (2005). Do physiological data relate to traditional usability indexes? In A. Donaldson (Ed.), *Proceedings of the 17th Australia conference on computer-human interaction: Citizens online: Considerations for today and the future* (pp. 1–10). ACM.

Lu, F., Okabe, T., Sugano, Y., & Sato, Y. (2014). Learning gaze biases with head motion for head pose-free gaze estimation. *Image and Vision Computing, 32*(3), 169–179.

Lukanov, K., Maior, H. A., & Wilson, M. L. (2016). Using fNIRS in usability testing: Understanding the effect of web form layout on mental workload. In A. Druin & J. Kaye (Eds.), *Proceedings of the 2016 CHI Conference on Human Factors in Computing Systems* (pp. 4011–4016). ACM.

Majaranta, P. & Bulling, A. (2014). Eye tracking and eye-based human–computer interaction. In S. Fairclough & K. Gilleade (Eds.), *Advances in physiological computing* (pp. 39–65). New York: Springer.

Makeig, S., Gramann, K., Jung, T.-P., Sejnowski, T. J., & Poizner, H. (2009). Linking brain, mind and behavior. *International Journal of Psychophysiology, 73*(2), 95–100.

Marshall, C., & Rossman, G. B. (2014). *Designing qualitative research* (6th ed.). Newbury Park, California: Sage.

Mayer, R. E. (2014). Incorporating motivation into multimedia learning. *Learning and Instruction, 29*, 171–173.

Mayer, R. E. & Estrella, G. (2014). Benefits of emotional design in multimedia instruction. *Learning and Instruction, 33*, 12–18.

Mirza-Babaei, P., Long, S., Foley, E., & McAllister, G. (2011). Understanding the contribution of biometrics to games user research. In M. Copier, A. Waern, & H. W. Kennedy (Eds.), *Proceedings of the 2011 DiGRA international conference: Think, design, play*. DBLP.

Nasby, W. & Yando, R. (1982). Selective encoding and retrieval of affectively valent information: Two cognitive consequences of children's mood states. *Journal of Personality and Social Psychology, 43*(6), 1244–1253.

Oaksford, M., Morris, F., Grainger, B., & Williams, J. M. G. (1996). Mood, reasoning, and central executive processes. *Journal of Experimental Psychology. Learning, Memory, and Cognition, 22*(2), 476–492.

Park, B., Flowerday, T., & Brünken, R. (2015). Cognitive and affective effects of seductive details in multimedia learning. *Computers in Human Behavior, 44*, 267–278.

Park, B., Knörzer, L., Plass, J. L., & Brünken, R. (2015). Emotional design and positive emotions in multimedia learning: An eyetracking study on the use of anthropomorphisms. *Computers & Education, 86*, 30–42.

Pekrun, R., Frenzel, A. C., Goetz, T., & Perry, R. P. (2007). The control-value theory of achievement emotions: An integrative approach to emotions in education. In P. A. Schutz & R. Pekrun (Eds.), *Emotion in education* (pp. 13–36). Cambridge, MA: Academic Press.

Plass, J. L., Heidig, S., Hayward, E. O., Homer, B. D., & Um, E. (2014). Emotional design in multimedia learning: Effects of shape and color on affect and learning. *Learning and Instruction, 29*, 128–140.

Podsakoff, P. M., MacKenzie, S. B., & Podsakoff, N. P. (2012). Sources of method bias in social science research and recommendations on how to control it. *Annual Review of Psychology, 63*, 539–569.

Poole, A. & Ball, L. J. (2005). Eye tracking in human-computer interaction and usability research: Current status and future prospects. In C. Ghaoui (Ed.), *Encyclopedia of human computer interaction* (pp. 211–219). Hershey, Pennsylvania: IGI.

Reisenzein, R. (2017). Varieties of cognition-arousal theory. *Emotion Review, 9*(1), 17–26.

Scharinger, C., Soutschek, A., Schubert, T., & Gerjets, P. (2015). When flanker meets the n-back: What EEG and pupil dilation data reveal about the interplay between the two central-executive working memory functions inhibition and updating. *Psychophysiology, 52*(10), 1293–1304.

Seibert, P. S. & Ellis, H. C. (1991). Irrelevant thoughts, emotional mood states, and cognitive task performance. *Memory & Cognition, 19*(5), 507–513.

Sweller, J. (1994). Cognitive load theory, learning difficulty, and instructional design. *Learning and Instruction, 4*(4), 295–312.

Um, E., Plass, J. L., Hayward, E. O., & Homer, B. D. (2012). Emotional design in multimedia learning. *Journal of Educational Psychology, 104*(2), 485–498.

Veneri, G., Pretegiani, E., Rosini, F., Federighi, P., Federico, A., & Rufa, A. (2012). Evaluating the human ongoing visual search performance by eye tracking application and sequencing tests. *Computer Methods and Programs in Biomedicine, 107*(3), 468–477.

11 Exploring the Evolution of Instructional Design and Technology

Disciplinary Knowledge through Citation Context Analysis

Wendy Ann Gentry and Barbara Lockee

Introduction

Academic publication plays an important role in disseminating relevant insights and research findings. Typically, articles, books and other forms of written discourse build upon prior knowledge and citations play a critical role in defining these inter-publication relationships (Angrosh, 2012). These connections help researchers become members of the scholarly community (Kamler & Thomson, 2006), position their research in relation to prior work, and influence the direction of the discipline by building on the research of others.

Against this background, the authors situate academic discourse and citation within the larger system of Instructional Design and Technology (IDT) disciplinary knowledge, and position these as a theoretical framework to explore the discipline with a mixed method approach called citation context analysis (CCA). CCA is a combination of bibliometric analysis and content analysis that explores the relationships between cited and citing documents and the content which is transferred from one to the other through citation (Ritchie, 2008); it may be used to analyze cited concepts based on the text surrounding citations (Small, 1978). When content analysis is performed within the citation context, researchers are able to explore the "intellectual lineage for a given idea" (Angrosh, Cranefield, & Stanger, 2014, p. 36), uncover the influence of concepts over time (Chang, 2013b; McCain & Salvucci, 2006), and provide citation classifications (Cronin, 1984). IDT scholars (Reeves & Oh, 2017; West & Borup, 2014) have recently noted the need for IDT research that focuses on the exploration and synthesis of literature, resulting in the development of new conceptual and theoretical knowledge in our field. The application of CCA as a research methodology seeks to address this need.

A better understanding of the application of concepts through citation will alert IDT researchers to concepts and arguments that may have become overlooked over time and the mix of those that have come in and out of favor. This provides an opportunity for researchers, experienced and novice alike, to reflect on their own practice and consider how their efforts have influenced the direction of the discipline and what changes they can make going forward to benefit IDT research and practice. To achieve these objectives, this chapter provides an introduction to CCA, an overview of related research, and a seven-step framework to help researchers apply the method in their own work.

Overview of CCA

CCA is a combination of bibliometric analysis and content analysis that explores the relationships between cited and citing documents and the content which is transferred through citation (Ritchie, 2008). Bibliometric analysis studies relationships between bibliographic elements included in publication such as authors, journals, and articles (Havemann & Scharnhorst, 2010). Content analysis is "a research method that uses a set of procedures to make valid inferences from text" (Weber, 1990, p. 9) for the purpose of creating "a numerically based summary of a chosen message set" (Neuendorf, 2002, p. 14). Through the analysis of citation-related text, researchers can uncover content which is transferred during the citation process (Anderson, 2006; Golden-Biddle, Locke, & Reay, 2006; Lounsbury & Carberry, 2005; Mizruchi & Fein, 1999), document the influence of theory (Lounsbury & Carberry, 2005), and identify knowledge claims (Anderson, 2006).

Citation counts are often used as indicators of influence, importance, and quality of authors, articles, journals, areas of focus, and disciplines, and do not take into account the direction of the information flow (Borgman & Furner, 2002). A review of literature in IDT reveals that bibliometrics have primarily been used to identify influential articles, authors, books, and journals. Content analysis of IDT scholarly publication has been historically performed in conjunction with bibliometrics and focused heavily on the citing article in isolation in order to identify research and publication trends.

Early Applications of CCA Methods

Research which explores direction of the information flow and relationships between the cited and citing articles (Borgman & Furner, 2002) can be segmented into three broad classifications: citer motivation surveys and interviews (White, 2004), citation context classification (Small, 1982), and citation content analysis (Small, 1982). These classifications are not mutually exclusive and have been applied in citation study literature reviews by Angrosh (2012), Bornmann and Daniel (2008), Liu (1993), and Ritchie (2008). CCA falls within the combined categories of citation context classification, used to identify relationships between the cited and citing documents, and citation content analysis, which explores the content of prior work which is incorporated through citation (Ritchie, 2008).

Moravcsik and Murugesan (1975; Murugesan & Moravcsik, 1978) performed the first comprehensive CCA to identify citation classifications for research evaluation (Bornmann & Daniel, 2008). These and similar studies inspired researchers to explore citation contexts and the content that is transferred through citation in greater detail. For example, researchers categorized citations based on use (Chang, 2013a; Chubin & Moitra, 1975; Kacmar & Whitfield, 2000; Mizruchi & Fein, 1999), created summaries of key concepts and multi-tiered classification systems (Golden-Biddel et al., 2006; McCain & Salvucci, 2006; Sieweke, 2014), and examined the contribution of concepts over time (Anderson & Sun, 2010; Pooley, 2015; Walsh & Ungson, 1991).

McCain (2011) explains that researchers may explore citations to a single publication or set of publications related to a subject, theory, research method, or concept and classify findings by topic and time. However, as McCain puts it, "studies of this kind ... are rare" (p. 1413). To address this gap, Gentry (2016) created a typology of theory use in IDT publication by tracing the application of theory in the *Educational Technology Research and Development* (*ETRD*) journal from 1953 to 2012.

Introduction to CCA Methods

Taken together, bibliometric analysis and content analysis provide an integrative framework for CCA application in IDT academic publication. Given the breadth of CCA research questions and application contexts, methods vary from one study to the next. The following seven steps adapted from Neuendorf (2002) are intended to serve as a framework to begin planning:

1. Develop theoretical framework.
2. Identify variables.
3. Define citation contexts.
4. Develop sampling procedures.
5. Create codes and codebook.
6. Develop coding procedures.
7. Analyze and report results.

In Step 1, Develop Theoretical Framework, the authors introduce a complex adaptive system (CAS) as a framework to explore IDT disciplinary knowledge and boundaries as well as two components that serve as a foundation of IDT academic publication, discourse, and citation. The goal of this approach is to align CCA to IDT disciplinary knowledge and provide a simple foundation to introduce the breadth and depth of research opportunities available to IDT.

Step 1: Develop Theoretical Framework

In Step 1, researchers explore prior research to develop their own theoretical framework and research questions (Neuendorf, 2002). These selections provide focus and boundaries to the study. To help researchers consider and refine research opportunities, this chapter introduces a CAS framework for exploring CCA within the context of IDT. Next, the discussion moves to two key elements of CCA, including discourse and citation. Taken together, this theoretical framework explores the topic through multiple perspectives that include its components, dimensions, and role of each in impacting IDT disciplinary knowledge. Exploring CCA from these varying perspectives is intended to serve as a starting point for researchers considering the application of CCA in their own work.

A Complex Adaptive Systems Framework for Exploring IDT Disciplinary Knowledge

Systems theory provides an explanation of the emergence of knowledge, and underlines the importance of collaboration between individuals and a community (Kimmerle, Moskaliuk, Cress, & Thiel, 2011). Similarly, disciplinary knowledge, an output of academic discourse described as "the ways of thinking and using language," builds the "social roles and relationships which create academics and students and which sustain the universities, the disciplines, and the creation of knowledge itself" (Hyland, 2009, p. 1). The term *complex* comes from the Latin term *"complexus,* meaning to entwine"; used as an adjective for a system it refers to "interconnected or interwoven parts" (Boardman & Sauser, 2008, p. 188). This definition ideally captures the interconnections of scholarly discourse elicited through the CCA methodology featured herein. Exploring these concepts in unison provides an opportunity to consider the varying ways that citations support the development of the IDT discipline.

Becher and Trowler (2001) describe a discipline as an academic, knowledge community, often identifiable by the boundary of an academic department. A discipline's autonomy is dependent upon its ability to maintain boundaries and conditions for participation, such as contributing to the advancement of knowledge through academic publication (Medina, 2013). This opens opportunities for researchers to apply CCA to examine how IDT concepts are put into practice in other disciplines.

IDT may be described as a practice science with a knowledge base shaped by both theoretical and practical components; simply stated, "a knowledge base is what a field has learned about itself over time" (Richey, Klein, & Tracey, 2011, p. 4). This knowledge base is revealed through IDT academic publication which may be explored through CCA. Disciplinary knowledge is socially constructed (Becher & Trowler, 2001) through chains of citations; journal articles form a network of publication, continually incorporating prior work into publication and incrementally building on their findings.

Publication "builds its own walls—the boundary between science and society, the boundary between science and non-science ... and the boundaries of the discipline" as a result of the ongoing operation of the system (Fujigaki, 1998, p. 10). When articles include citations from another consistent set of related journals, clusters are created from these citing relationships (Leydesdorff, Cozzens, & Van den Besselaar, 1994) and results in additional boundaries between scientific and nonscientific journals (Fujigaki, 1998).

This prior work opens opportunities for researchers to use CCA to study the boundaries of IDT and the degree to which concepts or theories shared through citation across disciplinary borders have impacted the breadth or depth of the discipline.

Components of Disciplinary Knowledge in IDT Academic Publication

Two critical components that situate citation within the larger system of IDT disciplinary knowledge include discourse and citation. An introduction to these concepts and the role that each play in the production of disciplinary knowledge is provided in the sections to follow.

Discourse

Discourse is a "systematically organized set of statements which give expression to the meanings and values of an institution" (Kress, 1989, p. 7). Discourse is situated in stable forms of social activities (Fairclough, 2003). Within the context of CCA, these include text-based artifacts such as conference proceedings or academic articles. There are three dimensions of discourse developed by Fairclough (1992) that researchers may consider when refining their focus: text, discursive practice, and social practice.

TEXT DIMENSION OF DISCOURSE

The text dimension refers to written and spoken forms of communication used to support interaction (Fairclough, 2003). At this level, citation context can reveal the influence of prior work on subsequent research (Paul, 2000). For example, Winsor (1993) combines an analysis of citation patterns and the rhetorical use of citations, finding that a widely cited, controversial article in biology was often incorporated without acceptance of its core arguments. Examining the context of citations, that is the text surrounding citations, Small and Greenlee (1980) concluded that articles which are highly cited are generally cited in relation to a single central idea that the original article introduces. However, Cozzens (1982) finds that articles can have a "split citation identity" representing two distinct concepts over time (p. 233).

DISCURSIVE PRACTICE DIMENSION OF DISCOURSE

The discursive practice dimension mediates the relationship between the text and social practice dimensions; "hence it is only through the discursive practice—whereby people use language to produce and consume texts— that texts shape and are shaped by social practice" (Jorgensen & Phillips, 2002, p. 69). Through writing, researchers influence the direction of an area of study by building on the work of others.

SOCIAL PRACTICE DIMENSION OF DISCOURSE

Social practice is the broader context in which the text is produced, which includes practices of academicians and practitioners as well as the relationships that shape university and industry practices (Kamler & Thomson, 2006). For example, in seeking publication and respect within the discipline, researchers may feel the pressure to apply methods, research instruments, and methods of analysis that are specific to their discipline (Klahr, 2002). For example, CCA is a method applied in other disciplines but has not yet become common within IDT. For this reason, research in other disciplines may offer opportunities to expand how we explore IDT.

Citation

A citation is the collection of words and indexing methods, such as the author and publication year, which correlates to a list of references (Borgman, 1989; Powley & Dale, 2007). Citations are situated in both "a rhetorical system, through which scientists try to persuade each other of their knowledge claims; and a reward system, through which credit for achievements is allocated" (Cozzens, 1989, p. 440). According to this perspective, the ownership of science is shared by a community. However, others consider that discoveries belong to the researchers and that citing the work of another is a way of compensating the original creator (Cozzens, 1989). In addition to good etiquette, citations can also represent the "war of words" in which "publications are weapons in a struggle among scientists to persuade each other of the validity of knowledge claims, and thereby to establish dominant positions in the community" (p. 440). CCA provides a strategy to explore the content that is incorporated across publications through citation, and in doing so may help researchers unfold debated topics such as media studies, and debunked concepts such as learning styles in greater detail. Doing so could unveil opportunities to open conversations not only within IDT, but also across its boundaries.

CITATION AS A BOUNDARY OBJECT

Research findings and communication among researchers play a key role in the production of disciplinary knowledge, but as Star and Griesemer (1989) explain, this process is more complex than it may first appear and researchers must "translate, negotiate, debate, triangulate, and simplify in order to work together" (pp. 388–389).

Medina (2013) argues that the differences between social worlds highlight the value of "negotiation and debate" which occurs between actors and allow for cooperation across borders without general agreement (Merton, 1973, p. 36).

These processes are facilitated by boundary objects—a term used to describe objects that "maintain a common identity" even when adapted for varied target settings—and play a critical role in "developing and maintaining coherence across intersecting social worlds" (Star & Griesemer, 1989, p. 393). Library databases, citations, research articles, and standardized citation practices are all examples of boundary objects (Martens, 2004).

CITATION AS A FEEDBACK MECHANISM

The success of an individual researcher is measured by the quality and quantity of publication (Merton, 1973). Publication quality is difficult to measure because it cannot be determined solely through the examination of the published ideas, but is instead based on what other researchers do with the published ideas (Latour, 1987). While the quantity of publication is easier to determine, Merton cautions that the pressure for publication can "transform the sheer number of publications into a ritualized measure of scientific or scholarly accomplishment" (Merton, 1973, p. 316). Nonetheless, the number of researchers who utilize a published idea through citation is used as a gauge to quality (Latour, 1987).

CITATION AS ARGUMENT

Scientific thinking, a form of problem solving, is formed through the coordination of theory and evidence through the process of argumentation (Belland, 2013; Kuhn & Pearsall, 2000). Argumentation is the process researchers use to generate theory, challenge and support claims, communicate and refine knowledge, refute criticisms, and solve ill-structured problems (Belland, Glazewski, & Richardson, 2008; Golanics & Nussbaum, 2008; Osborne, 2010; Toulmin, Rieke, & Janik, 1979; von Aufschnaiter, Erduran, Osborne, & Simon, 2008). In academic publication, knowledge claims are supported by arguments shared through citation at the sentence level (Cozzens, 1989; Toulmin, 2003). An argument is a series of statements to support a conclusion and a term and serves as a signpost for the reader (Lumer, 2005). CCA can help IDT researchers explore the varying ways that concepts are incorporated into arguments within publication and in doing so open opportunities to support graduate students learning the craft.

A deeper understanding of the dimensions and components of disciplinary knowledge increases the opportunity for researchers to explore the past through prior publication while defining new ways to adjust the trajectory of IDT.

Step 2: Identify Variables

With the theoretical framework in hand, the next step is to identify the variables for the study. A variable is a construct that varies by case or unit (Neuendorf, 2002). Variables may be described as either manifest or latent. Manifest content is measurable or countable (Gray & Densten, 1998), such as the keywords in a journal article or the number of citations included in a single sentence. In contrast, latent content is measured by one or more indicators but cannot be measured directly (Hair, Anderson, Tatham, & Black, 1998), such as the manner in which a citing article incorporates information from a cited article through citation. When content analysis is performed within the citation context, researchers are able to explore variables across time. For example, Gentry (2016) defines cognitive theory as a variable and explores the varying ways it is applied in *ETRD* over a 60-year period. Variables are identified through a review of literature and are ultimately up to the discretion of the researcher.

Step 3: Define Citation Contexts

In Step 3, the researcher identifies the citation contexts collected during the study. A citation context is the reference made to a document, such as a research article, industry white paper, book, or conference proceedings, to provide justification for an argument or other support in a paper. It is recommended that researchers review context samples to make sure they are suitable for the variables selected in Step 2 and with the research questions defined in Step 1.

Zhang, Ding, and Milojević (2013) warn that the selection process can be challenging and propose that researchers consider the diversity, consistency, and flexibility of the contexts. Diversity refers to selecting the disciplinary boundaries. For example, researchers may select citation contexts for a single publication within a discipline, or choose instead to select contexts across a broad range of publications. Decisions about consistency refer to the selection of genre(s) such as journals, books, or conference proceedings. Lastly, the principle of flexibility refers to the semantic or syntactic categories (Zhang, Ding, & Milojević, 2013). To collect an accurate representation of the variables, consider collecting sentences or full paragraphs before and after the citation. For example, contexts may include a few words before and after a reference, multi-sentence passages, sections and paragraphs where the citation is located (Angrosh, Cranefield, & Stanger, 2013; Eto, 2013; Herlach, 1978; Paul, 2000). Due to the breadth and depth of these options, the accessibility of the selected artifacts should be considered.

Step 4: Develop Sampling Procedures

In Step 4, Sampling Procedures, researchers identify how the citation contexts will be located and extracted (Neuendorf, 2002). Data to support CCA varies by genre, and contexts may be extracted from journal articles downloaded from library databases, reference lists provided on library websites, books, and transcripts, among others. The process for extracting text, images or other records from a webpage is known as web content mining (Ambika & Latha, 2014). There are a number of tools for mining web content, a few include: Automation Anywhere, Mozenda, Web Content Extractor, and WebMiner (Ambika & Latha, 2014). After the samples are collected, Cobo, López-Herrera, Herrera-Viedma, and Herrera (2011) recommend that researchers take care in addressing duplicate and misspelled data that can hamper analysis.

Step 5: Create Codes and Codebook

In Step 5, the codes and related codebook are created to enable the researcher to label and sort the data. Codes are selected based on the research questions and are a first step in bringing meaning to the data. According to Zhang et al. (2013), balancing the specificity and generalizability of a code can be challenging; it "should be comprehensive but not too complicated, specific but not too detailed, be broadly applicable but not too general" (p. 1496). Similarly, Chelimsky (1989), recommends that codes are: 1) exhaustive so that the details relevant for the study could be categorized, 2) mutually exclusive so that each coded item related to no more than one category, and 3) independent so the assignment of a code for a unit would not be affected by codes assigned to other units.

Classification schemes are abundant. For example, over a 14-year period (1965 to 1979) ten citation classification schemes were developed through content analysis, each with four to 29 categories to document citation motivation (Baldi, 1998). However, researchers have also developed classifications that summarize how information contained in a cited article is incorporated into another through citation and in doing so to reveal "how prior work shapes ongoing knowledge development" (Golden–Biddle et al., 2006, p. 237). Classification schemes are not mutually exclusive. For example, the appendix provided in Camacho-Minano and Nunez-Nickel (2009) includes a review of over 125 research studies providing citation function typologies developed through qualitative analysis and taxonomies developed through quantitative analysis (Bailey, 1994).

A researcher may incorporate a portion of the prior effort while combining it with additional elements that may oppose the original approach (Moravcsik & Murugesan, 1975; Murugesan & Moravcsik, 1978). Mizruchi and Fein (1999) found that, of the citing articles studied, 72% briefly mentioned the cited article without further discussion, 12%

discussed a concept from the cited article, and the remaining 16% tested at least one of the constructs. Similarly, Kacmar and Whitfield (2000) found that 92% of the analyzed citations incorporated prior work with negligible discussion, while the remaining 8% incorporated prior work as a key focus. Chubin and Moitra (1975) classified citations as either affirmative (four types) or negational (two types) and found that the majority of cited full-length articles were affirmative but not directly connected to the content of the citing article. Each of these efforts includes a classification which relates to the acknowledgment of prior work without additional comment and demonstrate that prior research is incorporated through citation to varying levels of detail. IDT researchers may expand on these or other coding schemes to explore citation contexts and the content that is transferred through citation in greater detail.

Step 6: Develop Coding Procedures

In Step 6, the coding procedures are developed. Following Schreier (2012), a pilot study that tests the coding frame on sample citation contexts to be used for the main coding is recommended as a first step. After the coding procedures are modified as needed, the study can begin. Researchers can choose to review citation contexts randomly by a specific grouping such as a journal, or by time. These decisions can directly impact research findings and should be made with care. For example, starting with the earliest citation date and containing longitudinally until all citation contexts for a selected concept are complete allows the researcher to recognize trends that may not have been uncovered during final analysis.

Reliability

Reliability is defined as "the extent to which a measuring procedure yields the same results on repeated trials" (Neuendorf, 2002, p. 112). Sieweke (2014) and Schreier (2012) recommend calculating an intra-coder agreement rate to test for reliability as follows:

Percentage of agreement

$$= \frac{\text{Number of units of coding on which the codes agree}}{\text{Total number of units of coding}} \times 100$$

Validity

A codebook is considered "valid to the extent that the categories adequately represent the concepts under study" (Schreier, 2012, p. 175). Manifest variables are more standardized and easier to understand by different people, while latent variables may carry multiple meanings (Schreier, 2012).

Face validity and content validity are the most important types of validity for research studies which focus on the description of material rather than on making inferences that extend beyond the material (Schreier, 2012). Face validity is the extent to which the coding scheme appears to measure what is intended; it is also referred to as the "what you see is what you get" validity (Neuendorf, 2002, p. 115), and is primarily a concern for studies which use an inductive approach for developing codes (Schreier, 2012). Content validity measures the degree that a coding scheme covers all the dimensions of a variable, and is most applicable for studies using a deductive approach for developing codes (Schreier, 2012). Recall from Step 2, Identify Variables, that the codes for the latent variable for the study were developed through an inductive approach which begins with the details and ends with generalizations. As a result, face validity is of primary concern. Creating detailed specifications for applying each code for latent variables can improve face validity.

Step 7: Analyze and Report Results

During the final step, the results are analyzed and reported in response to the research questions (Neuendorf, 2002).

Conclusion

Scholarly discourse and citation serve as a preliminary framework to explore the evolution of disciplinary knowledge. While citation counts are a widely recognized, yet imperfect, measure of influence (Kacmar & Whitfield, 2000), Golden-Biddle et al. (2006) argue that establishing the impact of a body of work requires that one explores the extent of content use, as well as the content that is transferred through citation. Through CCA, researchers can extend IDT disciplinary knowledge by exploring the materialization of concepts over time. This innovative methodology holds promise in eliciting the origins of trends and important contributions to perspectives and practices in our field.

References

Ambika, M. & Latha, K. (2014). Web mining: The demystification of multifarious aspects. *International Review on Computers and Software*, 9(1), 135–141.

Anderson, M. (2006). How can we know what we think until we see what we said?: A citation and citation context analysis of Karl Weick's "The social psychology of organizing". *Organization Studies*, 27(11), 1675–1692.

Anderson, M. H. & Sun, P. Y. T. (2010). What have scholars retrieved from Walsh and Ungson (1991)? A citation context study. *Management Learning*, 41(2), 131–145.

Angrosh, M. A. (2012). *Enhancing citation context based information services through sentence context identification.* Dunedin: University of Otago.

Angrosh, M. A., Cranefield, S., & Stanger, N. (2014). Contextual information retrieval in research articles: Semantic publishing tools for the research community. *Semantic Web, 5,* 261–293.

Angrosh, M. A., Cranefield, S., & Stanger, N. (2013). Context identification of sentences in research articles: Towards developing intelligent tools for the research community. *Natural Language Engineering, 19*(4), 481–515.

Bailey, K. D. (1994). *Typologies and taxonomies: An introduction to classification techniques.* Thousand Oaks, CA: Sage.

Baldi, S. (1998). Normative versus social constructivist processes in the allocation of citations: A network-analytic model. *American Sociological Review, 63*(6), 829–846.

Becher, T. & Trowler, P. R. (2001). *Academic tribes and territories: Intellectual enquiry and the culture of disciplines* (2nd ed.). Philadelphia, PA: The Society for Research into Higher Education.

Belland, B. R. (2013). Mindtools for argumentation, and their role in promoting ill-structured problem solving. In J. M. Spector, B. B. Lockee, S. E. Smaldino, & M. C. Herring (Eds.), *Learning, problem solving, and mindtools: Essays in honor of David H. Jonassen* (pp. 229–246). New York, NY: Routledge.

Belland, B. R., Glazewski, K. D., & Richardson, J. C. (2008). A scaffolding framework to support the construction of evidence-based arguments among middle school students. *Educational Technology Research and Development, 56*(4), 401–422.

Boardman, J. & Sauser, B. (2008). *Systems thinking: Coping with 21st century problems.* Boca Raton, FL: CRC Press.

Borgman, C. L. (1989). Bibliometrics and scholarly communication: Editor's introduction. *Communication Research, 16*(5), 583–599.

Borgman, C. L. & Furner, J. (2002). *Scholarly communication and bibliometrics.* Paper presented at the Annual Review of Information Science and Technology.

Bornmann, L. & Daniel, H. (2008). What do citation counts measure? A review of studies on citing behavior. *Journal of Documentation, 64*(1), 45–80.

Camacho-Minano, M. & Nunez-Nickel, M. (2009). The multilayered nature of reference selection. *Journal of the American Society for Information Science and Technology, 60*(4), 754–777.

Chang, Y. (2013a). A comparison of citation contexts between natural sciences and social sciences and humanities. *Scientometrics, 96*(2), 535–553.

Chang, Y. (2013b). The influence of Taylor's paper, question-negotiation and information-seeking in libraries. *Information Processing and Management, 49*(5), 983–994.

Chelimsky, E. (1989). *Content analysis: A methodology for structuring and analyzing written material.* Washington DC: United States General Accounting Office.

Chubin, D. & Moitra, S. (1975). Content analysis of references: Adjunct or alternative to citation counting? *Social Studies of Science, 5*(4), 423–441.

Cobo, M. J., López-Herrera, A. G., Herrera-Viedma, E., & Herrera, F. (2011). Science mapping software tools: Review, analysis, and cooperative study among tools. *Journal of the American Society for Information Science and Technology, 62*(7), 1382–1402.

Cozzens, S. (1982). Split citation identity: A case study from economics. *Journal of the American Society for Information Science (Pre-1986), 33*(4), 233.

Cozzens, S. (1989). What do citations count? The rhetoric-first model. *Scientometrics*, 15(5–6), 437–447.

Cronin, B. (1984). *The citation process: The role and significance of citations in scientific communication*. London: Taylor Graham.

Eto, M. (2013). Evaluations of context-based co-citation searching. *Scientometrics*, *94* (2), 651–673.

Fairclough, N. (1992). *Discourse and social change*. Malden, MA: Blackwell.

Fairclough, N. (2003). *Analyzing discourse*. New York, NY: Routledge.

Fujigaki, Y. (1998). Filling the gap between discussions on science and scientists' everyday activities: Applying the autopoiesis system theory to scientific knowledge. *Social Science Information*, *37*(1), 5–22.

Gentry, W. A. (2016). Citation context analysis of theory use in instructional design and technology academic articles (Unpublished doctoral dissertation). Virginia Tech, Blacksburg, VA.

Golanics, J. D. & Nussbaum, E. M. (2008). Enhancing online collaborative argumentation through question elaboration and goal instructions. *Journal of Computer Assisted Learning*, *24*(3), 167–180.

Golden-Biddle, K., Locke, K., & Reay, T. (2006). Using knowledge in management studies: An investigation of how we cite prior work. *Journal of Management Inquiry*, *15*(3), 237–254.

Gray, J. H. & Densten, I. L. (1998). Integrating quantitative and qualitative analysis using latent and manifest variables. *Quality & Quantity*, *32*, 419–431.

Hair, J., Tatham, R., & Black, W. (1998). *Multivariate data analysis*. Englewood Cliffs, NJ: Prentice Hall.

Havemann, F. & Scharnhorst, A. (2010). Bibliometric networks. In C. Stegbauer & R. Haubling (Eds.), *Handbuch Netzwerkforschung* (pp. 799–823). Heidelberg, Germany: Springer Verlag.

Herlach, G. (1978). Can retrieval of information from citation indexes be simplified? Multiple mention of a reference as a characteristic of the link between cited and citing article. *Journal of the American Society for Information Science*, *29*(6), 308–310.

Hyland, K. (2009). *Academic discourse: English in a global context*. New York, NY: Continuum International Publishing Group.

Jorgensen, M. W. & Phillips, L. (2002). *Discourse analysis as theory and method*. Thousand Oaks, CA: Sage.

Kacmar, K. M. & Whitfield, J. M. (2000). An additional rating method for journal articles in the field of management. *Organizational Research Methods*, *3*(4), 392–406.

Kamler, B. & Thomson, P. (2006). *Helping doctoral students write: Pedagogies for supervision*. New York, NY: Routledge.

Kimmerle, J., Moskaliuk, J., Cress, U., & Thiel, A. (2011). A systems theoretical approach to online knowledge building. *AI & Society*, *26*(1), 49–60.

Klahr, D. (2002). *Exploring science: The cognition and development of discovery processes*. Cambridge, MA: MIT Press.

Kress, G. (1989). *Linguistic processes in sociocultural practice*. Oxford: Oxford University.

Kuhn, D. & Pearsall, S. (2000). Developmental origins of scientific thinking. *Journal of Cognition & Development*, *1*(1), 113–129.

Latour, B. (1987). *Science in action: How to follow scientists and engineers through society*. Cambridge, MA: Harvard University Press.

Leydesdorff, L., Cozzens, S., & Van den Besselaar, P. (1994). Tracking areas of strategic importance using scientometric journal mappings. *Research Policy, 23*(2), 217–229.

Liu, M. (1993). Progress in documentation the complexities of citation practice: A review of citation studies. *Journal of Documentation, 49*(4), 370–408.

Lounsbury, M. & Carberry, E. (2005). From king to court jester? Weber's fall from grace in organizational theory. *Organizational Studies, 26*(4), 501–525.

Lumer, C. (2005). The epistemological theory of argument: How and why? *Informal Logic, 25*(3), 213–242.

Martens, B. (2004). *Theories at work: Functional characteristics of theories that facilitate their diffusion over time* (Unpublished doctoral dissertation). Syracuse University, Syracuse, NY.

McCain, K. (2011). Eponymy and obliteration by incorporation: The case of the "Nash Equilibrium". *Journal of the American Society for Information Science and Technology, 62*(7), 1412–1424.

McCain, K. & Salvucci, L. (2006). How influential is Brooks' law? A longitudinal citation context analysis of Frederick Brooks' The Mythical Man-Month. *Journal of Information Science, 32*(3), 277–295.

Medina, L. (2013). *Center and peripheries in knowledge production.* New York, NY: Routledge.

Merton, R. (1973). *The sociology of science: Theoretical and empirical investigations.* Chicago, IL: University of Chicago Press.

Mizruchi, M. & Fein, L. (1999). The social construction of organizational knowledge: A study of the uses of coercive, mimetic, and normative isomorphism. *Administrative Sciences Quarterly, 44*, 653–683.

Moravcsik, M. & Murugesan, P. (1975). Some results on the function and quality of citations. *Social Studies of Science, 5*(1), 86–92.

Murugesan, P. & Moravcsik, M. (1978). Variation of the nature of citation measures with journals and scientific specialties. *Journal of the American Society for Information Science, 29*(3), 141–147.

Neuendorf, K. (2002). *The content analysis guidebook.* Thousand Oaks, CA: Sage.

Osborne, J. (2010). Arguing to learn in science: The role of collaborative, critical discourse. *Science, 328*(5977), 463–466.

Paul, D. (2000). In citing chaos: A study of the rhetorical use of citations. *Journal of Business and Technical Communication, 14*(2), 185–222.

Pooley, J. D. (2015). Mnemonic multiples: The case of the columbia panel studies. *Journal of the History of the Behavioral Sciences, 51*(1), 10–30.

Powley, B. & Dale, R. (2007). *High accuracy citation extraction and named entity recognition for a heterogeneous corpus of academic papers.* Paper presented at the Natural Language Processing and Knowledge Engineering, Sydney, Australia.

Reeves, T. C. & Oh, E. G. (2017). The goals and methods of educational technology research over the last quarter century. *Educational Technology Research & Development, 65*(2), 325–339. doi:10.1007/s11423-016-9474-1

Richey, R., Klein, J., & Tracey, M. (2011). *The instructional design knowledge base: Theory, research, and practice.* New York, NY: Routledge.

Ritchie, A. (2008). *Citation context analysis for information retrieval* (Unpublished doctoral dissertation). University of Cambridge, United Kingdom.

Schreier, M. (2012). *Qualitative content analysis in practice.* Thousand Oaks, CA: Sage.

Sieweke, J. (2014). Pierre Bourdieu in management and organization studies—A citation context analysis and discussion of contributions. *Scandinavian Journal of Management, 30*(4), 532–543.

Small, H. (1978). Cited documents as concept symbols. *Social Studies of Science, 8*(3), 327–340.

Small, H. (1982). Citation context analysis. In B. Dervin & M. Voight (Eds.), *Progress in communiation studies* (Vol. 3, pp. 287–310). Norwood, NJ: Ablex.

Small, H. & Greenlee, E. (1980). Citation context analysis of a co-citation cluster: Recombinant-DNA. *Scientometrics, 2*(4), 277–301.

Star, S. L. & Griesemer, J. R. (1989). Institutional ecology, "translations" and boundary objects: Amateurs and professionals in Berkeley's museum of vertebrate zoology. *Social Studies of Science, 19*(3), 387–420.

Toulmin, S. (2003). *The uses of argument.* Cambridge, NY: Cambridge University Press.

Toulmin, S., Rieke, R., & Janik, A. (1979). *An introduction to reasoning.* New York, NY: Macmillan.

von Aufschnaiter, C., Erduran, S., Osborne, J., & Simon, S. (2008). Arguing to learn and learning to argue: Case studies of how students' argumentation related to their scientific knowledge. *International Journal of Science Education, 45*, 101–131.

Walsh, J. & Ungson, G. (1991). Managerial and organizational cognition: Notes from a trip down memory lane. *Organizational Science, 16*(1), 57–91.

Weber, R. (1990). *Basic content analysis.* Newbury Park, CA: Sage Publications, Inc.

West, R. E. & Borup, J. (2014). An analysis of a decade of research in 10 instructional design and technology journals. *British Journal of Educational Technology, 45*(4), 545–556.

White, H. D. (2004). Citation analysis and discourse analysis revisited. *Applied Linguistics, 25*(1), 89–116.

Winsor, D. (1993). Constructing scientific knowledge in Gould and Lewontin's "The spandrels of San Marco". In J. Selzer (Ed.), *Understanding scientific prose* (pp. 203–231). Madison, WI: University of Wisconsin Press.

Zhang, G., Ding, Y., & Milojević, S. (2013). Citation content analysis (CCA): A framework for syntactic and semantic analysis of citation content. *Journal of the American Society for Information Science and Technology, 64*(7), 1490–1503.

12 Learning Environments Visual Mapping

Sonia Tiwari and Yu-Chen Chiu

Introduction

Learning Sciences research often studies learning in a specific learning environment, such as formal learning environments like classrooms (Fraser, 2015), outdoor informal environments such as parks or nature centers (Zimmerman & Land, 2014), indoor informal environments such as museums (Falk & Dierking, 2018), personal learning environments such as social media (Dabbagh & Kitsantas, 2012) etc. The authors argue that while it is useful to focus on a single learning environment to study the nuances in depth, there is also scope for other forms of research to help generate a wholesome view of learning experiences, as the sum of its parts. Learning environments are a complex ecosystem that encompasses the physical, social, and cultural aspects of a learner's life. This chapter suggests a new methodology to collect participatory data from all stakeholders across settings in everyday life, to holistically examine how the learning environments interconnect to generate diverse learning opportunities.

Scholars studying school climate have been interested in finding the relationships between school climate and students' academic performance (Berkowitz, Moore, Astor, & Benbenishty, 2017). However, more research is needed to determine which levels and dimensions of school climate are influencing students' learning in school. Authors suggest that the use of Learning Environment Visual Mapping (LEVM) may help identify additional factors at play within school climate, or home/neighborhood environment—that may not be apparent through conventional data collection methods such as questionnaires, surveys, or interviews alone. The LEVM method offers children to represent their learning environments through sketches and short notes, but also offers parents/guardians and teachers to represent their view of the learning environments. The analysis then combines these representations to generate a more zoomed-out view of a student's learning environments—where their interconnectedness is made visible.

Theoretical Background

A Holistic View on Learning Environments

In the Learning Sciences, scholars have been interested in understanding what is happening in the learning environment and how the design of the learning environment is affecting students' learning performance. "Learning environment" has been commonly used in across different fields in social sciences. However, what elements are included or studied in a learning environment vary in different fields. Sawyer (2014), in *The Cambridge Handbook of the Learning Sciences*, identifies the following elements that constitute a learning environment: 1) people in the environment (i.e., teachers, learners, and others), 2) computers in the environment, 3) architecture and layout of the room and the physical objects in it, and 4) social and cultural environment. Other scholars have conceptualized learning environment with the idea of "spatiality" which focuses on how the social and the physical in a space interact with each other to influence students' learning (McGregor, 2004; Monahan, 2002; Soja, 1989). Building upon the sociocultural view of learning (Vygotsky & Cole, 1978), we define learning environment with a holistic lens that takes social, cultural, and material aspects into consideration.

We also see learning environment as expanded, flexible, and merging in terms of time and place where learning happens in settings in addition to classroom and school but also home, community, and other informal learning environments. With the rising interest in bridging formal and informal learning environments, many researchers have looked into how students acquire and bring knowledge, skills, and identities in and across spaces. Moje and colleagues (2004), adopting the theoretical lens of Third Spaces (Gutiérrez, Baquedano-López, & Tejeda, 1999), examined the ways in which students develop their disciplinary literacies at school, community, home, and peer group, and how students' discourses that take place in those spaces interact and relate with one another. Schultz and Hull (2008) investigated students' literacy practices in and out of school in the United States. Building upon existing literature on learning across settings, we seek to innovate methodologies and tools that can help study how students learn across varied environments from different perspectives.

Visual Mapping as a Research Methodology to Study Children's Learning Environments

Bransford et al. (2006) state that we are in a "decade for synergy" in terms of education research and the sciences of learning. They discuss how key fields such as informal learning, formal learning, implicit learning, and the brain have been mutually influencing each other and how the relationships are important in shaping research in distinctive fields. To better study learning that occurs across settings, some researchers have focused on advancing methodologies that can depict a fuller picture of how individuals learn in diverse learning environments from varied perspectives. For instance, other than traditional on-site observation, some researchers have used technological tools such as cameras, GoPros, GPS, or other recording devices to capture learners' talk and interaction in one or multiple learning settings (Barron, 2007; Falloon, 2018) To investigate how children learn at home, Vygotsky and Cole (1978) developed the Home Learning Environment Survey (HLE) that contains three sections: 1) demographics section about parents' education, ethnicity, preferred language at home, relationship with children, 2) parent's awareness of children's math development, and 3) parents describe types of activities their child engaged in the previous week—alone, with other children, and with adults. Stimulated recall interviews (SRIs)—a technique of reviewing video data with participants as a tool for allowing participants to view themselves and describe their experiences from a first-hand perspective—is also used in studies to examine people's experiences in different learning spaces (Bryan, Bay, Shelden, & Simon, 1990; Lyle, 2003; Takeuchi & Bryan, 2019).

"Visuals" are commonly used as a tool and data source in research where mapping, photography, filming, drawing, and maps, etc. are widely applied in ethnographic or education research studies to understand the various aspects of people's lives (Amsden & VanWynsberghe, 2005; Powell, 2010; Powell & Serriere, 2013). Luna Hernández (2009), for instance, conducted an ethnography using participant-generated photos to study the lived experience of people in poverty. Powell (2010), on the other hand, discusses the use of "mapping" in modern ethnographic research to understand the relationships between place, people's lived experience and community. In participatory research or visual ethnography, visual/arts-based methods such as participant-created photography or drawings are often adopted to engage children and youth in research to understand issues of interests from their perspectives (Groundwater-Smith, Dockett, & Bottrell, 2015). In research engaging children as co-designers of their learning environment, children's "visual voices" are also valued in designing learning environments through "the view of children" (Burke, 2007). Hutchison (2011), through her study using children-generated videos to examine children's homework practices in different countries, argues that visual ethnographic methods leveraging participant-created visual representations could be a form of participatory research that allows researchers to understand children's experience from their points of view. Visual representations provide different forms of data source other than paper-based assessment or observation which have the potential to include children and youth of diverse backgrounds, and along with discussion or follow-up interview, to interpret the meanings of the artifacts that they create. In other research investigating youth's mobilities and learning, "mapping" is not only an approach for teaching children and youth spatial literacy and community issues, but also a qualitative research tool (Amsden & VanWynsberghe, 2005; Gordon, Elwood, & Mitchell, 2016; Leander, Phillips, & Taylor, 2010). For instance, relevant research studies have engaged youth in using mobile technologies (e.g., Digital maps, Google Maps, GPS, etc.) and other media to map out community collective experiences, histories, and social issues located within the environment they live in (Rubel, Hall-Wieckert, & Lim, 2017; Santo, Ferguson, & Trippel, 2010). Through mapping activities, researchers and youth are able to identify key community issues and reflect on personally relevant experiences situated across spaces and can engage in conversations and actions that build deeper community understandings and opportunities for social change (Santo et al., 2010). By using maps produced by children outlining the environments that they live in, researchers are able to examine the relationships between physical environments, spatial elements, social values, and personal experience. Maps, in this case, can serve as a powerful representation tool to obtain a more multidimensional picture of children's learning environments.

Thus, with our interest in understanding where, what, and how children learn in their everyday spaces, we adapt visual representations and mapping practices used in prior scholarship in ethnographic and qualitative research to develop a holistic approach combining visual mapping with learning environment surveys to better look into what the learning environment looks like for each individual child from multiple dimensions.

Methodology and Data Instruments

We propose using visual mapping as the primary instrument and questionnaires as supplement data to depict children's everyday learning environments. Here are the three instruments that we use to collect information on children's overall learning environments: 1) Child's visual map of their learning environments, 2) Learning environment survey for teachers, and 3) Learning environment survey for parents/legal guardians.

Data Collection

Visual Map

Students (Grade 4+) are provided with a Visual Map in class, and asked to draw stick figures or any other images representing their learning activities in three settings: Home, School, Other Places. The purpose of having students draw the Visual Maps is to understand students' learning environments from their perspectives and experiences. Students are also asked to write keywords or simple annotations next to their drawings to explain the gist of their ideas. Teachers or researchers will be on site to give instructions on the task and help clarify questions if needed. To facilitate the visual mapping activities, teachers or researchers are provided with some prompts to guide students on recalling their learning experiences within those spaces. Possible prompts include:

- Where do you learn in school/home/other places?
- What do you usually learn/do in those spaces?
- Who are also present in those spaces?
- What kinds of technology or materials do you use when learning in those spaces?

Figure 12.1 is an example template for the Visual Map. After the students finish their drawings, each student is asked to briefly explain the drawing. Their responses are recorded and are used along with their drawings for data analysis.

Learning Environment Questionnaire For Teachers

In addition to the Visual Maps collected from children, questionnaires will also be collected from teachers to understand classroom environment, technology, and other learning resources in class, learning activities that take place in classrooms or other spaces in school. The responses will be used to supplement the analysis of the Visual Map created by students. Figure 12.2 is an example survey for teachers.

Task: Draw the most important people, technology/tools, learning activities, and spaces (your room/class etc.) within **Home, School,** and **Other Places you visit frequently.** Try to draw **ACTIONS** (people doing something, not standing still). Also add a few words to describe your drawings.

Your Home	Your School

Other Places you love to visit (for example: museum/grandparents'/summer camp/ scout club etc.)

Figure 12.1 Visual Map template

Learning Environment Survey for Teachers

Part 1. General information on teacher's teaching

Q1: What subject do you teach in school? _____

Q2: How long have you been teaching?

- ☐ Less than a year
- ☐ 1–5 years
- ☐ 6–10 years
- ☐ 10+ years

Q3: How would you describe your school location?

- ☐ Urban
- ☐ Suburban
- ☐ Rural

Q4: What grade(s) do you teach? _____

Q5: How many students (average) do you teach in a class?

- ☐ 5–10
- ☐ 10-20
- ☐ 20–30
- ☐ More than 30

Part 2. Learnings spaces in classrooms

Q6: Please briefly illustrate or describe how you arrange the learning spaces in your classroom. (e.g., How do you arrange tables, chairs, or other resources in your classroom? Where do you sit/stand while teaching?)

Q7: Please briefly describe the typical structure of a lesson that you would have in your class. (i.e., What are some typical activities you would have when teaching a class?)

Q8: What learning tools/technologies are *often used* in your teaching and students' learning in the classroom? (choose all that apply)

- ☐ Textbooks
- ☐ Handouts
- ☐ PowerPoints
- ☐ Videos/photos
- ☐ Music
- ☐ Audio text
- ☐ iPads or computers for students to use
- ☐ Some learning platforms/websites online
- ☐ Blogs
- ☐ Other:_____

Figure 12.2 Example Learning Environment Questionnaire for Teachers

Q9: How would you describe your teaching style and the learning atmosphere in your class?

Part 3. Learning spaces in other spaces in school
Q10: Based on your observation, *what* do students do during class breaks?

Q11: Based on your observation, *where* do students usually hang out during class breaks? (can be spaces in or outside the classroom)

Q12: Based on your understanding, what are other learning spaces in school that students usually go to?

Figure 12.2 (Cont.)

Learning Environment Questionnaire For Parents

In addition to children's perspectives on their learning environments, we also use the help of parents to capture how and what students learn at home or other environments outside of school. To collect individual data about student demographics, architecture of home/child's room, technologies and other learning resources at home, social and cultural environment at home, neighborhood and their culture at large. Figure 12.3 is an example questionnaire for parents.

Data Analysis

Analysis Map

We generate a wholesome view of the learning environment across settings for each student, by adding keywords to an Analysis Map for Learning Environments (see Table 12.1), categorizing observations in four categories that define a learning environment—people, technology, architecture, culture.

Learning Environment Questionnaire for Parents

Part 1. Demographic information

Q1: What is your relationship with the child

- ☐ Mother
- ☐ Father
- ☐ Grandfather
- ☐ Grandmother
- ☐ Other legal guardian:_____

Q2: How would you describe the location of your home?

- ☐ Urban
- ☐ Suburban
- ☐ Rural

Q3: What is your occupation? _____

Q4: What is the highest degree or level of school you have completed?

- ☐ Elementary school
- ☐ High school
- ☐ Vocational/technical training
- ☐ Bachelor's degree
- ☐ Master's degree
- ☐ Professional degree
- ☐ Doctorate degree

Q5: What is your age?

- ☐ 20–25
- ☐ 26–30
- ☐ 31–35
- ☐ 36–40
- ☐ 41–45
- ☐ 46–50
- ☐ 50–55
- ☐ 55–60

Q6: What are the family members that live in the household?

Q7: How many children do you have? What are their respective ages?

Q8: What is the preferred language at home?

Q9: Please select the racial/ethnic identity that you think best describe you and the child: You:

- ☐ Non-Hispanic Black
- ☐ Non-Hispanic White
- ☐ Hispanic or Latinx
- ☐ Asian, Hawaiian or Pacific
- ☐ Islander
- ☐ American Indian or Native
- ☐ American
- ☐ Biracial or multiracial
- ☐ Other:_____

Figure 12.3 Learning Environment Questionnaire for Parents

Child:
- ☐ Non-Hispanic Black
- ☐ Non-Hispanic White
- ☐ Hispanic or Latinx
- ☐ Asian, Hawaiian or Pacific
- ☐ Islander
- ☐ American Indian or Native
- ☐ American
- ☐ Biracial or multiracial
- ☐ Other:_____

Part 2. Children's learning at home
Q10: Where does your child usually do homework/study at home?
- ☐ Living room
- ☐ Child's own bedroom
- ☐ Dining room
- ☐ Other:_____
Q11: Do you or your partner do schoolwork with your child?
- ☐ Yes, seldom
- ☐ Yes, sometimes (1–2 days a week)
- ☐ Yes, often (more than 3 days a week)
- ☐ No
Q12: Which family member(s) interact with or participate in the child's learning the most?

Q13: What are other learning spaces for your child at home, and what resources/ technologies do these spaces have?

Q14: What are some other learning activities your child does or you do with your child at home? (Can be school or non-school related. Choose all that apply.)
- ☐ Schoolwork
- ☐ Watch educational videos
- ☐ Play educational games
- ☐ Story time
- ☐ Play toys
- ☐ Other:_____

Q15: What do your family do in your leisure time?

Q16: How would you describe your parenting style?

Q17: How would you describe your child's personality?

Q18: Please describe the types of activities your child did in the previous week. (i.e., what did they do? Did they do it alone or with other children/adults?)

Figure 12.3 (Cont.)

Part 4. Children's learning in other places

Q19: Does your child participate in any after-school activities?

☐ Yes

☐ No

Q20: If you respond yes to Q19, What types of after-school activities does your child participate in? (Choose all that apply.)

☐ Sports:_____

☐ Arts:_____

☐ Language:_____

☐ Science:_____

☐ Community service:_____

☐ Other:_____

Q21: If you respond yes to Q19, how often does your child engage in after-school activities?

☐ Once a week

☐ Twice a week

☐ Three times a week

☐ More than three times a week

Figure 12.3 (Cont.)

The learning environment includes:

- People in the environment (teachers, learners, and others).
- Technology in the environment.
- Architecture and layout of the room and the physical objects in it.
- Social and cultural environment.

We also observe the *type of learning activities* that occur in each setting, to better understand how the environment can support them:

- Visual (spatial): using pictures, images, and spatial understanding.
- Aural (auditory-musical): using sound and music.

Table 12.1 Analysis Map for Learning Environments

Setting	People	Technology	Architecture	Culture	Learning
Home					
School					
Other					

- Verbal (linguistic): using words, both in speech and writing.
- Physical (kinesthetic): using your body, hands, and sense of touch.
- Logical (mathematical): using logic, reasoning, and systems.
- Social (interpersonal): prefer to learn in groups or with other people.
- Solitary (intrapersonal): prefer to work alone and use self-study.

The types of learning activities are ranked as (1) primary, (2) secondary, (3) tertiary.

Sample Data

Sample data of drawing exercise by a 4th grade student (Figure 12.4) suggests that at home, this student has access to resources such as Chromebook, the Discovery Channel on TV, Khan Academy Kids on an iPad or phone type mobile device, books and people such as mother/grandmother and a pet dog. Drawings of the school suggest a seating arrangement where students face each other, there's a projector and bookshelf. The student also points out play at the playground dome. Other places this student learns is at a natural history museum, craft fair with wood-working demonstration, cub scout, nature etc.

After comparing data from the drawing exercise, teacher and parent questionnaires, the Analysis Map for this student looks like the completed Table 12.2. The researchers were able to identify key insights from multiple data sources, and organized the information in an easy-to-read format. For this particular student, we see that although the home environment is very liberal, the school environment by contrast is more strict and has fewer technology resources than home.

Implications and Future Research

The authors hope that by using the Learning Environment Visual Mapping method, it would be possible to get a summarized at-glance view of the interconnected nature of a student's learning environment. The process of data collection is designed in a non-linear way, meaning the three data sources (1) Visual Map (drawing exercise for students) (2) Questionnaire for teachers, and (3) Questionnaire for parents—can all be collected simultaneously or in any order. Each of the three data sources not only bring in diverse perspectives, they also offer additional clarification to each other's learning experiences. For instance, a child's drawing revealing visits to an art festival, combined with the parents' interests in traveling and attending art and craft festivals—may give us an insight into how interests from the home environment carry over to activities in the school and neighborhood. It may also be possible to study how the limitations in one environment can be made up for in other environments. For instance, a child who has fewer technological resources at school may have access to more resources at home.

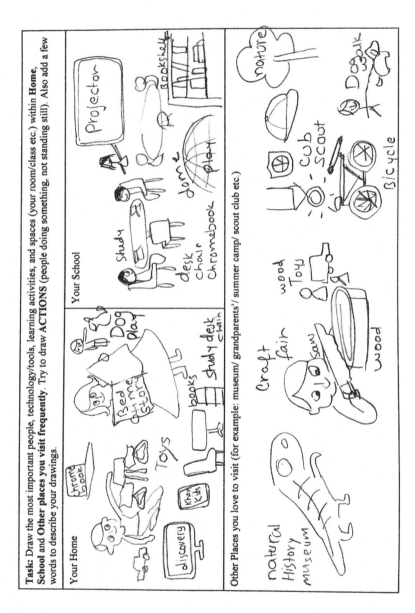

Figure 12.4 Sample data of drawing exercise for 4th grade students

Table 12.2 Analysis Map for Learning Environments for Student A

Setting	People	Technology	Architecture	Culture	Learning
Home	Mother and father (higher ed), dog	Chromebook, iPad, TV, LeapFrog learning tablet	Own room, small study desk, bookcase, reading nook, toy shelf	Laid back, informal, few rules, self-regulated, gets help from dad for homework, reads story with mom	(1) social, verbal (2) solitary (3) physical
School	Friends, teacher, para, principal	Chromebook, projector	Round tables and chairs facing each other, projector, bookcase, library, science lab, playground, assembly hall, corridors	Somewhat strict, restricted, short recess, emphasis on STEM, poor emphasis on sports	(1) Logical, Social (2) Verbal, Visual (3) Physical
Other	Neighbors, grandparents, cousins	TV	Community center, grandparents' house	Diverse neighborhood, tolerant and supportive	(1) social (2) physical (3) visual

There are a few challenges that may be experienced with the LEVM method, such as reliance on a researcher's prompts for the Visual Map exercise with children. Children may not fully comprehend what to draw, or may have limited drawing skills. The authors recommend to offer alternative keyword descriptions for children who may not be comfortable drawing. The other challenge is organization of the data, as there are three sources of data for every student. As the number of participants increase, it may become challenging to maintain an organized documentation. The Analysis Map may not accurately capture the truth of the learning environments, as the researchers are relying on keywords. Authors recommend maintaining additional descriptive notes to support their keyword assignment. For example, a researcher may rank "social learning" as primary type of learning in "other" section, however, it may differ from one environment to another (grandparents' place, public library, community center, etc. are all examples that are currently represented by the same "other" category.) It may then be helpful to use a specific learning environment for comparison, such as to create a separate row for community center, or public library etc. which are relevant to the participants.

In the future, these insights may be used to generate data visualizations for educators and researchers to take into account the diversity of learning environments, and match their teaching with naturally occurring learning opportunities for the students. Teachers may have access to an LEVM Analysis Map for each student, and the ability to generate a cumulative map for the entire class. The teacher may then choose to make use of the people/technologies/architecture/culture of these environments to support learning across settings. For example, for a class where the majority of students have elderly members in the family—may utilize intergenerational learning opportunities, or classes where all students have access to mobile devices at home, may be assigned interactive homework using mobile technologies. Similar insights may be used at a district, state, or national level—where the average of several profiles could be used to update policy level decisions. For example, districts where "logical" learning is constantly falling in the tertiary level of the Analysis Map across all settings, may be intervened with better resources or alternative ways of teaching and learning, in order to support student learning.

The authors hope that the LEVM method will be tested and challenged by many researchers and evolve over time into a more insightful tool to support research in Learning, Design, and Technology.

References

Amsden, J. & VanWynsberghe, R. (2005). Community mapping as a research tool with youth. *Action Research, 3*(4), 357–381. doi:10.1177/1476750305058487

Barron, B. (2007). Video as a tool to advance understanding of learning and development in peer, family and other informal learning contexts. In R. Goldman, R. Pea, & B. Barron (Eds.), *Video research in the learning sciences* (pp. 159–185). New York, NY: Routledge.

Berkowitz, R., Moore, H., Astor, R. A., & Benbenishty, R. (2017). A research synthesis of the associations between socioeconomic background, inequality, school climate, and academic achievement. *Review of Educational Research, 87*(2), 425–469. doi:10.3102/0034654316669821

Bransford, J., Vye, N., Stevens, R., Kuhl, P., Schwartz, D., Bell, P., ... Sabelli, N. (2006). Learning theories and education: Toward a decade of synergy. In P. Alexander & P. Winne (The LIFECenter) (Eds.), *Handbook of educational psychology* (pp. 209–244). Mahwah, NJ: Lawrence Erlbaum.

Bryan, T., Bay, M., Shelden, C., & Simon, J. (1990). Teachers' and at-risk students' stimulated recall of instruction. *Exceptionality: A Special Education Journal, 1*(3), 167–179.

Burke, C. (2007). The view of the child: Releasing "visual voices" in the design of learning environments. *Discourse: Studies in the Cultural Politics of Education, 28*(3), 359–372. doi:10.1080/01596300701458947.

Dabbagh, N. & Kitsantas, A. (2012). Personal learning environments, social media, and self-regulated learning: A natural formula for connecting formal and informal learning. *The Internet and Higher Education*, *15*(1), 3–8.

Falk, J. H. & Dierking, L. D. (2018). *Learning from museums*. Lanham, MD: Rowman & Littlefield.

Falloon, G. (2018). Researching students across spaces and places: Capturing digital data "on the go". *International Journal of Research & Method in Education*, *41*(1), 53–68.

Fraser, B. (2015). Classroom learning environments. In R. Gunstone (Eds.), *Encyclopedia of science education* (pp. 154–157). New York: NY: Springer, Dordrecht.

Gordon, E., Elwood, S., & Mitchell, K. (2016). Critical spatial learning: Participatory mapping, spatial histories, and youth civic engagement. *Children's Geographies*, *14*(5), 558–572.

Groundwater-Smith, S., Dockett, S., & Bottrell, D. (2015). Innovative Methods. In *Participatory research with children and young people* (1st ed. ed. pp. 101–138). London: SAGE Publications Ltd.doi: 10.4135/9781473910751.

Gutiérrez, K. D., Baquedano-López, P., & Tejeda, C. (1999). Rethinking diversity: Hybridity and hybrid language practices in the third space. *Mind, Culture, and Activity*, *6*(4), 286–303.

Hutchison, K. (2011). Homework through the eyes of children: What does visual ethnography invite us to see? *European Educational Research Journal*, *10*(4), 545–558. doi:10.2304/eerj.2011.10.4.545.

Leander, K. M., Phillips, N. C., & Taylor, K. H. (2010). The changing social spaces of learning: Mapping new mobilities. *Review of Research in Education*, *34*(1), 329–394.

Luna Hernández, J. (2009). Photo-ethnography by people living in poverty near the Northern border of Mexico. *Forum Qualitative Sozialforschung/Forum: Qualitative Social Research*, *10*, 2. doi:10.17169/fqs-10.2.1310.

Lyle, J. (2003). Stimulated recall: A report on its use in naturalistic research. *British Educational Research Journal*, *29*(6), 861–878.

McGregor, J. (2004). Space, power and the classroom. *Forum*, *46*(1), 13–18.

Moje, E. B., Ciechanowski, K. M., Kramer, K., Ellis, L., Carrillo, R., & Collazo, T. (2004). Working toward third space in content area literacy: An examination of everyday funds of knowledge and discourse. *Reading Research Quarterly*, *39*(1), 38–70.

Monahan, T. (2002). Flexible space and built pedagogy: Emerging IT embodiments. *Inventio*, *4*(1), 1–19.

Powell, K. (2010). Making sense of place: Mapping as a multisensory research method. *Qualitative Inquiry*, *16*(7), 539–555. doi:10.1177/1077800410372600.

Powell, K. & Serriere, S. (2013). Image-based participatory pedagogies: Reimagining social justice. *International Journal of Education & the Arts*, *14*(15). Retrieved from www.ijea.org/v14n15/.

Rubel, L. H., Hall-Wieckert, M., & Lim, V. Y. (2017). Making space for place: Mapping tools and practices to teach for spatial justice. *Journal of the Learning Sciences*, *26*(4), 643–687. doi:10.1080/10508406.2017.1336440.

Santo, C. A., Ferguson, N., & Trippel, A. (2010). Engaging urban youth through technology: The youth neighborhood mapping initiative. *Journal of Planning Education and Research*, *30*(1), 52–65.

Sawyer, R. (2014). Introduction. In R. Sawyer (Ed.), *The Cambridge handbook of the learning sciences* (pp. 1–18). Cambridge: Cambridge University Press. doi:10.1017/CBO9781139519526.002.

Schultz, K. & Hull, G. (2008). Literacies in and out of school in the United States. In B. V. Street & N. Hornberger (Eds.), *Encyclopedia of literacy and education* (Vol. 2, pp. 239–250). New York: Springer.

Soja, E. W. (1989). *Postmodern geographies: The reassertion of space in critical social theory.* London: Verso.

Takeuchi, M. A. & Bryan, V. (2019). Video-mediated interviews to reveal multiple voices in peer collaboration for mathematics learning in groups. *International Journal of Research & Method in Education, 42*(2), 124–136.

The design of learning environments. (1999). In J. D. Bransford, Ann L. Cocking, & R. Rodney (Ed.), *How people learn: Brain, mind, experience, and school.* National Academies Press. ProQuest Ebook Central Retrieved from http://ebookcentral. proquest.com/lib/pensu/detail.action?docID=3375627.

Vygotsky, L. S. & Cole, M. (1978). *Mind in society: The development of higher psychological processes.* Cambridge, MA: Harvard University Press.

Zimmerman, H. T. & Land, S. M. (2014). Facilitating place-based learning in outdoor informal environments with mobile computers. *TechTrends, 58*(1), 77–83.

13 Learning Analytics

The Emerging Research Method for Enhancing Teaching and Learning

Tiantian Jin

Introduction

Since learning analytics (LA) was recognized as an independent discipline, it has exhibited extraordinary impact and drawn attention within the field of learning and teaching. However, as an emerging research community, it is still an immature area that people are not familiar with yet, including its definitions, taxonomies, techniques, analytic models, and applications. Additionally, LA's connection with and differentiation from educational data mining (EDM) is a common question. In this chapter, the author will provide an overview of LA and EDR and compare two disciplines in various contexts through a review of relevant literature. Moreover, recommendations for applying LA models in practice and the challenges learning design and technology (LDT) stakeholders face when utilizing LA in education will be discussed.

What Is Learning Analytics?

As digital education has flourished over the past decades, along with emerging "big data" of learning, institutions have new opportunities to measure, predict, and improve learning. Accompanying these new opportunities were "how to" questions. As a response, researchers and developers from the educational field developed learning analytics (LA). Initially, LA was coined as "the measurement, collection, analysis, and reporting of data about learners and their contexts, for purposes of understanding and optimizing learning and environments in which it occurs" in the First International Conference on Learning Analytics and Knowledge (LAK) in 2011. Slightly later, the Society for Learning Analytics (SoLAR) was founded. The first graduate program focused on LA was built by Ryan Baker in 2015 at Teachers College, Columbia University.

Learning Analytics Methods and Techniques

Unlike traditional educational research, the data used in LA research are mostly generated in digital learning environments (e.g., distance education, learning management systems, digital courseware, MOOCs, and LOOCs, etc.) rather than in physical environments (e.g., face-to-face classroom environments). Learning analytics seeks to use the intensive educational data to advance learning, teaching, and learning environments by improving educational assessment, ways for understanding education, and selection and planning of interventions. As an emerging field of study, LA is considered an interdisciplinary area that embraces methods and approaches related to machine learning, business intelligence, artificial intelligence, statistics, data mining, data visualization, psychology, social network analysis, semantics, and e-learning (Bienkowski, Feng, & Means, 2012; Dawson & Siemens, 2014; Siemens, 2013). Baker and Inventado (2014) identified four major categories of LA methods, including prediction methods, relationship mining, structure discovery, and discovery with models.

Prediction Methods

Prediction methods are used to develop a parsimonious model with a limited data set to infer students' learning performance and behaviors. By building an accurate prediction model, researchers can discover what specific factors should receive attention, as they might affect some critical events. For example, a prediction model constructed from LA techniques can extrapolate the optimal learning progression for novice students taking a particular course (Corbett & Anderson, 1995). Prediction models can also be used to determine future outcomes (Dekker, Pechenizkiy, & Vleeshouwers, 2009; San Pedro, Baker, Bowers, & Heffernan, 2013). In a climate where graduation rates are front and center, a prominent goal of educational institutions is to identify at-risk students and intervene before they fail a class or drop out of college (Dekker et al., 2009). Baker and Inventado (2014) categorized prediction methods into three types: classification, regression, and latent knowledge estimation. In classification, the predicted variables are either binary or categorical variables. Decision trees, random forests, decision rules, step regression, and logistic regression are popular classifiers that are typically cross-validated in the LA community. Regarding regressors, linear regression and regression trees are the two most popular methods. The predicted variables are continuous variables. The latent knowledge estimation is a special case of classification. In latent knowledge estimation, students' knowledge is not directly measured but inferred from their patterns of correctness of related skills. Two classic algorithms that are often used are Bayesian networks (Martin & VanLehn, 1995; Shute, 1995) and Bayesian Knowledge Tracing (Corbett & Anderson, 1995).

Relationship Mining

When conducting relationship mining, researchers aim to identify relationships in learner behavior patterns and diagnose student difficulties. To achieve that goal, researchers discover in a large data set which variables are most strongly associated with another variable, or which relationships between two groups of variables are the strongest. Four types of relationship mining are normally used in LA, which include association rule mining, sequential pattern mining, correlation mining, and causal data mining (Baker & Inventado, 2014). The purpose of association rule mining is to find "if-then" relationships. If one event happens, then another event will be found. The objective of sequential pattern mining is to identify temporal relationships between events. In correlation mining, researchers want to discover whether variables are positively or negatively linearly correlated. The goal of causal data mining is to determine whether one event causes another event. Based on different areas of interest, researchers choose the most appropriate type of relationship mining technique to use.

Structure Discovery

Structure discovery differs from prediction models in that the predicted outcome has been labeled before starting a model development. Instead, in structure discovery, researchers conduct exploratory research without knowing the structure of the data. Three structure discovery algorithms are commonly used: clustering, factor analysis, and domain structure discovery. Clustering is mostly conducted when researchers attempt to categorize data. In an optimal set of clusters, the similarity between each data point and other points in that cluster should be stronger than the similarity between that data point and other points in other clusters. Unlike clustering that groups and splits data points, factor analysis is used to group and split variables to discover an optimal set of latent factors that consists of the least number of variables, but still maintains a good fit. As the name implies, domain structure discovery is considered when researchers aim to disclose which items relate to specific skills. As an exploratory approach, researchers conducting structure discovery generally place less weight on validation than on prediction.

Discovery with Models

In discovery with models, researchers attempt to discover the relationship between models instead of between data, variables, or items. In this case, a prediction model developed in an analysis can become a component in another model or analysis. Moreover, a discovery with models can be used to leverage the generalization of a prediction model across contexts. For example, prediction models of gaming the system, off-task behavior, and carelessness across a full year of educational software data were used to study the differences in these behaviors between urban, rural, and suburban schools in the same region (Baker & Gowda, 2010).

Learning Analytics Process

As defined, LA is an iterative process where various stakeholders, such as students, instructors, administrators, data scientists, statisticians, researchers, programmers, instructional designers, and user experience and interface designers, may be involved at different stages. Campbell and Oblinger (2007) defined academic analytics as an engine that makes decisions or guides actions in five steps: capture, report, predict, act, and refine. Similarly, Siemens (2013) suggested an LA cycle composed of seven components that include collection, storage, data cleaning, integration, analysis, representation and visualization, and action. In both models, the process starts with data collection.

However, one important component that should precede data collection, but is often overlooked, is data source identification. Depending on different research purposes, the data sources that are required can vary. The complete LA cycle is illustrated in Figure 13.1. To date, the three most common sources of data that populate an LA cycle include: (1) student information systems (SISs), (2) learning management systems (LMSs), and (3) open online courses. Data collected by sensors can increase the quality and depth of analysis, but manually entered data are not uncommon. Once data are collected, they will be stored in an appropriate place and then cleaned. Data cleaning can be a time-consuming process and requires human judgment. However, if there is a well-designed plan before data collection (for example, researchers have a clear plan about how to tag and pull data), efforts and time on data cleaning can be significantly reduced, which in turn will condense the length of an iteration. As data may be collected at different times and from multiple organizations, researchers sometimes must integrate multiple data sets into one before conducting an analysis. Once all preparation work is completed, data scientists will analyze the data with appropriate techniques. In an LA cycle, determining how best to present or visualize results from the analysis is also an essential consideration. An effective visualization can facilitate stakeholders' understanding and reception of results, and ultimately assist in their decision-making and reaction to the findings. The last step in one iteration is to take action to enhance student success and institutional achievement. These actions may take various formats, such as sending alerts and warnings to schools regarding students' drop-out possibilities, providing students with tips for what has helped other students with similar backgrounds achieve success, or improving the learning system. Once the action is executed, corresponding feedback will be generated, which will lead to new data. A new iteration will then begin. In the new cycle, the process can be refined based on the success of the previous cycle.

The components of an LA cycle are designed to be used in a flexible manner. For instance, if a project only acquires one data set, then there is no need for integration in its model. Moreover, an effective LA cycle should be a top-down approach that relies on support from the organizational level rather than merely from students and/or instructors (Siemens, 2013).

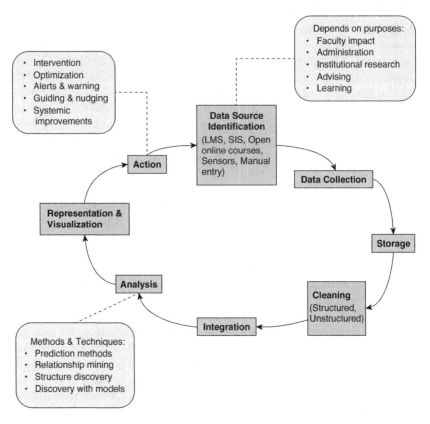

Figure 13.1 LA Cycle

Adapted from "Learning analytics: The emergence of a discipline," by G. Siemens, 2013, The American Behavioral Scientist, 57(10), p. 1392.

Applications and Benefits of LA

As an emerging discipline, LA leverages educational stakeholders' new perspectives when investigating learning and teaching, as well as new possibilities of learning experiences. Learning analytics has been applied to education in various areas and benefited learners, instructors, and institutions (Bienkowski et al., 2012; Pistilli, Willis, & Campbell, 2014).

Applications and Benefits for Learners

An initial benefit that LA provides to learners is the possibility to offer targeted courses and tips that align with their needs. To drive this offering are the data and analysis, which discover potential student groups with similar characteristics and reactions to a particular strategy that yields academic success (Romero, Ventura, Espejo, & Hervás, 2008). Those characteristics and reactions can be embedded into recommendations for students who need guidance. Moreover, in the learning experience, LA is used to measure and track learners' performance and actions, which helps identify knowledge gaps and mastery. Depending on these gaps and mastery, personalized recommendations on content and social connections can be identified and delivered to students, as well as adaptive content provisions.

In addition, LA empowers students to improve their learning behavior, which can lead to a better learning outcome. One major task in LA is to collect and analyze real-time information from technology tools, such as LMS, e-learning, and mobile learning, and convert the "findings" into an intuitive interaction to encourage student change. The ability to convert raw data into a student nudge or guide is advantageous in establishing a truly flexible and rich learning experience (Phillips et al., 2011). Furthermore, data of learners' reactions to the nudges, as well as the extent of success followed by their reaction, can be used to discover future learning and teaching strategies.

Beyond academic education, LA extends its benefits to learners' employment. With big data and analytics techniques, LA can identify post-education employment, unemployment, and undetermined situations. Such insight can assist individuals target available education and training that more closely aligns with current and future employment market needs (Jantawan & Tsai, 2013).

Applications and Benefits for Instructors

In the prior educational environment, instructors were not able to gauge the learning of their students for long periods of time, sometimes even until the end of a semester. With LA, now instructors can access this student information more immediately. Course monitoring systems are examples of tools that allow instructors to track students' progress and actions, and also determine the weaknesses of particular students. This insight enables instructors to devote more attention to students who require additional assistance (Greller & Drachsler, 2012). Furthermore, student data also serve as a diagnostic tool and informs instructors of any areas in the curriculum that may need to be improved or adjusted. Instructional feedback generated directly by students or by the system provides instructors a real-time aid in the teaching process to facilitate enhanced instructor–student interactions. Even though LA provides data-driven tools or suggestions to help instructors make quick changes that can be measured based on student learning outcomes (Pistilli et al., 2014), it does not mean that LA can necessarily yield ideal pedagogy (van Harmelen & Workman, 2012).

Learning analytics also benefits and expedites the process of pedagogical exploration and innovation. In traditional educational models, testing a pedagogical shift takes a long time. The testing results are usually limited by access to large sample sizes and the granulation level of data that can be collected and analyzed. Learning analytics allows instructors to tag parameters in granular data that can assess the effectiveness of a pedagogical shift within a large group of students in a short time frame. As a result, the cycle of a pedagogical innovation is greatly shortened; instructors are informed more rapidly with rich evidence.

Applications and Benefits for Institutions

Applications of LA can be viewed at different levels. For example, when focused on students and instructors, the application of LA is considered micro-analytics. When institutions use LA to concentrate on improving the operating efficiency of the institution or comparing performance with other peer institutions, the application of LA is macro-analytics (Buckingham Shum, 2012). Student retention is an important indicator of how well an institution focuses its engine to ensure its students become successful (Pistilli et al., 2014). Learning analytics provides a quick and compelling measure of actions (such as, how well a curriculum is adjusted, and how effective recruitment policies are developed) that can affect retention rate. All the assessing data can be utilized to support systemic change in institutions (Long & Siemens, 2011). Based on student retention, an institution can further demonstrate its institutional accountability (EDUCAUSE, 2010).

In addition to assessing retention, LA plays an essential role in prediction and intervention. Using big data and analysis based on the prior record of students, institutions frequently focus on determining whether a current student is at risk and will be retained. Once an at-risk student is detected, institutions can receive an early warning and investigate the cause—whether the problem is at a student, instructor, or institutional level. As a response, institutions can implement interventions aimed to retain the student, considering recommendations generated through analysis of previous successful cases that demonstrated similar characteristics.

Challenges of LA

Being widely recognized and applied in education, LA is also facing significant challenges and concerns that need to be addressed. Many researchers (e.g., Bienkowski, Feng, & Means, 2012; Nunn, Avella, Kanai, & Kebritchi, 2016; Siemens, 2013) have reviewed those challenges from various perspectives. In this article, we focus on three aspects: quality of data, privacy and ethical issues, and stakeholders' collaboration.

Learning analytics is a research tool that relies heavily on data and, therefore, the quality of data can determine the success of an LA project. Digital education and new technologies facilitate the collection of enormous amounts of data through different collection models. However, without sufficient prior research and preparation, data collected may not be able to accurately serve the research purposes. For instance, if researchers did not conduct an adequate literature review prior to collecting data, the parameter data that can best describe a key variable of their study was not programmed to be logged while students were interacting with the e-learning system. Even with massive data, it is impossible to progress the study. Another factor that impacts the data quality is the granularity of the data point. How granular the data point must be to best assess the desired phenomenon is always a concern of analytics researchers. Besides, data collected through diverse systems may cause uncertainty of data interoperability[1] as well (Bienkowski, Feng, & Means, 2012). Along with continued emerging technology (e.g., new learning devices), data interoperability problems may stay constant.

Another considerable challenge of LA is privacy and ethical issues. Personalized interaction and user modeling require learners' personal information—their needs, learning actions, and performance—to realize a customized learning experience. How to safely store this information and who owns the data become immediate concerns. Moreover, it has been acknowledged that all of these personal data can generate large economic and societal values beyond academic benefits (World Economic Forum, 2011). Therefore, more ethical and legal complexities get involved. In addition, Sclater (2014) demonstrated more concerns, including data interpretation, data preservation, data sharing with outside parties, and proper training of staff members regarding the handling of data. Considering all of these different issues, institutions must achieve a balance between legally and ethically safeguarding student privacy and using data to achieve educational goals (Nunn et al., 2016).

The previous two challenges pertain to data and its application, and the last concern discussed in this article focuses on people—the stakeholders involved in LA projects. A successful analytics project can barely be accomplished by one person. As mentioned before, an LA project requires accessing, cleaning, integrating, analyzing, and visualizing data before sensemaking and taking action. That means that if one individual wants to accomplish the process alone, she must possess the full range of skills (e.g., familiarity with study designing and planning, programming, statistical knowledge, data visualization tools, analytics models) and attributes (e.g., familiarity with the data and the domain represented in those data) required to make sense of numerous data sets, which is rare (Manyika et al., 2011). Moreover, access to server logs and databases is usually not completely granted to a single individual. Therefore, a learning analytics project is a cross-departmental collaborative task involving multiple stakeholders. Some researchers focus more on the challenge of gathering experts in various field. However, the author is more concerned with how well stakeholders can collaborate to achieve educational goals. After all, it is not necessarily that an institution can produce a satisfying outcome, even though it has the "capability".

Learning Analytics and Educational Data Mining

Educational data mining (EDM) is a discipline that is often discussed in tandem with LA, and they can be seen in two ways: either as research communities or as areas of research inquiry (Baker & Inventado, 2014). From the perspective of research communities, EDM and LA can be viewed as intertwined research communities. Some researchers even take the position that EDM encompasses LA, as EDM emerged earlier than LA in mid-2000. In 2011, the International Educational Data Mining Society (IEDMS) was founded, who defined EDM as "an emerging discipline, concerned with developing methods for exploring the unique types of data that come from educational settings, and using those methods to better understand students, and the settings which they learn in" (International Educational Data Mining Society, 2011). The same year, LA emerged as a distinct discipline. A timeline of key events for both EDM and LA communities is shown in Table 13.1.

People often confuse how LA and EDM differ from each other since the two communities share strong commonalities, such as research interests, goals, and techniques. However, from the perspective of an area of scientific inquiry, LA and EDM focus on different research questions and usually generate different deliverables, despite the considerable overlap between them. Calling out the differences between LA and EDM is not the goal of comparing these two fields. However, pointing out what separates the two communities can improve researchers' understanding of each and when it is appropriate to use each one. Their distinctions revolve more around the focus of the respective research questions and the frequency of using each technique (Siemens & Baker, 2012), and less about a philosophical or adversarial split (Baker & Inventado, 2014). According to multiple conference talks, research, and articles in both communities (Baker & Inventado, 2014; Behrens, 2012; Bienkowski, Feng, & Means, 2012; Siemens & Baker, 2012; Siemens, 2013), distinctions between LA and EDM are categorized as origins, concerns and research questions, disciplines, role of automated discovery, adaptation and personalization, holism and reduction, and techniques and methods.

Origins

Even though LA and EDM have similar, multidisciplinary roots, some are stronger towards one community than the other. Learning analytics has origins in semantic web, "intelligent curriculum," outcome prediction, and systemic interventions, while EDM is more connected to educational software and student modeling.

Concerns and Research Questions

Improving education is the shared mission for both communities, but each considers some specific concerns more strongly than the other. For

Table 13.1 Key Events for Both EDM and LA Community

Time	EDM related events	LA related events
1995	Corbett & Anderson paper on Bayesian Knowledge Tracing—key early algorithm that is still prominent today	
2000	First EDM-related workshop	
2001	Zaiane theoretical paper on potential of EDM methods 2005	
2005	First workshop using term "educational data mining"	
2006	First published book on EDM: *Data mining in e-learning*, Romero & Ventura	
2008	First international conference on Educational Data Mining	
2009	*Journal of EDM* publishes first issue—first issue has 189 citations as of this writing (15.75 citations per article per year) 2010	
2010	First handbook on EDM published, Romero, Ventura, Pechenizkiy, & Baker	
2011	International Educational Data Mining Society founded	First Learning Analytics and Knowledge conference held
2012		Society for Learning Analytics founded
2013		First learning analytics summer institute
2015		First learning analytics graduate program established by Ryan Baker at Teachers College Columbia University
2017		*Handbook of Learning Analytics* (first edition) launched

Note: Adapted from *Learning Analytics: From Research to Practice*, by J. A. Larusson and B. White (2014), p. 62. New York, NY: Springer New York.

example, LA is more concerned with sensemaking and action, whereas EDM is more focused on developing methods, such as automated methods. Another perspective states that LA pertains more to aspects of education beyond learning, while EDM is associated more with learning as a research topic.

Disciplines

Learning analytics is considered to envelope more disciplines than EDM. In addition to computer science, machine learning, artificial intelligence, statistics, psychology, and the learning sciences, LA is also related to information science and sociology.

Role of Automated Discovery

In general, LA research focuses more on leveraging human judgment in processes where automated discovery serves as a tool to accomplish the goal. On the contrary, in EDM research, automated discovery is the key and human judgment is a tool.

Adaptation and Personalization

In line with the greater focus on human judgment, LA studies are designed more to inform and empower instructors and learners. Educational data mining studies, on the other hand, are more used for automated adaptation that is conducted by computer systems without human judgment.

Holism and Reduction

In LA, researchers more typically attempt to understand systems as wholes. By contrast, EDM researchers usually want to reduce phenomena to their components and analyze each component and the relationships between them.

Techniques and Methods

Origins and research questions ultimately drive researchers' preferred or more frequently used methods. For prediction models, LA researchers tend to focus on classical approaches of classification and regression more often than on latent knowledge estimation. Moreover, LA research tends to predict larger constructs (i.e., dropping out and course failure), while EDM research predicts smaller constructs (i.e., boredom). Relationship mining and discovery with models are more commonly employed in EDM than in LA. In structure discovery, EDM researchers typically emphasize specialized or domain-specific structure discovery, whereas LA researchers may emphasize network analysis or social network analysis. In addition, text analysis, text mining, and discourse analysis are conducted more often in LA than EDM.

Conclusion

This chapter provided insight into what learning analytics is, how it can applied in the field of learning design and technology (LDT), and what benefits and

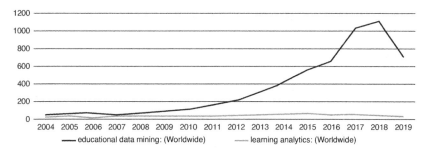

Figure 13.2 Search interest in EDM (orange line) and LA (blue line) during 2004–2019

Note: Data source is from Google Trends, where the earliest data can be traced is in 2004. Data for 2019 only include data from January to August.

challenges may be met during the application process. Even though EDM, as a conjoined community, emerged and developed earlier than LA, interest in LA has substantially exceeded EDM in recent years (Figure 13.2).

As such, applications of LA in education, including LDT, can be anticipated to continue to explode. However, one considering the use of LA should understand that it is not a one-size-fits-all endeavor. Instead, it is a goal-directed practice and not as useful for educational research pursuits that are exploratory in nature (van Barneveld, Arnold, & Campbell, 2012). Therefore, a successful LA practitioner will possess several essential attributes. In addition to the appropriate technical skills and knowledge, researchers will know the correct way to use the data and analytics techniques, carefully consider the various factors that lead to an interpretation of the data, and, finally, make the most reasonable decision.

Note

1 Data interoperability refers to a property of a system whose input/output data flow and formats are completely understood by other systems so that data from such systems can be integrated or exchanged seamlessly for analysis (Bienkowski, Feng, & Means, 2012).

References

Baker, R. & Gowda, S. (2010). An analysis of the differences in the frequency of students' disengagement in urban, rural, and suburban high schools. In *Proceedings of the 3rd International Conference on Educational Data Mining* (pp. 11–20).

Baker, R. S. & Inventado, P. S. (2014). Educational data mining and learning analytics. In J. A. Larusson & B. White (Eds.), *Learning analytics: From research to practice* (pp. 61–75). New York: Springer New York. doi:10.1007/978-1-4614-3305-7_4.

Bienkowski, M., Feng, M., & Means, B. (2012). *Enhancing teaching and learning through educational data mining and learning analytics: An issue brief.* U.S. Department of Education Office of Educational Technology. Retrieved from http://tech.ed. gov/wp-content/uploads/2014/03/edm-la-brief.pdf.

Buckingham Shum, S. (2012). *Learning analytics.* UNESCO policy brief. Retrieved from http://iite.unesco.org/pics/publications/en/files/3214711.pdf.

Campbell, J. P. & Oblinger, D. G. (2007). Academic analytics. Educause. Retrieved from http://net.educause.edu/ir/library/pdf/pub6101.pdf.

Corbett, A. & Anderson, J. (1995). Knowledge tracing: Modeling the acquisition of procedural knowledge. *User Modeling and User-Adapted Interaction, 4*(4), 253–278.

Dawson, S. & Siemens, G. (2014, September). Analytics to literacies: The development of a learning analytics framework for multiliteracies assessment. *International Review of Research in Open and Distance Learning, 15*(4), 284–305.

Dekker, G., Pechenizkiy, M., & Vleeshouwers, J. (2009). Predicting students drop out: A case study. In: *Proceedings of 2nd International Conference on Educational Data Mining* (pp. 41–50).

EDUCAUSE. (2010, April). 7 things you should know about analytics. *Creative Commons Attribution.* Retrieved from https://library.educause.edu/-/media/files/library/2010/4/eli7059-pdf.pdf.

First International Conference on Learning Analytics and Knowledge. (2011, July 22). First International Conference on Learning Analytics and Knowledge 2011. Retrieved February 28, 2019, from https://tekri.athabascau.ca/analytics/.

Greller, W. & Drachsler, H. (2012). Translating learning into numbers: A generic framework for learning analytics. *Journal of Educational Technology and Society, 15*(3), 42–57.

International Educational Data Mining Society. (2011). *International educational data mining society.* Retrieved February 28, 2019, from http://educationaldatamining. org/.

Jantawan, B. & Tsai, C. (2013). The application of data mining to build classification model for predicting graduate employment. *International Journal of Computer Science and Information Security, 11*(10), 1–7.

Larusson, J. A. & White, B. (Eds.). (2014). *Learning analytics: From research to practice.* New York: Springer New York. doi:10.1007/978-1-4614-3305-7.

Long, P. & Siemens, G. (2011, September/October). Penetrating the fog: Analytics in learning and education. *EDUCAUSE Review, 46*(5), 31–40.

Manyika, J., Chui, M., Brown, B., Bughin, J., Dobbs, R., Roxburgh, C., & Byers, A. H. (2011). *Big data: The next frontier for innovation, competition, and productivity.* McKinsey Global Institute. Retrieved from www.mckinsey.com/business-functions/mckinsey-digital/our-insights/big-data-the-next-frontier-for-innovation.

Martin, J. & VanLehn, K. (1995). Student assessment using Bayesian nets. *International Journal of Human Computer Studies, 42*(6), 575–592.

Nunn, S., Avella, J. T., Kanai, T., & Kebritchi, M. (2016). Learning analytics methods, benefits, and challenges in higher education: A systematic literature review. *Online Learning, 20*(2), 13–29. doi:10.24059/olj.v20i2.790.

Phillips, R., Maor, D., Cumming-Potvin, W., Roberts, P., Herrington, J., Preston, G., & Moore, E. (2011). Learning analytics and study behavior: A pilot study. In G. Williams, P. Statham, N. Brown & B. Cleland (Eds.), *Changing Demands, Changing Directions. Proceedings ascilite Hobart 2011.* (pp.997–1007).

Pistilli, M. D., Willis, J. E., & Campbell, J. P. (2014). Analytics through an institutional lens: Definition, theory, design, and impact. In *Learning analytics: From research to practice.* doi:10.1007/978-1-4614-3305-7_5.

Romero, C., Ventura, S., Espejo, P. G., & Hervás, C. (2008). Data mining algorithms to classify students. *Educational Data Mining 2008: The 1st International Conference on Educational Data Mining, Montréal, Québec, Canada, June 20- 21,2008 Proceedings, 8-17.* Retrieved from www.educationaldatamining.org/EDM2008/uploads/proc/full%20proceedings.pdf#page=8.

San Pedro, M., Baker, R., Bowers, A., & Heffernan, N. (2013). Predicting college enrollment from student interaction with an intelligent tutoring system in middle school. In: *Proceedings of the 6th International Conference on Educational Data Mining* (pp. 177–184).

Sclater, N. (2014, November). *Code of practice for learning analytics: A literature review of the ethical and legal issues.* Retrieved from http://repository.jisc.ac.uk/5661/1/Learning_Analytics_A-_Literature_Review.pdf.

Shute, V. J. (1995). SMART: Student modeling approach for responsive tutoring. *User Modeling and User-Adapted Interaction, 5*(1), 1–44.

Siemens, G. (2013). Learning analytics: The emergence of a discipline. *The American Behavioral Scientist, 57*(10), 1380–1400. doi:10.1177/0002764213498851.

Siemens, G. & Baker, R. S. J. D. (2012). Learning analytics and educational data mining: Towards communication and collaboration. *Proceedings of the 2nd International Conference on Learning Analytics and Knowledge.* ACM. doi:10.1145/2330601.2330661.

van Barneveld, A., Arnold, K. E., & Campbell, J. P. (2012). Analytics in higher education: Establishing a common language. *EDUCAUSE Learning Initiative, 1,* 1–11. Retrieved from http://net.educause.edu/ir/library/pdf/ELI3026.pdf.

van Harmelen, M. & Workman, D. (2012, November). Analytics for learning and teaching. *JISC CETIS, 1*(3), 1–40. Retrieved from http://publications.cetis.ac.uk/2012/516.

World Economic Forum. (2011). *Personal data: The emergence of a new asset class.* Retrieved from www3.weforum.org/docs/WEF_ITTC_PersonalDataNewAsset_Report_2011.pdf.

14 Futurama

Learning Design and Technology Research Methods

Enilda Romero-Hall, Ana Paula Correia, Robert Maribe (Rob) Branch, Yasemin Demiraslan Cevik, Camille Dickson-Deane, Bodong Chen, Juhong Christie Liu, Hengtao Tang, Lucas Vasconcelos, Nicola Pallitt, and Briju Thankachan

Introduction

This chapter serves as an examination and projection of developments in learning design and technology research methods in the next decade and beyond, as provided by scholars and practitioners in the field. For this chapter, members of the community were asked to focus on the probable nature of learning design research methods in the near future to outline their perspectives on where learning design research is going or ought to be going. Why do we engage in this prediction of the future? Perhaps we share these perspectives because it allows us to feel optimistic about what is to come, it gives the opportunity for reflection on what has happened and how it can improve, and it is an outlet for progressive ideas that have gone unexplored.

Historical comments, current strengths, and weaknesses, trends, or overlapping statements were not edited or removed. Also, as mentioned in this book (Romero-Hall, 2020), the term *learning design and technology* is used as an umbrella term that refers to instructional design, instructional design and technology, educational technology, and instructional technology.

Ana Paula Correia, Ph.D.
The Ohio State University

When asked to predict the future, I like to look back into the history of the field. An analysis of the last 15 years of studies published in the *Educational Technology Magazine* shows that research in educational technology has oscillated between two methodologies: qualitative and quantitative. The controversy regarding qualitative versus quantitative approaches is ongoing in our field and stems from the intellectual debate between objectivism and relativism (Smith & Heshusius, 1986). Looking into the future, I believe that this conflict will evolve into additional collaboration and thoughtful strategies to harmonize both approaches.

As Smith and Heshusius (1986, p.11) explain in the context of educational research in the mid-eighties:

> In the end the two sides may be close to speaking different languages-a neutral scientific or value-free language versus a value-laden language of everyday discourse. Since it is not clear at present what kind of *via media* could be worked out between the two languages, it is all the more important that we make every effort to keep the conversation open.

I would argue that the *via media* that Smith and Heshusius (1986) are referring to are the current societal problems that we face nowadays. At this very moment, we are facing a viral pandemic and reimagining ways to respond to one of the most devastating issues that humans have ever faced. The COVID-19 worldwide outbreak is bringing researchers together to address problems with a multitude of methodologies. The scientific language that one speaks no longer matters; what matters is to approach the problem from different methods and arrive at a solution that can be quickly and effectively deployed to individuals, groups, and communities and scale-up globally.

Efforts to bridge theory and practice in the instructional design field date to 2000 with Reeves' seminal article on "Socially Responsible Educational Technology Research" (Reeves, 2000). This was followed by Reeves, Herrington, and Oliver (2005) who designate design-based research as a socially responsible approach to instructional technology research in higher education. The most recent edition of the *Handbook of Research in Educational Communications and Technology* is organized "to focus on the learning *problems* we are trying to solve with educational technologies, rather than to focus on the *things* we are using to solve those problems." (Bishop, Boling, Elen, & Svihla, 2020, para 1). The transformative impetus to put societal problems at the core of the instructional design work is also captured on the civic-minded instructional designer framework (Yusop & Correia, 2012). This framework asserts a paradigm that any instructional design work has social implications in three interrelated contexts: micro, macro, and mega. The micro context refers to a person's immediate environments, such as his or her community, workplace, or school; the macro context refers to a person's extended environment, e.g., the district and country of residence, while the mega context refers to the global environment in which a person is immersed. Additionally, an instructional designer is viewed as a potential agent of social change who has the transformative power to bring about good to the society at large. The term "civic-minded instructional designer" is proposed, referring to a professional who: (a) has the public interest and a sense of civic responsibility at the forefront of their work, (b) is attentive, responsible, and responsive to the emergent instructional needs of the members of the community, and (c) utilizes their knowledge and skills in instructional design to improve learning and performances of others.

Translating theory into practice is a demand in today's world. Taking scientific findings from a single methodological approach is no longer a viable approach. Scientists will come together from any intellectual dispositions and related methodologies to collaborate in finding scientific solutions and, as importantly to turn them into implementation to address current problems.

The National Institutes of Health defines translational research as turning observations in the laboratory, clinic, and/or community into interventions that promote well-being (National Center for Advancing Translational Research, 2015). They go on to explain that

> translational research includes two areas of translation. One is the process of applying discoveries generated during research in the laboratory, and in preclinical studies, to the development of trials and studies in humans. The second area of translation concerns research aimed at enhancing the adoption of best practices in the community. Cost-effectiveness of prevention and treatment strategies is also an important part of translational science.
>
> (National Institutes of Health, 2007, para 32)

In summary, the future of research methods in the instructional design field is situated in the realm of translational research with translation consisting of a set of thoughtful steps to ensure the implementation of evidence-based practices. The evidence consists of scientific findings and results from different methodological approaches. As Heleta (2016) advocates, "academics need to start playing a more prominent role in society instead of largely remaining observers who write about the world from within ivory towers and publish their findings in journals hidden behind expensive digital paywalls" (para 19). The future is here, and the world educational problems call for research methods that look at phenomena from a variety of epistemological assumptions. It is not time to debate which assumptions are better, but instead to work together to use evidence-based instructional design practices to address pressing societal challenges.

Robert Maribe (Rob) Branch, Ed.D.
University of Georgia

The notion of predicting anything is risky; however, the opportunity to prophesy the direction of instructional design research is intriguing. The role of soothsayer notwithstanding, I will attempt to forecast the future state of instructional design research based on historical patterns, recent trends, and current issues of learning, design, and technology.

First, the scope of instructional design will increase from a narrow academic discipline to a broad field of practice. While there will remain scholarly theories of instructional design, there will be a noticeable increase in the instructional design practitioner role through all aspects of educational institutions and learning services organizations throughout industry, governments, and social agencies as well. The theory and practice of instructional design have been around for over 70 years, yet I remember formally entering the field of educational technology 30 years ago, specializing in instructional design, and having to explain the term to practically anyone I met, including scholars and educational professionals. During that time, instructional design was rarely listed as a classified listing in *The Chronicle of Higher Education*. Now, instructional design listings are included in practically every issue, and the *Chronicle*'s front-page article for the February 9, 2016 edition was entitled: "Instructional Design: Demand Grows for a New Breed of Academic." Thus, instructional design research will generate empirical data that can be easily applied by instructional design practitioners.

Future instructional design research will be based on access to real-time data, and conducted by interdisciplinary research teams. The days of an individual locked away for weeks at a time searching for a solution to a well-defined problem will be practically non-existent. Statistical modeling methods may still be relevant, but future instructional design research will feature research methodologies such as mixed methods (quantitative and qualitative), Q Methodology, and design-based research.

The conceptual frameworks that will guide future instructional design research will be based on learner-centered paradigms, complexity theory, and the law of requisite variety. Pedagogical practices are moving away from teacher-centered approaches to cultivating innovative student-centered learning spaces. Instructional design is a social construction, comprised of independent complicated entities, each performing interrelated functions while moving toward common goals, and thus complex. Such complex situations require equally complex strategies. This idea is consistent with the law of requisite variety, which states that in order to facilitate the quantity and diversity of a situation properly, you must have an equal quantity and diversity of responses. Future instructional design research will need to produce results that inform educators and practitioners about successful strategies for managing the complexity of spaces designed for teaching and learning.

Several indisputable core principles have emerged during the past decade that characterizes instructional design, most prominent among these principles is that true instructional design is process-oriented, context responsive, and measurable outcomes. Moreover, the development of enhanced global communications, digital technologies, artificial intelligence, augmented reality, data analytics, and techno-biometric interfaces will require sophisticated instructional design models. Such models are yet to be invented. Likewise, compatible instructional design research is only now being realized, which is very promising. Finally, future instructional design research will need to complement the research conducted by scholars in the learning sciences. Instructional design and learning sciences research should focus on the application of psychological theories and philosophical orientations that address the way diverse student populations learn.

Yasemin Demiraslan Cevik, Ph.D.
Hacettepe University

In a rapidly changing field, like ours, in particular, we cannot know exactly what will happen in the future. However, we can make some estimations regarding the future or develop expectations in line with the history of the field, research trends, and current needs. In examining the history of the field, we observe that media comparisons and ATI research, which used experimental methods until the 1990s in the field of Instructional Technology (IT) were popular. Later, interest in the use of research methodologies (e.g., design studies) allowing the examination of interactions between technology, design, and learning in authentic settings increased (Winn, 2002). Today, studies aiming to make sense of the complex relationships between the learner and the environment along with those which use multiple perspectives and new methods (e.g., learning analytics, data mining, and modeling) together are remarkable. Review studies provide very useful information in today's evaluations. Thanks to these studies, the field can be examined from a holistic point of view, what subjects have been saturated, the research topics needed, and current research trends are determined, and predictions for the future can be made. Accordingly, as the results obtained from several international review studies show, in terms of research methods in the field of IT:

- There has been a dramatic increase in descriptive/interpretive studies. This result may be an indication that such studies/goals are now more accepted in the field. Considering the methods, descriptive (quantitative) studies have been conducted the most, followed by those who used mixed and qualitative methods.
- It is noteworthy that there was a considerable decline in the number of theoretical/synthesis studies, design/development studies, literature review studies and action research type studies; however, there were not many studies done with critical/postmodern purposes.
- Participants were mostly selected from higher education, most likely because they are more easily accessible. Then, there were studies conducted with students K–12 and teachers. Studies performed with school administrators, parents, adults, and private sector employees were few.
- The convenience and purposeful sampling methods were used the most.
- The data collection tools that were used the most were surveys, scales, tests and interviews.

- In analysis of the data, descriptive statistics and content analysis were preferred (i.e., Hew, Kale, & Kim, 2007; Kılıç Çakmak et al., 2016; Ozcinar, 2009; Reeves & Oh, 2016; Shih, Feng, & Tsai, 2008; West & Borup, 2014).

In investigating the research trends in the field of IT in Turkey, it is noteworthy that the results of the studies are quite similar to those conducted at the international level (i.e., Küçük, Aydemir, Yıldırım, Arpacık, & Göktaş, 2013; Sert, 2010; Şimşek et al., 2009).

In this regard, concerning research methodologies, I can offer two basic views on the question of what IT studies should look like.

First of all, different research methodologies should be used. Paradigm wars are discussions about which research tradition is the best. This war in educational research has been between quantitative and qualitative methodologies, however recently, mixed methodology has also been involved. There is no consensus on which one is better or more suitable. Educational researchers need to use all the research methods at their disposal. Each methodology is suitable for different types of research questions and provides different types of evidence to support learning. However, particularly the use of qualitative and mixed methodologies, which are fewer in number, can be increased.

Secondly, methodologies that will provide tangible educational benefits should be emphasized. The problem regarding the effect of educational research on practice has long been known (Tompsett, 2013). As Reeves (1995) highlighted, instead of studies which are short-term, controlled, artificial and do not meet educational needs (pseudoscience), those which are based on real needs, are long-term and those which are conducted with multiple assessment methods will contribute better to education. Therefore, we need studies that are authentic and realistic, cooperate with practitioners, and produce useful, concrete information for them. In such studies, giving detailed information about the research process (participants, data collection, data analysis, etc.) and sharing the data can contribute to conducting similar research and interpreting the results. Furthermore, more precise information on the conditions and context of results can be obtained (Richey, 1998; Roblyer, 2005). While determining the participants for this kind of research, attention should be paid to working with groups other than undergraduate students and on trying different (e.g. critical) methods.

However, conducting theory development studies in which the validity of the design models and their processes are tested is also quite important. According to Reigeluth (2013), the most important contributors to the field are not research studies but design theories. Therefore, emphasis should be placed on creating and developing such design theories (Şimşek, 2013). Using design-based research methodology, a research agenda should be created for the purpose of developing these design theories. According to Kim, Lee, Merrill, Spector, and van Merrienboer (2008), the increase in design-based and developmental research is a positive step forward for the field developing into a science of instruction.

As a result, we, as educators, do not focus on the problems that concern us, but more on what others produce (new technologies). As Reeves and Oh (2016) have noted, let us stop for a while and think about the contribution our research has on our practice and how little of an effect it actually has. Let us give up the technological determinism, and focus on the study of social, economic, political and cultural contexts related to the use of educational technologies (Oliver, 2011). Last but not least, let us try to make changes in practice through creating mutual dialogues with practitioners and helping them interpret their research results (Hannafin, 1985; Richey, 1998; Schrum et al., 2005).

Camille Dickson-Deane, Ph.D.
University of Technology Sydney

Learning designs that transcend force majeures by adjusting and accommodating needs whilst still being sustainable and contextual will be the true measure of our field. These are the times when we should be thinking about how we truly measure what is designed and what those measures mean for the field and of course, for learning. My response is guided by questions—questions which I think we can ask not only ourselves, but also the research the field produces.

Learning Science as a field has knowledge which intersect numerous fields such as cognitive psychology, software development, neuroscience, information architecture, project management, interaction design, and many more. When discussing research in the instructional design field, the field of Learning Science plays a key part where most have assumed that only Education should be considered. Instructional design is yet to reach a century of existence and has since become more synonymous with technology, which can be seen as unfortunate or a blessing in disguise. Either way, as the increased societal need to have ubiquitous access to information is an expectation along with education sectors expansion to offer more online and distance learning opportunities, the disciplinary knowledge has expanded to include Technology—Education Technology. To suggest that with time, instructional design research methods should or should not also evolve, means that we need to ask: has our understanding of how people learn, how we design for such learning and how we measure that, evolved?

Measuring learning and performance requires our methods to, not necessarily be more sophisticated, but more truthful to the measure. It is with truth that we will gain meaning. In order to accomplish this, it means that those in the field need to consider drawing from other disciplines as a way of refining what we know, and how we know, in order to give it value through research. ID research and practice secretly draws from fields such as Marketing, Management, Health Sciences, and Information

Technology to address learning and performance from a social, emotional, and socioemotional point of view—areas which were not seen as purposeful in our research literature until recent. As social revolutions continue to probe at our understanding of learning, it reminds us that human existence does not simply require us to change our approaches, but literally demands that we remember that this is so humans can continue to thrive and exist. Professor Emeritus Tom Reeves stated some years ago, and I paraphrase: "it is important that we begin to research the things that matter". He made this statement as he referenced the United Nations' Sustainable Development Goals as a way for the field to move forward. As such, I too adopt Reeves notions of "are we researching what matters?" and extrapolate it to: "are we *willing* to research what matters?" Scholarly research is costly, and as scholars we are pushed to publish quickly and publish often. Researching what matters, will not be quick and easy and good meaningful research is always costly.

Continuing to acknowledge and reaffirm the tenets of human learning and the ideologies of how characterizations of those who learn are tested, is still important but never really addressed. Most studies report on general demographics such as socioeconomic status, age, gender, race, and ethnicity which is quite confounding in that we have known for years that these are not great measures for the ability for our brains to operate. So, are the commonly used demographics true characterizations of those who learn? Very few research studies normalize cognitive constructs (Jonassen & Grabowski, 2012) as general demographics simply because our methods are tied to the belief that *differences for learning* are based on what we see as opposed to what we can do. In order to affect change, we need to focus on the demographics of the brain. Those associated in instructional design, do not design based on whether the person is male or female but rather we design for what can be observed— actions associated with learning. As we design for "learning and performance" remembering that the change which occurs must be more tangibly measured. This is so we do not simplify measurements by having someone say they think or perceived they have learned. Being true to the tenets is pertinent.

"Learning is change"

Alexander, Schallert, and Reynolds (2009)

Finally, remembering that the power of the unit of analysis of one is not a condemnation of validity and reliability, but that we should not generalize research in an effort to industrialize our learning methods. The digital age has since taught us, actually, reminded us, of how different we all are and that the only similarities we have is that we all have a brain and a context in which this exists. Whilst we have these similarities what we do as we interact with technologies create numerous contextualized interactions of learning that are mapped to the demographics of one brain. The challenge is: Does the current research fully describe learning and performance based on the specificities of a context? Not truly describing a context is exacerbated by the use of technology and analytics to quantify research data. Learning with and behind computer screens should challenge the field to do better research.

The following four questions force us to take a position on where research stands today, and forge ahead for what we know the future will hold:

1. Has our understanding of how people learn, how we design for such learning and how we measure that, evolved?
2. Are we *willing* to research what matters?
3. Are the commonly used demographics true characterizations of those who learn?
4. Does the current research fully describe learning and performance based on the specificities of "A" context?

Instructional design research should test sustainable designs by collecting rich data showing changes in behavior and demonstrating the contexts in which learning has occurred. This is what the future of our field should look like, the movement towards sustainable contextual learning designs with the research to support such.

Bodong Chen, Ph.D.
University of Minnesota

It was 15 years ago when I took my undergraduate course on Systematic Instructional Design at Beijing Normal. On a page that introduces the Dick and Carey model, I circled the word "system" and wrote in puzzlement: "What does a *system* mean?" Today, after traversing several research communities including educational technology, learning sciences, and learning analytics, I pivot this discussion again on the word *systems*. I wonder: How much progress has the field(s) of *instructional systems and design* (ISD) made in unpacking systems? What research methods are needed to advance its current goals? Below I discuss three ideas without any intent of comprehensively surveying research methods in the field (cf. Reeves & Oh, 2017).

First of all, we need research methods that shed light on complex processes involved in learning. A systems perspective of learning may consider complex processes happening in a student's brain, within a classroom where students collaborate on projects, in a school that integrates a new technology, or in an educational regime that attempts to scale an AI platform built for adaptive learning. Learning, and the contexts that shape learning, are necessarily complex. Future work needs to do a better job at surfacing the sophisticated interplays among various elements in these systems. The abundance of learning data and the improved access to computational tools create conditions for ISD researchers to examine systems-oriented questions from new angles. In particular, we can turn to research methods that can computationally analyze large amounts of "digital trace data"—given learning is increasingly digital and networked—to examine micro-level patterns that cannot be picked up by traditional methods. Educational data mining and learning analytics are positioned to help us apply computational methods to investigating learning phenomena, connect research in learning across levels and across settings, and make an impact in practice (Buckingham Shum, 2012). For instance, to study the use of a social media platform in online courses, a novel network-analysis method—*Relational Event Modeling*—is used to holistically gauge the influence of individual, social, temporal, and instructional factors on peer interaction using system logs (Chen & Poquet, 2020). Such modeling, when guided by learning theories, provides tools for researchers and design teams to consider multiple factors altogether instead of putting them into silos. Learning designers are now positioned to integrate learning analytics in the design process so that design decisions are informed by such computational analysis of learning processes (Persico & Pozzi, 2015). These computational methods are useful additions to ISD research to help the field incorporate the systems perspectives.

Richer data and computational methods are not "silver bullets" though. Because of ISD's deep commitments to practice and impact, the systems perspectives also require us to mobilize *design methods* so that the designed "products" will operate in the systems with fidelity. While *design-based research* (DBR) as a research methodology (Barab & Squire, 2004) is familiar to ISD scholars, *design research* and *design methods* as discussed in design disciplines (Bayazit, 2004; Laurel, 2003) are not widely understood in our field. Design methods that emphasize user involvement in design decisions are evident in the field. Given the increasing complexity of the learning systems (e.g., with dashboards, bots), we need to incorporate nascent design methods, such as fairness by design and value-sensitive design (Friedman, Hendry, & Borning, 2017), to help us consider fairness, values, and value tensions in complex systems.

Finally, the field also needs more critical perspectives to interrogate the political dimension of instruction and instructional systems. When new forms of digital inclusion and exclusion can now be deployed at scale on global platforms, more than ever we need to critically examine the interplay of nuanced factors in systems to discern who get to benefit from the use of technology (Selwyn et al., 2020). It was troubling to see no papers published in a top educational technology journal to advance critical/postmodern goals (Reeves & Oh, 2017). As critical pedagogy gains traction in contexts such as instructional design and open education (Farrow, 2017), we need critical perspectives and compatible research methods—no matter ethnographic or critical quantitative—to steer us clear of a dystopian future.

Juhong Christie Liu, Ph.D.
George Mason University

Predicting the future of educational research is in need and intriguing, as scholars like Krathwohl have asserted more than three decades ago (Farley, 1982). Anticipating trends of research to be conducted in learning design and technology (LDT) can be even more challenging because of the ever-evolving technologies and related affordances. However, the role that LDT research plays is instrumental in leading to more validated and reliable methods and results that can inform the analysis, design, and development of materials and environments scaffolding, guiding, and assessing learning. The unique practical perspectives of research in this field have also driven the optimal use of the constantly emerging technologies which shape and are being shaped by the human society.

At both micro- and macro-levels, the advancement of technologies, interdisciplinary relevance of LDT, increased cross-cultural collaboration, and reference to other fields of social science research can inform the future research in LDT. At the micro-level, ubiquitous connection with digital and networked devices and sensory technologies can enable the collection of data in diverse formats that have never been possible (Taljaard, 2016). For example, eye-tracking, electroencephalography (EEG), and wearable technologies like video capture and sensory chips can be easily adopted as data collection tools. Learning management systems generate user data untiringly. However, making sense of these data, as well as ethically processing them, will need newer skills, competencies, and ethical perspectives of data analysis (Spector, 2016). These increasingly affordable technologies for data capturing have also generated immense amounts of data from multiple dimensions, which requires clear discernment of selective inclusion so as to serve research purposes and questions as well as respectfully use research time and resources. The contexts of data collection can also create challenges. For example, virtual reality environments and interaction with artificial intelligence that can demand newer literacy to identify the variables of control, interventions, and methods of observation. Recordings of video conferencing for cross-cultural research may lose subtle cultural implication when being transcribed to text for analysis. These are the challenges as well as opportunities for future LDT research at the micro-level.

At macro-level, interdisciplinary and global collaboration will drive LDT research to broadened and deepened dimensions (Ashby & Exter, 2019; Azevedo & Aleven, 2013). LDT is located in the junction of specific disciplines and needs in relation to the science of learning. Metacognition development and related assessment of learning will all anticipate newer perspectives, methods, and interpretations. The interdisciplinary LDT collaborations themselves deserve reflection, analysis, and evaluation of the process, factors, stages, and outcomes for improvement and broader adoption (Buus et al., 2019). These can also include studies of effectiveness and impact of interdisciplinary learning. As funding agencies support more interdisciplinary and capacity building projects, they also look for valid and reliable results with foci on various levels. For instance, recommendations of efficacy, effectiveness and scale-up research are provided by funding agency research guidelines (NSF, IES, & USDOE, 2018). These can drive references to research results in the adoption of instruments from other social science and STEM research.

Hengtao Tang, Ph.D.
University of South Carolina

I highly admire the editor's foresight in initiating this effort to build up a forward-thinking understanding of the future of research methods in instructional design and technology (IDT). Predicting the future is complicated but crucial for our field, especially at this point when emerging technology has been widely integrated in education. The last decade has seen an increase in technology-enriched learning environments; however, this is not only attributed to the advance in technology but also to the implications inferred from empirical research geared towards the effective integration of emerging technology in education. Research in our IDT field has long-term dedications to the effectiveness and the efficiency of technology integration in various educational contexts, and in the next several years, to supplement and augment the use of technology in education is likely to be a major trend of IDT research (Romero-Hall, Hsiao, & Gao, 2018). IDT research has been closely bundled with technology, so when making the predictions of future research methods, I resonate with Mayer's (2003) idea of issue-driven research and thus I have also considered how research methods in the IDT field can adapt to the evolution of technology. Based on the trend in IDT research and also technology advance, I have the following speculations about the future research methods in our IDT field.

My first speculation is that future IDT research methods might be driven by a need to accurately understand learning in a technology-enhanced setting. Artificial intelligence (AI) is one of the most popular technologies in the media hype, affording IDT researchers with opportunities for making accurate predictions of learning outcome or progress based on a large volume of data. Some AI algorithms have been used in IDT research to offset the limitation of self-reported data and classify the latent patterns that self-reported data cannot reveal (Tang, Xing, & Pei, 2018; Xing, Tang & Pei, 2019). Future IDT research methods might bring together AI research to seek for ways to grasp a more granular understanding of learning, such as its temporality and multi-modality.

My second speculation is that future research methods might focus on the practical merits of IDT research. With this being said, I specifically talk about the practical implications geared towards design and development of technology-enhanced interventions and/or scaffolds. Design-based research (Barab & Squire, 2004) needs to be spotlighted in regard to its role in investigating the effectiveness of technology-enhanced intervention and exploring ways to optimize its design. We might also see that action research (Mertler, 2019) can be another increasingly used approach in IDT research. The growing prominence of the fifth generation (5G) wireless technology unlocks unlimited possibilities for online education. In the next few years, the number of online Ed.D. programs may increase, and the number of professionals enrolled in online programs may also escalate. For the pursuit of practical merits of IDT research, empowering professionals as researchers in action research can be a viable option (Arslan-Ari, Ari, Grant, & Morris, 2018).

My third speculation results from the increasing interdisciplinary colla-boration in the IDT field. Actually, the IDT field itself is an interdisciplin-ary domain. For future research methods, we might increasingly see the merge between research methods from different domains into a more comprehensive one, such as quantitative ethnography (Shaffer, 2017). By combining interdisciplinary research methods, we can thus disentangle the massive qualitative data using quantitative methods beyond the border between qualitative and quantitative research. In addition to bringing together cross-disciplinary methods, we might need to address how to select research methods in interdisciplinary inquiries. My personal recom-mendation is to select appropriate methods with a systematic understanding of the context.

In closing, I hope to add that I also agree with Romero-Hall et al. (2018) that we need to "understand the importance of mixed methods, the richness of qualitative inquiry, and the limitations of findings based on location context" (p. 424). For future IDT research methods, the long-term dedication to the effectiveness and efficacy of technology in that specific context will persist. In other words, technologies come and go, but the pursuit for effectiveness and efficacy in a specific context will go on for IDT research.

Lucas Vasconcelos, Ph.D.
University of South Carolina

When I was invited to provide insights on where instructional design research is going, I immediately felt the weight and responsibility of such a lofty task. Narrowing down my insights to the scope of this publication and the word limit was challenging given the wide range of possibilities. To get there, I paused for introspection and reflection about instructional design research. As a visual person, I wrote down several keywords and attempted to organically connect them to construct a narrative. One of the keywords that struck me was *epistemology*. At that point, I understood that I wanted to convey my values and beliefs about where impactful instruc-tional design research is going.

My reflective experience about instructional design research did not focus on innovative educational technologies, instructional design models or approaches, target populations, learning theories, or specific designs for teaching and learning. These are certainly important elements, but they were not at the forefront. Rather, the keywords I came up with revolved around equity, access, culture, inclusion, social justice, and democracy. In summary, my reflection about instructional design research relied on its potential contribution to a more equitable and just society. I soon realized that I would be writing this section about the fact that instructional design research is moving towards being more socially engaged and responsible. Specifically, future research endeavors ought to (a) be driven by real-world problems in modern society and (b) democratize access to quality teaching and learning by including more diverse populations.

It is not rare to find empirical studies that simply seek to test the effectiveness or impact of an instructional intervention on dependent variables within a controlled environment. This type of experimental or quasi-experimental research design certainly has merit. But the value of empirical studies should not be assessed solely based on a rigorous design. Beyond this, the question we need to consider is: Does the study test relationships between variables simply for the sake of doing it? Too many empirical studies that are published, even in top-tier journals, report research designs that are decontextualized and disconnected from pressing issues that affect educational settings, such as the reality found in schools and universities. Authors often fail to disclose what motivated their research, how the academic community and larger society benefit from findings, as well as the implications of findings for educational policy, research, and practice. This approach weakens or even thwarts the potential for empowerment, inclusion, and democratic access to quality teaching and learning experiences in instructional design research.

Top peer-reviewed journals and funding agencies have increasingly valued research that leverages educational technologies and instructional approaches in innovative ways to make a positive impact in education and promote social justice. Examples of such instructional design research topics include, but are in no way limited to: (a) increasing educational access to minorities and populations with special needs, (b) creating equitable experiences for learners with a diverse range of skills and interests, and (c) designing culturally sensitive and/or culturally situated instruction. Designing research that promotes social justice may seem daunting, especially for novice researchers and graduate students. While I would love to continue a reflection about this, I will limit myself to proposing that graduate programs should adopt a social justice framework to better prepare novice researchers on designing, implementing, and reporting research that uses instructional design and technologies to contribute to a more fair and just society.

Nicola Pallitt, Ph.D.
Rhodes University

Research in instructional design (ID) has diversified from being undertaken by those who teach ID, to those who practice ID in a range of spaces. Increasingly, instructional designers are studying their own practices and those of others in their professional community. As IDs come from a range of disciplinary and educational backgrounds across the world and are able to share diverse experiences online more easily, there is an awareness of ID as culturally situated and interdisciplinary. IDs as reflexive professionals bring their own positionalities and intersectionalities to bear as part of their research. Reflexivity extends beyond design to researching our practice. Educational technologies research, more broadly, is criticality informed by a range of perspectives and methodological approaches which is becoming a scholarly status quo rather than theoretically thin studies of practice. This entails going beyond technicist assumptions and linear approaches to ID research, to multifaceted engagements with what should be at the heart of ID: meaningful learning experiences.

ID evolves differently in different contexts. Professionals making use of ID are questioning some of the normative assumptions embedded in models and principles originating from the global north. What is ID? Who does it and what does it involve? ID is a label that some professionals do not identify with as their primary profession but identify with being doers of ID work. I found this to be the case in my own survey of learning design in African universities, where many participants shared that they do not have formal training in the field but are making use of ID in their teaching or as faculty developers. These individuals are often attracted to ID because of limited capacity in their institutions and the need to design learning experiences for contexts with wicked challenges (Pallitt, Carr, Pedersen, Gunness, & Dooga, 2018). As massification is a global phenomenon, professionals in African contexts have felt its effects and ID (while still invisible as part of many lecturers' "normal" work) forms part of a range of technology-mediated responses across the continent.

While big data and learning analytics present new opportunities for mixed methods and quantitative ID research, I believe there will always be a place for qualitative research and in particular, design-based and autoethnographic approaches. I think ID research designs are going to become more creative, as we are already seeing research methodology handbooks that provide alternatives to traditional methods. For example, online interviews using web conferencing tools where interviewees are able to share a virtual walkthrough of their designs. Using online tools for research in ethically sound, valid, and reliable ways is part of the journey ahead. ID researchers can be agile in how we approach data collection, many of the frameworks for analysis are still emerging or we need to look beyond the ID field for precedents. Interdisciplinary, cultural awareness, and agility are important qualities for IDs, not just as designers, but as researchers too.

Briju Thankachan, Ph.D.
The Ohio State University

Learning is a journey from one destination to another. During this journey, a good instructional design helps the learner to reach the destination more effectively and efficiently. In an instructional design research, it is important to analyze the factors/variables that impact learning and instruction and evaluate those factors to make informed instructional decisions. Five decades ago, Harvard University professor Dr. John Carroll (1963) identified five variables that influence learning. I believe those variables are still relevant to the instructional design research in the information age. Three are internal to the learner (aptitude, ability to understand instruction, perseverance) and two are external (opportunity and quality of instruction). Over the last three decades, many instructional design researchers focused on the external factors of learning and instruction, such as opportunity to learn (time allowed to learn), types of instructional materials and presentations. I believe identifying and analyzing internal factors such as the learner aptitude, ability to understand and perseverance will enhance the instructional design research and help the learner learn better.

Over the years, traditional instructional design researchers collected, self-reported, and observed data that influence learning and instruction. However, modern learning environments could analyze and synthesize internal characteristics of the learner as part of the learning analytics. For example, the learning management systems and apps can record the amount of time the learner is spending to actively engage the content. For example, the number of clicks, downloads, real-time viewer experience, etc.

In the coming decade, we will witness a tremendous growth in the instructional design research with the help of artificial intelligence in the cognitive and psychomotor domains of learning and instruction. However, to analyze the factors that influence the affective/humanistic domain of instruction and learning we still need the element of human interactions.

Reigeluth and Carr-Chellman (2009) defines instruction as "anything that is done purposely to facilitate learning" (p. 6). For future instructional design research, I propose to focus on the affective/humanistic domain of instruction where the interaction of content, learner, and instruction happens. The research question is—How can we measure level of proficiency in the affective/humanistic domain of learning and instruction?

Conclusion

The aim of this chapter was to provide projections about the future of research methods in the learning design and technology field in the next decade and beyond. This chapter is inspired by the article published by Farley (1982), titled "The Future of Educational Research" in the *Educational Researcher* journal.

As mentioned by many in this chapter, predicting the future can seem arrogant and chancy. But, we engage in it because these predictions can serve as an outlet for other scholars to think about what we have yet to accomplish and it can be an opportunity to figure out ways to address these needs in terms of research methods within our field. As predicted and encouraged by several, it is key that we move forward with research methods that truly allow learning design professionals to engage in evidence-based practice and result in tangible outcomes. Our efforts in research methods within our field should aim to continue to help reduce the gap between learning design and technology research and practice.

Several scholars also predict that future research practice and methods will be more interdisciplinary. The community of learning design and technology professionals is often connected with other education-related fields. However, an increased connection with other non-education fields can bring change, and dare we say "innovation," to further create interdisciplinary research methods. The learning design and technology field has its origin in theories and foundations from various fields such as communication, psychology, information technology, art and design, and business, among others. The idea that research methods will become more interdisciplinary is something that we are currently starting to experience. As we write this book, we are experiencing the COVID-19 pandemic. Learning design practitioners are in high demand in K–12 and institutions of higher education around the world, as they aid in the transition to online teaching and learning. However, learning design and technology professionals are also working in interdisciplinary teams (i.e. public health officials, epidemiologists, politicians, doctors, nurses, microbiologists, and others) to help educate the public through the design, development, evaluation, and dissemination of educational material that help the public stay inform and learn more about the COVID-19 pandemic. As this and other experiences occur, it is likely that similar teams of interdisciplinary scholars will work together using interdisciplinary research methods to explore different social phenomena.

Scholars also foresee access to real-time data. As researchers we tend to be protective of our data; however, in more recent times the publication process has increased a certain level of openness, in which authors are welcome to share data related to their studies. We can hope that advances on research methods increase access and transparency of research data. Scholars can also agree that new research methods will continue to evolve from their current state to perhaps allow for (a) more granular data collections, (b) diverse learning environments, (c) culture-specific contexts, or (d) technology driven methods. For example, as mentioned by Dr. Liu and as mentioned in various chapters in this book, we have already seen the implementation of eye-tracking, electroencephalography (EEG), and wearable technologies in research methodology in the learning design and technology field. The applications of these research methods are likely to change over time, their validation, and use for data collection. Similarly, as other learning environments emerge and/or our research questions change research methods will either adapt or surface. The goal in the future, as it is today, will be to continue to expose, understand, and disseminate research about the complexity of the learning process.

Expanding beyond the diversity of research methods, as scholars we also believe in fine tuning our methods, traditional or novel, to more accurately present a depiction of research questions presented. Predictions about the future of the field, in terms of research methods, are optimistic that as scholars our work will push forward with disruptive methods of research that go beyond learning and also address key cultural, socioeconomic, and political issues that are part of education. These are challenging ideas, since as scholars we are trained to shy away from controversial topics, yet with adequate research methods scholars can investigate with a critical perspective and in different contexts issues that are important not only to the learning design and technology community but also to society as a whole.

Key questions that we want to leave you with as you think about the future of research methods: What traditional or novel methods can you use to address critical topics in learning design and technology? What challenges do you foresee with using novel research methods? How can we become more critical of our own current practice with research methods? What can we do to improve education of research methods, traditional or novel, in our graduate programs?

References

Alexander, P., Schallert, D., & Reynolds, R. (2009). What is learning anyway? A topographical perspective considered. *Educational Psychologist, 44*(3), 176–192.

Arslan-Ari, I., Ari, F., Grant, M. M., & Morris, W. S. (2018). Action research experiences for scholarly practitioners in an online education doctorate program: Design, reality, and lessons learned. *TechTrends, 62*(5), 441–449.

Ashby, I. & Exter, M. (2019). Designing for interdisciplinarity in higher education: Considerations for instructional designers. *TechTrends, 63*(2), 202–208.

Azevedo, R., & Aleven, V. (2013). Metacognition and learning technologies: An overview of current interdisciplinary research. In R. Azevedo & V. Aleven (Eds.), *International handbook of metacognition and learning technologies* (pp. 1–16). New York, NY: Springer.

Barab, S. A. & Squire, K. (2004). Design-based research: Putting a stake in the ground. *Journal of the Learning Sciences, 13*(1), 1–14. doi:10.1207/s15327809jls 1301_1.

Bayazit, N. (2004). Investigating design: A review of forty years of design research. *Design Issues, 20*(1), 16–29.

Bishop, M. J., Boling, E., Elen, J., & Svihla, V. (Eds.). (2020). *Handbook of research in educational communications and technology* (5th ed.). New York: Springer. www. springer.com/gp/book/9783030361181.

Buckingham Shum, S. (2012). *UNESCO policy brief: Learning analytics*. Moscow: UNESCO Institute for Information Technologies in Education.

Buus, L., Frydendahl, J. A., Jensen, T. W., Jensen, T. F., Lillelund, K. B., & Falbe-Hansen, M. (2019). Designing for learning in an interdisciplinary education context. *Journal of Systemics, Cybernetics and Informatics, 17*(1), 169–185.

Carroll, J. (1963). A model of school learning. *Teachers College Record, 64*(8), 723–733.

Chen, B. & Poquet, O. (2020). Socio-temporal dynamics in peer interaction events. In *Proceedings of the Tenth International Conference on Learning Analytics & Knowledge*, 203–208. doi:10.1145/3375462.3375535.

Farley, F. H. (1982). The future of educational research. *Educational Researcher, 11*(8), 11–19. doi:10.2307/1175580.

Farrow, R. (2017). Open education and critical pedagogy. *Learning, Media and Technology, 42*(2), 130–146. doi:10.1080/17439884.2016.1113991.

Friedman, B., Hendry, D. G., & Borning, A. (2017). A survey of value sensitive design methods. *Foundations and Trends® in Human–Computer Interaction, 11*(2), 63–125. doi:10.1561/1100000015.

Hannafin, M. J. (1985). The status and future of research in instructional design and technology. *Journal of Instructional Development, 8*(3), 24–30.

Heleta, S. (2016). Academics can change the world – If they stop talking only to their peers. *The Conversation* (Updated March 31, 2017).

Hew, K. F., Kale, U., & Kim, N. (2007). Past research in instructional technology: Results of a content analysis of empirical studies published in three prominent instructional technology journals from the year 2000 through 2004. *Journal of Educational Computing Research, 36*(3), 269–300.

Jonassen, D. H., & Grabowski, B. L. (2012). *Handbook of individual differences learning and instruction*. Abingdon: Routledge.

Kılıç Çakmak, E., Özüdoğru, G., Bozkurt, Ş. B., Ülker, Ü., Ünsal, N. Ö., Boz, K., ... Gül, H. Ü. (2016). 2014 yılında eğitim teknolojileri alanındaki yayımlanan makalelerin incelenmesi (Examination of educational technology articles within 2014). *Eğitim Teknolojisi Kuram ve Uygulama, 6*(1), 80–108.

Kim, C., Lee, J., Merrill, M. D., Spector, J. M., & van Merrienboer, J. J. G. (2008). Foundations for the future. In *Handbook of research on educational communications and technology* (3rd ed., pp. 807–815). Abingdon: Routledge.

Küçük, S., Aydemir, M., Yıldırım, G., Arpacık, O., & Göktaş, Y. (2013). Educational technology research trends in Turkey from 1990 to 2011. *Computers & Education, 68*, 42–50.

Laurel, B. (2003). *Design research: Methods and perspectives.* MIT Press. Retrieved from books.google.com/books?id=xVeFdy44qMEC www.amazon.com/dp/026 2122634.

Mayer, R. E. (2003). The case for evidence-based practice and issue-driven research. *Educational Psychology Review, 15*(4), 367–373.

Mertler, C. A. (2019). *Action research: Improving schools and empowering educators* (6th ed.). Thousand Oaks, CA: SAGE Publications.

National Center for Advancing Translational Research. (2015). Exploring the translational science spectrum. Retrieved from https://ncats.nih.gov/director/oct-2015.

National Institutes of Health. (2007). *Definitions under Subsection 1 (Research Objectives), Section I (Funding Opportunity Description), Part II (Full Text of Announcement), of RFA-RM-07-007: Institutional Clinical and Translational Science Award (U54) Mar2007.* Retrieved from http://grants.nih.gov/grants/guide/rfa-files/RFA-RM-07-007.html.

National Science Foundation (NSF), Institute of Educational Science (IES), & US Department of Education (US DOE). (2018). *Companion guidelines on replication & reproducibility in education research.* Retrieved from https://ies.ed.gov/pdf/Compa nionGuidelinesReplicationReproducibility.pdf.

Oliver, M. (2011). Technological determinism in educational technology research: Some alternative ways of thinking about the relationship between learning and

technology. *Journal of Computer Assisted Learning*, *27*, 373–384. doi:10.1111/
j.1365-2729.2011.00406.x.

Ozcinar, Z. (2009). The topic of instructional design in research journals: A citation
analysis for the years 1980-2008. *Australasian Journal of Educational Technology*, *25*, 4.
doi:10.14742/ajet.1129.

Pallitt, N., Carr, T., Pedersen, J., Gunness, S., & Dooga, J. 2018. Learning Design in
African Higher Education. 13th International Conference on e-Learning (ICEL),
July 5–6, 2018, Cape Town, South Africa.

Persico, D. & Pozzi, F. (2015). Informing learning design with learning analytics to
improve teacher inquiry. *British Journal of Educational Technology*, *46*(2), 230–248.
doi:10.1111/bjet.12207.

Reeves, T. (2000). Socially responsible educational technology research. *Educational
Technology Magazine*, *40*(6), 19–28.

Reeves, T., Herrington, J., & Oliver, R. (2005). Design research: A socially responsible approach to instructional technology research in higher education. *Journal of
Computing in Higher Education*, *16*(2), 97–116.

Reeves, T. C. (1995). Questioning the questions of instructional technology
research. In M. R. Simonson & M. Anderson (Eds.), *Proceedings of the Annual
Conference of the Association for Educational Communications and Technology* (pp.
459–470). Anaheim: Research and Theory Division.

Reeves, T. C. & Oh, E. G. (2017). The goals and methods of educational technology
research over a quarter century (1989–2014). *Educational Technology Research and
Development*, *65*, 325–339. doi:10.1007/s11423-016-9474-1.

Reigeluth, C. M. & Carr-Chellman, A. (Eds.). (2009). *Instructional-design theories and
models: Building a common knowledge base: Vol. III*. Mahwah, NJ: Lawrence Erlbaum
Associates.

Reigeluth, C.M. (2013). *Instructional-design Theories and Models*. Abingdon, Oxon:
Routledge.

Richey, R. C. (1998). The pursuit of useable knowledge in instructional technology.
Educational Technology Research and Development, *46*(4), 7–22.

Roblyer, M. D. (2005). Educational technology research that makes a difference:
Series introduction. *Contemporary Issues in Technology and Teacher Education*, *5*(2),
192–201.

Romero-Hall, E., Hsiao, E. L., & Gao, F. (2018). The (Re) adaptability of research
methodologies in the instructional design & technology field. *TechTrends*, *62*(5),
424–426.

Romero-Hall, E. J. (2020). Research methods in learning design and technology:
A historical perspective of the last 40 years. In E. J. Romero-Hall (Ed.), *Research
methods in learning design and technology*. Abingdon: Routledge.

Schrum, L., Thompson, A., Sprague, D., Maddux, C., McAnear, A., Bell, L., &
Bull, G. (2005). Advancing the field: Considering acceptable evidence in educational technology research. *Contemporary Issues in Technology and Teacher Education*,
5(3/4), 202–209.

Selwyn, N., Hillman, T., Eynon, R., Ferreira, G., Knox, J., Macgilchrist, F., &
Sancho-Gil, J. M. (2020). What's next for Ed-Tech? Critical hopes and concerns
for the 2020s. *Learning, Media and Technology*, *45*(1), 1–6. doi:10.1080/
17439884.2020.1694945.

Sert, G. (2010). Öğretim teknolojileri eğitiminde yayınlanmış Türkiye adresli
makalelerin içerik analizi (Content analysis of educational technology research

conducted in Turkey). Yayımlanmamış yüksek lisans tezi (Unpublished MS Dissertation), Hacettepe Üniversitesi, Ankara, Türkiye.

Shaffer, D. W. (2017). *Quantitative Ethnography*. Madison, WI: Cathcart Press.

Shih, M., Feng, J., & Tsai, C.C. (2008). Research and trends in the field of e-learning from 2001 to 2005: A content analysis of cognitive studies in selected journals. *Computers & Education, 51*(2), 955–967. doi:10.1016/j.compedu.2007.10.004.

Şimşek, A. (2013). Interview with Charles M. Reigeluth: Applying instructional design to educational reform. *Contemporary Educational Technology, 4*(1), 81–86.

Şimşek, A., Özdamar, N., Uysal, Ö., Kobak, K., Berk, C., Kılıçer, T., & Ve Çiğdem, H. (2009). Current trends in educational technology research in Turkey in the new millennium. *Educational Sciences: Theory and Practice, 9*(2), 961–966.

Smith, J. K. & Heshusius, L. (1986). Closing down the conversation: The end of the quantitative-qualitative debate among educational inquirers. *Educational Researcher, 15*(1), 4–12.

Spector, J. M. (2016). Ethics in educational technology: Towards a framework for ethical decision making in and for the discipline. *Educational Technology Research and Development, 64*(5), 1003–1011.

Sustainable development goals: Sustainable development knowledge platform. (2015). Retrieved March 3, 2020, from https://sustainabledevelopment.un.org/?menu=1300.

Taljaard, J. (2016). A review of multi-sensory technologies in a Science, Technology, Engineering, Arts and Mathematics (STEAM) classroom. *Journal of Learning Design, 9*(2), 46–55.

Tang, H., Xing, W., & Pei, B. (2018). Exploring the temporal dimension of forum participation in MOOCs. *Distance Education, 39*(3), 353–372.

Tompsett, C. (2013). On the educational validity of research in educational technology. *Educational Technology & Society, 16*(3), 179–190.

West, R. E. & Borup, J. (2014). An analysis of a decade of research in 10 instructional design and technology journals. *British Journal of Educational Technology, 45*(4), 545–556.

Winn, W. D. (2002). Current trends in educational technology research: The study of learning environments. *Educational Psychology Review, 14*(3), 331–351.

Xing, W., Tang, H., & Pei, B. (2019). Beyond positive and negative emotions: Looking into the role of achievement emotions in discussion forums of MOOCs. *The Internet and Higher Education, 43*, 100690.

Yusop, F. & Correia, A.-P. (2012). The civic-minded instructional designers framework: An alternative approach to contemporary instructional designers' education in higher education. *British Journal of Educational Technology, 43*(2), 180–190.

Index

Locators in **bold** refer to tables and those in *italics* refer to figures.

Made in the USA
Coppell, TX
12 November 2020

41228567R00138